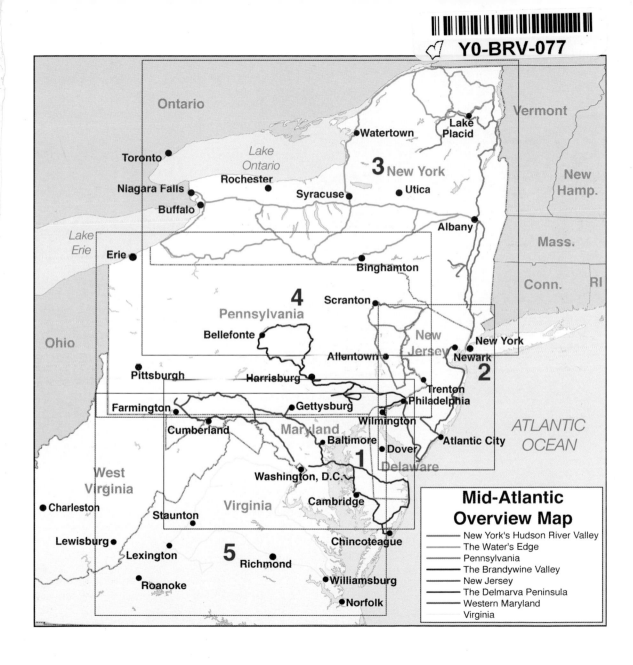

**Mid-Atlantic
Overview Map**

New York's Hudson River Valley
The Water's Edge
Pennsylvania
The Brandywine Valley
New Jersey
The Delmarva Peninsula
Western Maryland
Virginia

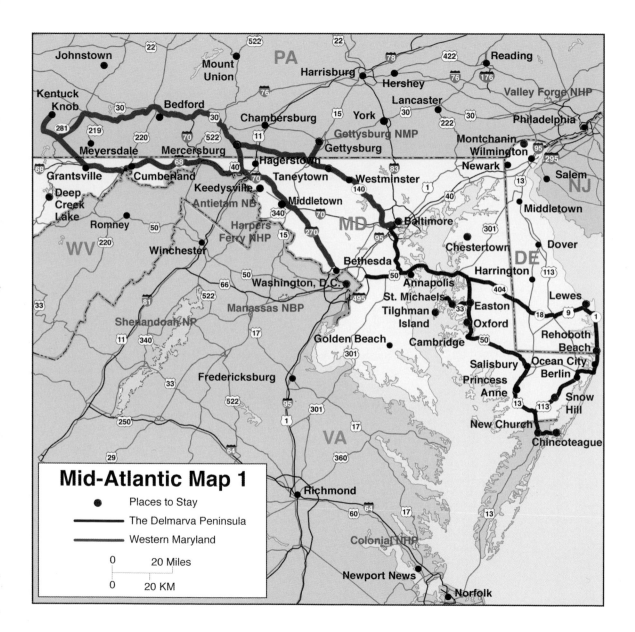

Mid-Atlantic Map 1

● Places to Stay

—— The Delmarva Peninsula

—— Western Maryland

0 — 20 Miles

0 — 20 KM

Mid-Atlantic Map 2

● Places to Stay

▬▬▬ New Jersey

0   20 Miles

0   20 KM

NY

CT

Milford

Delaware Water Gap NRA

Franklin

Peekskill

Andover

Stanhope

Yonkers

Hope

Morristown NHP

Newark

New York

NJ

Allentown

Gateway NRA

Long Beach

Stockton

New Brunswick

Reading

PA

Lambertville

Sandy Hook

Trenton

Spring Lake

Valley Forge NHP

Point Pleasant

Norristown

Bristol

Lavallette

Philadelphia

Cherry Hill

Barnegat Light

Wilmington

Hammonton

Salem

Batsto Village

Beach Haven

Vineland

Bridgeton

Atlantic City

DE

Woodbine

Ocean City

Dover

MD

Avalon

Cape May

North Wildwood

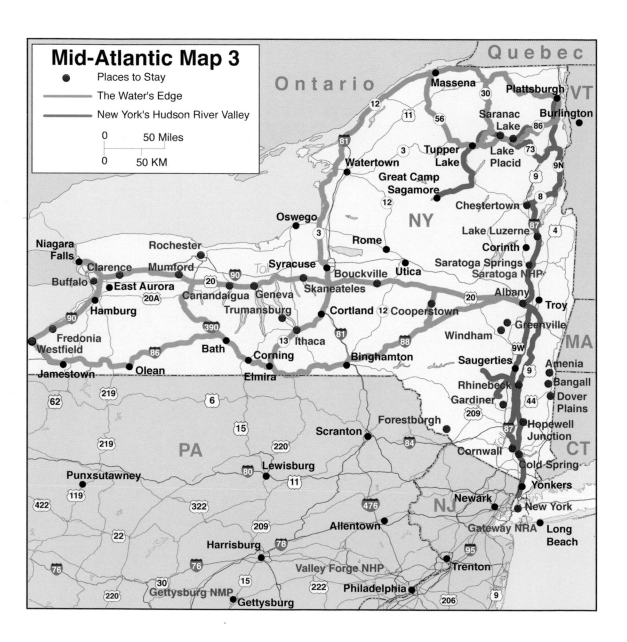

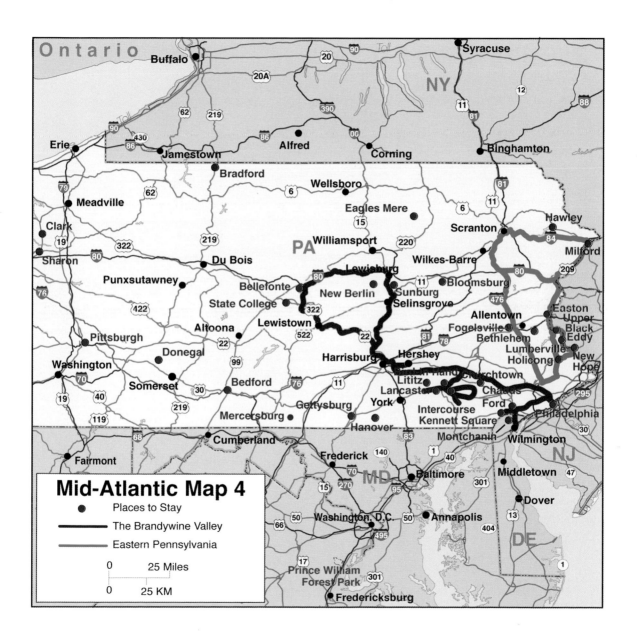

Ontario

Buffalo

Syracuse

NY

20A

20

90

Toll

12

88

62

219

390

Erie

430

90

86

Jamestown

86

Alfred

Corning

11

81

Binghamton

79

Meadville

62

Bradford

6

Wellsboro

81

Clark

19

Sharon

322

Du Bois

Williamsport

219

6

11

Eagles Mere

15

PA

220

Scranton

84

Hawley

Milford

209

80

Punxsutawney

Bellefonte

Lewisburg

New Berlin

Sunburg
Selinsgrove

Wilkes-Barre

Bloomsburg

476

Allentown

Easton
Upper
Black
Eddy

422

State College

322

Lewistown

522

80

11

78

81

Fogelsville

Bethlehem

Lumberville
Holicong

New
Hope

Pittsburgh

76

Altoona

22

99

Harrisburg

Hershey

Doylestown

Chadds

Philadelphia

Washington

70

Donegal

Somerset

30

219

40

19

119

Bedford

76

11

Gettysburg

Mercersburg

York

Lititz

Lancaster

Intercourse
Kennett Square

Ford

Montchanin

Wilmington

30

295

NJ

68

Hanover

83

Montchanin

Cumberland

Fairmont

Frederick

140

270

15

70

95

1

40

301

Middletown

47

Dover

13

Mid-Atlantic Map 4

● Places to Stay

—— The Brandywine Valley

—— Eastern Pennsylvania

0   25 Miles

0   25 KM

66

50

Washington, D.C.

50

Annapolis

404

DE

MD

Baltimore

17

Prince William
Forest Park

301

Fredericksburg

1

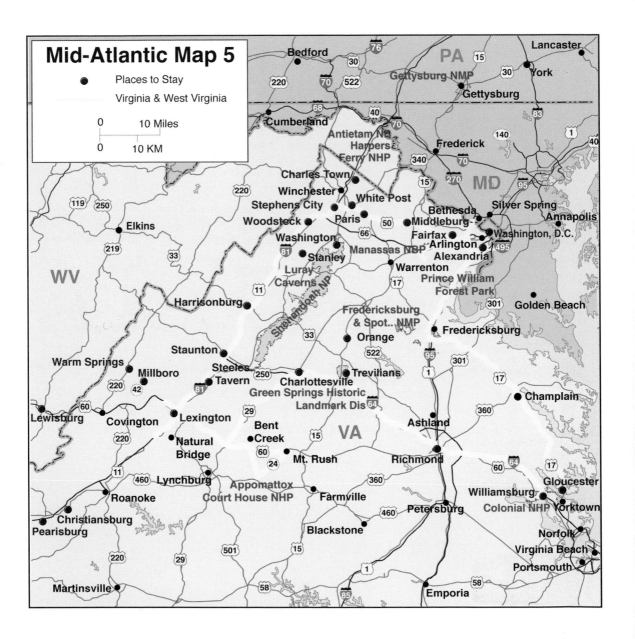

Mid-Atlantic Map 5

- Places to Stay

Virginia & West Virginia

0   10 Miles

0   10 KM

Bedford

Lancaster

PA

15

Gettysburg NMP

30

York

76

30

220

70

522

Gettysburg

83

68

Cumberland

40

70

140

1

Antietam Na...

Harpers
Ferry NHP

Frederick

40

340

70

MD

270

Charles Town

15

95

Winchester

Silver Spring

Stephens City

White Post

Bethesda

Annapolis

Woodstock

Paris

50

Middleburg

Washington, D.C.

Elkins

66

Fairfax

Washington

Arlington

495

119

250

Stanley

Manassas NBP

Alexandria

220

81

Luray
Caverns

Warrenton

WV

11

Prince William
Forest Park

219

Golden Beach

301

33

Harrisonburg

Fredericksburg
& Spot... NMP

Fredericksburg

33

Staunton

Orange

Warm Springs

Steeles
Tavern

522

95

301

Millboro

250

Trevilians

17

220

42

81

Charlottesville

Champlain

60

Green Springs Historic
Landmark Dis

360

Lewisburg

Lexington

64

Covington

29

Ashland

220

Bent
Creek

15

VA

Natural
Bridge

Richmond

60

64

60

Mt. Rush

17

24

Gloucester

11

460

Lynchburg

Williamsburg

Roanoke

Appomattox
Court House NHP

360

Colonial NHP

Yorktown

Farmville

Christiansburg

Petersburg

Pearisburg

460

Norfolk

220

29

Blackstone

Virginia Beach

501

15

Portsmouth

Martinsville

1

58

85

58

Emporia

Karen Brown's
MID-ATLANTIC
2007

Governor's Palace, Williamsburg

Contents

Dedicated to Mr. Tom Cox
and Eighth Grade Teachers everywhere
whose infectious passion for our country's heritage
has inspired our children and brought history to life.

Cover Painting: Governor's Palace, Williamsburg, Virginia

Authors: Karen Brown, Jack Bullard.

Editors: Clare Brown, Karen Brown, June Eveleigh Brown, Debbie Tokumoto.

Illustrations: Vanessa Kale Brown.

Color photos: Spring in Williamsburg, Battlefield at Gettysburg.

Cover painting: Jann Pollard.

Maps: Michael Fiegel and Rachael Kircher-Randolph.

Technical support: Gary Meisner.

Distributed by National Book Network, 15200 NBN Way, Blue Ridge Summit, PA 17214, USA. Tel: 717-794-3800 or 1-800-462-6420, Fax: 1-800-338-4500, Email: custserv@nbnbooks.com

A catalog record for this book is available from the British Library.

ISSN 1535-4067

 # Introduction

This book is the product of our searching out the best places to stay and the most interesting itineraries to travel in the states of New York, Pennsylvania, New Jersey, Delaware, Maryland, Virginia, and West Virginia and in the District of Columbia. There are distinct differences between the states and within each state there are areas that are markedly different in terrain, weather patterns, and tourist attractions. With so many diverse attractions, touring the entire region would require a considerable investment of time but with this guide travelers have the opportunity to tailor their trips according to what appeals most and how much time they have. One can argue for a visit to Washington, the nation's capital, for therein lies the history of our country; alternatively, a visit to New York City opens vistas in the fast lane of life ranging from museums to shopping to financial institutions. And then spread across the miles as one moves west, north, or south is a land with much history of the founding of America, a land of varying geography and culture, a land whose inhabitants have shaped its life and where the traditions of old continue on today.

Your entry into these Mid-Atlantic States will more than likely be through one of its major cities and quite probably, you will arrive by air. Since today's airfare structures are very complex, price at least a couple of alternatives to be sure that you are receiving the best value. Try to avoid renting a car while you visit the cities of New York, Philadelphia, and Washington because their public transportation systems are so extensive and well organized that you have no need of a car.

About Itineraries

Eight driving itineraries describe routes through the various regions of the Mid-Atlantic States. The itineraries are outlined on the hotel state maps found at the front of the book in the color map section and on the individual, more detailed, black-and-white map that precedes each itinerary. The overview map will help you visualize the routes of the various itineraries as they navigate a course through the Mid-Atlantic States. Each routing can easily be tailored to meet your own specific needs by leaving out some sightseeing if time is limited, or linking several itineraries together if you wish to enjoy a longer vacation. In addition, we list sightseeing attractions in the cities of New York, Philadelphia, and Washington.

CAR RENTAL

The itineraries are designed for travel by car unless your plan is to visit only the major cities of New York, Philadelphia, and Washington, in which case train or even bus transportation between cities is both fast and convenient. If you are staying in any of the major cities at the beginning of your trip, it is not necessary to pick up a rental car until you leave the city or just before any day trips by car, since public transportation systems are so convenient and all of the cities are great for walking. Consider asking your hotel if there is a car rental office inside the hotel or nearby. Sometimes car rental companies will deliver your car to your hotel.

DRIVING TIMES

The distances in the Mid-Atlantic States as you go from east to west in Maryland, Pennsylvania, or New York or from north to south from the Eastern Shore of Maryland to the northern parts of New York State are lengthy. To drive the length or the breadth of the region would take you at least a full day—and a long day at that. In many itineraries there are choices between traveling on the major highways where speed is of the essence and where distances can be covered quickly, or the alternative of taking the winding, scenic roads through the countryside and the towns along the way. To get the most enjoyment from your travel we recommend the slower, more picturesque routes where you have the opportunity to enjoy the special qualities of the area.

Erwinna Covered Bridge, Delaware

MAPS

A total of six colored maps are to be found at the front of the book. The overview map outlines our recommended driving itineraries as they cross through the Mid-Atlantic States. The overview is followed by a series of five detailed maps that show the itinerary routings, and places to stay by geographic state groupings. Fronting each itinerary is a black and white map that outlines the suggested route, detailing sightseeing suggestions and roads. These are simply renderings and not necessarily to scale. For detailed trip planning, it is essential to supplement these with comprehensive commercial maps. Rand McNally maps are available for purchase on our website, *www.karenbrown.com.*

PACING

At the beginning of each itinerary we suggest our recommended pacing to help you decide the amount of time to allocate to each one. The suggested time frame reflects what we believe will make for a pleasant and comfortable trip, allowing you time to enjoy not only the scenery but also the historic sights along the way. Allow more time if you want to do a lot of shopping or if you have a special interest in any particular area. Use our recommendation as a guideline only, and choreograph your own itinerary based on how much leisure time you have and whether your preference is to move on to a new destination each day or settle in and use a particular inn as your base.

WEATHER

This is a region where weather varies greatly—not only from season to season, but also with the geography. You may not get the weather you expect during your trip—but oftentimes this adds to the enjoyment of your stay. While the weather may be changeable, there are certainly some guidelines that will be helpful to the traveler. In the winter months of December through March, you can expect everything from snow and ice to sleet and freezing rain. Temperatures often get down to zero and below, and yet there may be days and even weeks when there is little snow and just brisk cold weather. Traditionally, in the latter half of January there is even a period of warm weather, deceiving everyone into believing that winter is over. The spring months of March, April, and May are wonderful, with each of the Mid-Atlantic States sprouting forth with bulbs of every description and flowering shrubs and trees. The newness of everything with the freshness of spring green is hard not to love. Occasionally, however, there is a taste of winter weather that will remind you that the decision to bring a coat on your trip was indeed a very good one. Summer is a lazy time of year and generally has great weather, but there will be rain showers. Summer can also get hot and humid—on those days you'll welcome the pair of shorts and short-sleeved shirt that you brought and you'll be grateful that your rental car and your hotel are air-conditioned. Many a traveler will say that the Mid-Atlantic States are best in the spring and fall when the days are long and warm. Fall brings the added bonus of the changing colors of the foliage.

Introduction—About Itineraries

About Inn Travel

We use the term "inn" to cover everything from a simple bed and breakfast inn to a hotel in one of the major Mid-Atlantic cities. A wide range of overnight accommodations is included in this guide: some are great bargains, others very costly; some are in cities, others in remote locations; some are quite sophisticated, others extremely simple; some are decorated with opulent antiques, others with furniture from grandma's attic; some are large hotels, others have only a few rooms. The common denominator is that each place has some special quality that makes it appealing. The descriptions are intended to give you a honest appraisal of each property so that you can select accommodation based on personal preferences. The following pointers will help you appreciate and understand what to expect when traveling the "inn way."

BATHROOMS

Almost all the overnight accommodations recommended in this book have an en suite bathroom for each bedroom. Some inns will offer guestrooms that share a bath with other guestrooms, or rooms that have private baths down the hall. We point out in the inn description if each guestroom does NOT have a private bathroom. We do not specify whether the bath is equipped with shower, tub-shower, tub, or Jacuzzi, so inquire what the term "with bathroom" means when making your reservation.

BREAKFAST

A trademark of many inns is their morning repast—many cookbooks have been authored by innkeepers. Breakfast is almost always included in the room rate, but we definitely mention if it is NOT. Although innkeepers take great pride in their delectable morning offerings, know that breakfast can range from a gourmet "waddle-away" feast to muffins and coffee. Sometimes breakfast is a Continental in the privacy of your room or a hot breakfast with others in the dining room. Breakfast times vary—some innkeepers serve a hot breakfast at a specified time, while others replenish a buffet on a more leisurely schedule. Breakfasts are as individual as the inns themselves.

CANCELLATION POLICIES

Hotels and inns have different policies for cancellation based on the fact that most hotels accommodate many corporate business travelers whose plans often change on short notice. Some hotels are now beginning to make a charge of $25 or more if the guest departs earlier than the date given at the time the reservation was made. Although policies vary, inns, by definition, have only a few rooms and when a reservation is made, the owner/innkeeper counts on receiving that revenue. Most inns usually require you to cancel at least a week in advance of the arrival date and some inns charge a small fee if the reservation is canceled in order to cover their administrative costs. If you cancel within a specified number of days prior to your planned arrival, you may be required to pay for the first night if the room cannot be re-rented. Some inns have even more stringent policies, so be sure to enquire about them at the time you make your reservation.

CHECK-IN

Inns are usually very specific about check-in time—generally between 3 and 6 pm. Let the inn know if you are going to arrive late and the innkeeper will make special arrangements for you, such as leaving you a door key under a potted plant along with a note on how to find your room. Also, for those who might arrive early, note that some inns close their doors between check-out and check-in times. Inns are frequently staffed only by the owners themselves and that window of time between check-out and check-in is often the one opportunity to shop for those wonderful breakfasts they prepare in addition to running their own personal errands.

CHILDREN

Many places in this guide do not welcome children. Inns cannot legally refuse accommodation to children but, as parents, we really want to stay where our children are genuinely welcome, so ask when making reservations. In the inn descriptions on our website (*www.karenbrown.com*) we have an icon that indicates at what age children are welcome.

COMFORT

Comfort plays a deciding role in the selection of inns and hotels recommended. Firm mattresses, a quiet setting, good lighting, fresh towels, scrubbed bathrooms—we do our best to remember the basics when considering our recommendations. The charming decor and innkeeper will soon be forgotten if you do not enjoy a good night's sleep and comfortable stay. Be aware, however, that some inns in areas with hot summers do not always have the luxury of air conditioning, especially those in older buildings. Air conditioning is a standard feature of most hotels.

CREDIT CARDS

Whether or not an establishment accepts credit cards is indicated at the bottom of each description by the symbol ▭. Even if an inn does not accept credit card payment, it will perhaps request your account number as a guarantee of arrival.

CRITERIA FOR SELECTION

It is very important to us that an inn or a hotel has charm—ideally the property should be appealing, perhaps in an historic building, beautifully decorated, lovingly managed, and in a wonderful location. Few inns or hotels meet every criterion, but all our selections have something that makes them special and are situated in enjoyable surroundings—we have had to reject several lovely inns because of a poor location. Many are in historic buildings, but remember that the definition of "historic" may depend on the century in which the state came into being. Many inns are newly constructed and may be in buildings built to look old. Small inns are usually our favorites, but size alone did not dictate whether or not a hostelry was chosen. Most are small but sometimes the only place to stay in a "must-visit" area is a splendid hotel of great character and charm. We have tried to include properties with a variety of size, decor, and ambiance to suit a variety of tastes and pocketbooks.

FOOD

The majority of places featured in this guide do not have restaurants but usually there are restaurants close by. Almost all of the inns include breakfast in the tariff: quite often a sumptuous one. Frequently, in addition to breakfast, tea or wine and hors d'oeuvres are served in the afternoon. Sometimes, if you request in advance, a picnic lunch can also be prepared. If you have any special dietary requirements, most innkeepers will gladly try to accommodate your needs. It is best to mention any special requests at the time of making your reservation both as a courtesy and from a practical point of view so that the innkeeper can have on hand any special items that you might need.

ICONS

We have introduced these icons in the guidebooks and there are more on our website, *www.karenbrown.com*. ❋ Air conditioning in rooms, ⬆ Beach nearby, � Breakfast included in room rate, ✎ Children welcome, ⚱ Cooking classes offered, CREDIT Credit cards accepted, ☎ Direct-dial telephone in room, 🐕 Dogs by special request, 🛗 Elevator, 🏋 Exercise room, 🔥 Fireplaces in some bedrooms, ⵖ Mini-refrigerator in rooms, P Parking available, 🍴 Restaurant, ⊘ Some non-smoking rooms, ⚘ Spa, ≈ Swimming pool, 🎾 Tennis, 🖼 Television with English channels, ⚭ Wedding facilities, ♿ Wheelchair friendly, 🏌 Golf course nearby, 🚶 Hiking trails nearby, 🐎 Horseback riding nearby, ⛷ Skiing nearby, 🏊 Water sports nearby, 🍷 Wineries nearby.

Icons allow us to provide additional information about our recommended properties. When using our website to supplement the guides, positioning the cursor over an icon will in many cases give you further details. For easy reference an icon key can be found on the last page of the book.

PROFESSIONALISM

The inns and hotels we have selected are run by professionals. There are many homes that rent out extra bedrooms to paying guests but this was not what we were looking for and they are not included in our guide. We have recommended only inns that have privacy for the guests and where you do not have to climb over family clutter to reach the bathroom.

RESERVATIONS

The best way to make a reservation is changing. We used to just pick up the phone and call but with the advent of the worldwide web, it is now possible to view many properties, including the bedrooms, "on line" and then make a reservation electronically. Phoning is still a good way to discuss the various differences in available accommodation and the inn's policies. Please try not to call during breakfast hours. Also, inns are often homes, so late-night calls are not appreciated. Another convenient and efficient way to request a reservation is by fax: if the inn has a fax, we have noted the number after the telephone number. Be aware that the majority of inns in this guide require a two-night stay on weekends and over holidays.

RESPONSIBILITY

Our goal is to outline itineraries in regions that we consider of prime interest to our readers and to recommend inns and hotels that we think are outstanding. All of the inns or hotels featured have been visited and selected solely on their merits. Our judgments are made on the charm of the property, its setting, cleanliness, and, above all, the warmth of welcome. Each has its own appeal, and we try to present you with a very honest appraisal. However, no matter how careful we are, sometimes we misjudge a property's merits, or the ownership changes, or unfortunately sometimes standards are not maintained. If you find an inn or hotel is not as we have indicated, please let us know, and accept our sincere apologies.

ROOM RATES

It seems that many inns and hotels play musical rates, with high-season, low-season, midweek, weekend, and holiday rates. We have quoted the projected 2007 high-season, general range of rates for two people, from the lowest-priced bedroom (singles usually receive a very small discount) to the most expensive suite, including breakfast. The rates given are those quoted to us. Please use these figures as a guideline and be certain to ask at the time of booking what the rates are and what they include. We have not given prices for "special" rooms such as those that can accommodate three people traveling together. Discuss with the reservation desk rooms and rates available before making your selection. Of course, several inns and hotels are exceptions to our guidelines and whenever this is the case we mention the special situation (such as breakfast not being included in the rate). Please be aware that local tourist taxes are not included in the rates quoted and can be very high—frequently around 10%.

SMOKING

Most inns and hotels have extremely strict non-smoking policies. A few permit smoking in restricted public areas or outside, but in general it is best to assume that smoking is not appropriate. If smoking is of great concern, be sure to ask the inn or hotel specifically as to their policy about smoking in the garden, on the deck, or in a specially designated public area.

SOCIALIZING

In this Mid-Atlantic guide we have included both inns and hotels and socializing ranges from being one of the family to sharing an organized cocktail hour. Breakfast in inns may be served at a set time when the guests gather around the dining-room table or it may be served buffet-style over several hours where guests have the option of either sitting down to eat alone or joining other guests at a larger table. Breakfast in hotels is generally available for several hours and you sit at your own table. Some inns or hotels will bring a breakfast tray to your room, while some inns serve breakfast only in the dining room. After check-in, many inns and some hotels offer afternoon refreshment, such as tea and cakes or wine and hors d'oeuvres, which may be seen as another social opportunity.

Some inns and hotels set out the refreshments buffet style where guests are invited to meander in and out, mixing or not mixing with other guests as they choose, and then others orchestrate a more structured gathering, often a social hour, with the hotelier presiding. Choose the property that seems to offer the degree of privacy that you desire.

WEBSITE

Please supplement this book by looking at the information provided on our Karen Brown Website (*www.karenbrown.com*), which serves as an added dimension to our guides. Most of our favorite inns are featured on the site (web participation is an inn's choice) and on their web page you can usually link to their email so that making a reservation is a breeze. Also featured on our site are comments, feedback, and discoveries from you, our readers; information on our latest finds; post-press updates; contest drawings for free books; special offers; unique features such as recipes and favorite destinations; and special savings offered by certain inns.

WHEELCHAIR ACCESSIBILITY

If an inn has *at least* one guestroom that is accessible by wheelchair, it is noted with the symbol ♿. This is not the same as saying it meets full ADA standards.

Elfreth's Alley, Philadelphia

Introduction—About Inn Travel

New York, New York!
It's a Wonderful Town

New York is much more than wonderful: it's an experience—there's none other like it, and you must not miss it. It's the energy of New York that clothes every moment of every day, with buildings that soar toward the stars and buildings that echo a city's history, museums as fine as they come, hotels fit for a king or small, quiet and intensely personal, restaurants of unsurpassed quality and cafés for coffee, shops of great treasures and tiny trinkets, music of symphonies and single voices, theater for every interest, and sports activities of every description—all set in broad avenues and the narrow streets of its villages, in grand parks and quiet corners. All of this is New York, and it is all so special that any visitor to the Mid-Atlantic States not familiar with its wonders must include at least a taste from its great menu.

The Statue of Liberty

The history of New York dates back to the days of tribes of Indians—long before George Washington—but it's the 19th, 20th, and 21st centuries that have given it the reputation that it enjoys today. New York City, often thought of as the capital of America, has been at the center of the country's economic and cultural life, made all the more dynamic by the city's size, its ethnic diversity, and a population more than double that of any other American town. It's situated much like a keyhole to a house, opening directly to the Mid-Atlantic States and, more importantly, to all of the United States.

Suggested Pacing: Travelers need to focus, just like a camera, on those parts of New York of interest to them and those to be left out of the picture. Itineraries can be built to focus on its historical background, on its arts, on its museums, or on the resources that know no end. The first-time visitor to New York, in my opinion, needs to taste a little of all that's there and for this a three-day visit will probably be enough. New York is nicely divided into areas surrounding its core of Mid-Town and from this center one can attend theater and musical concerts of every type, visit museums and go shopping, travel to the heart of the financial district, and eat beyond all imagination.

Getting to New York is easy, for air, rail, and bus transportation all come together in or just outside the city. The three major airports—LaGuardia and John F. Kennedy just to the east, and Newark a few miles away in New Jersey—provide the entry points for most of the city's visitors but there is also good railroad access from the north, the south, and the west.

Once you're in New York, getting around the city is easy since there are bus and subway public transportation systems, taxis, and cars (the latter being the most expensive and cumbersome). There are sightseeing tours on double-decker buses and tourist trolleys—a wonderful way to see New York either from on high or on an old-fashioned trolley. If you're lucky enough to be touring in the area of Central Park and some of the surrounding areas, perhaps even in the area of Times Square, there could be nothing more romantic than a horse-drawn carriage.

For many, one of best ways to begin to appreciate all that New York City has to offer is to take a **Circle Line Cruise** around the island of Manhattan. These regularly scheduled cruises last three hours and narrative is provided as you cruise by the many interesting and historical sights. Cruises depart from the terminal located at Pier 83 on 12th Avenue, just north of 42nd Street. (212-563-3200)

The skyline of New York is one of its major attractions and highlights. While visiting the city, try to find some vantage point from which to see the magnificent buildings silhouetted against the sky.

For the traveler, touring New York City is best and most easily done by deciding which of the many types of attractions are of the greatest interest and organizing the days visiting those attractions in the Mid-Town, Downtown, and Uptown areas of Manhattan. Mid-Town is generally described as the area between 34th and 59th Streets between Broadway and 1st Avenue; Downtown as the area below 34th, and Uptown as that part of Manhattan above 59th Street. There is such a wealth of things to do that the abundance will be your friend and time to see it all, your enemy.

Arguably, there are more sights and things to do in Mid-Town than either Downtown or Uptown. Travelers often find that they spend all their time in the Mid-Town area, which more than satiates the normal areas of interest—though your special interest might well lie in yet another part of the city.

MID-TOWN

This area of New York City is popular with tourists for its concentration of cultural and architectural attractions, shopping, and restaurants. Walk as much as you can, on any one of its many wonderful avenues between 34th and 59th Streets—Fifth Avenue with its glorious and world-famous shops; Madison Avenue with its galleries and boutiques; Park Avenue with its flower-planted median and great residential and commercial buildings; and Sixth Avenue (also known as the Avenue of the Americas). Crossing them all are 42nd and 57th Streets, the most major of all the cross-town streets in the Mid-Town area.

Empire State Building: Built in the first half of the 20th century, an architectural statement, with an observatory and a view that you won't want to miss unless you're not big on heights. (350 Fifth Avenue between 33rd and 34th Streets, 212-736-3100.)

New York Public Library: The marble lions in front are only the beginning of things of interest in this building, which houses some of the most famous and rare historical documents of our history. One-hour guided tours available. (476 Fifth Avenue between 40th and 42nd Streets, 212-661-7220.)

Ice Skating at Rockefeller Center

Rockefeller Center:
A commercial and retail complex of many buildings with gardens and water fountains and in the holiday season the site of a spectacular Christmas tree and skating rink (a restaurant at other times of the year). (Located between 48th and 51st Streets and Fifth and Sixth Avenues.)

General Electric Building:
Architecturally one of the best of the Rockefeller Center buildings. Home of the Rainbow Room restaurant on the 65th floor. (570 Lexington Ave, SW corner of 51st Street, 30 Rockefeller Plaza.)

Museum of Modern Art:
For those interested in the modern arts of painting, sculpture, photography, etc., there is no better museum anywhere in the world. (11 West 53rd Street, 212-708-9400.)

United Nations: One of the most important international organizations of our world. A great place to visit, to tour, and to be humbled. 45-minute guided tour only, no children under 5. (First Avenue, between 42nd and 48th Streets, 212-963-8687.)

Radio City Music Hall: A great tourist attraction with movies, and stage shows featuring the famous Rockettes. One-hour guided tour available. (1260 Avenue of the Americas, between 50th and 51st Streets, 212-247-4777.)

St. Patrick's Cathedral: New York's first and foremost Roman Catholic Cathedral, itself an architectural gem not to be missed by those with an interest in this area. (Fifth Avenue between 50th and 51st Streets, 212-753-2261.)

NBC Studios: One-hour guided tours of the National Broadcasting Company studios, located at the Rockefeller Center. (5th Ave., between 51st and 54th Sts, 212-664-4444.)

Grand Central Terminal: This major transportation complex is an architectural masterpiece in the Beaux Arts style. (Park Avenue and 42nd Street.)

Chrysler Building: Another of New York's architectural gems in the art deco style. Towering at 1045 feet, it was the tallest building in New York when it was constructed in 1930. (405 Lexington Avenue and 42nd Street.)

Theater District: The heart of the city's theater on Broadway from 40th to 53rd Streets.

Times Square: In the heart of the Theater District; best known for its lighted billboards at night.

UPTOWN

Within the area known as Uptown is the Upper East Side; Fifth Avenue, Madison Avenue, Park Avenue, and Lexington Avenue—each are different in character. Within this area you will find magnificent homes, the most fashionable boutiques, galleries of antiques and art, and commercial hotels and corporations. Highlights of this area are detailed on the following page.

Central Park: A spectacular swath of green comprising some 843 acres located between 59th and 110th Streets and between Fifth Avenue and Central Park West. Within the park are ponds, lakes, trails for hiking, biking, and horseback riding, carriage rides, and an ice-skating rink (used for roller skating in the summer).

Lincoln Center: This complex of five theater and concert buildings is the site of performances of music, drama, and dance. One-hour guided tours of performance halls only—reservations recommended. (Tours start at concourse level of Metropolitan Opera House.) (Between West 62nd and 65th Streets, and Columbus and Amsterdam Avenues, 212-875-5350.)

MUSEUMS

There can hardly be another city in the world with as many or such prestigious museums: an entire visit to New York can be built around visiting these.

Whitney Museum of Art: A museum focused on contemporary artists. (945 Madison Avenue, at 75th Street, 212-570-3676.)

Metropolitan Museum of Art: The largest museum in the western world houses more than one can conceive. Among the highlights are the American Wing and the collection of Impressionists and Post-Impressionists. (Fifth Avenue, from 80th to 84th Streets, 212-535-7710.)

The Frick Collection: A personal favorite, this museum is actually a 40-room mansion within whose walls you find art objects of every description. No children under 10. (1 East 70th Street at 5th Avenue, 212-288-0700.)

American Museum of Natural History: A monumental museum focusing on all aspects of natural history, a fabulous museum for children. (Central Park West, between 77th and 81st Streets, 212-769-5100.)

Solomon R. Guggenheim Museum: Housed in a building design by architect Frank Lloyd Wright, this building is as interesting for its architecture as for its art. Guided tours available. (1071 Fifth Avenue between 88th and 89th Streets, 212-423-3500.)

Museum of the City of New York: The history of the city of New York. (Fifth Avenue and 103rd Street, 212-534-1672.)

Cooper-Hewitt National Design Museum: A museum devoted to the decorative arts. (2 East 91st Street at Fifth Avenue, 212-849-8300.)

The Jewish Museum: A collection of Judaica spanning 4,000 years. (1109 Fifth Avenue, 212-423-3200.)

Museum of American Folk Art: The best of all forms of American folk art. (2 Lincoln Square between West 65th and 66th Streets, 212-977-7298.)

If you can tear yourself away from the museums, be sure to visit the **Cathedral of St. John the Divine**, a Gothic-style cathedral of enormous proportions, the seat of the Episcopal Diocese of New York. (West 112th Street and Amsterdam Avenue, 212-316-7540.)

DOWNTOWN

Lower Manhattan, also known as Downtown, goes all the way from 34th Street down to Battery Park, the lower tip of Manhattan.

The city's, and for that matter the world's, financial district is in this area. While **Wall Street** is most well known, there are many historical buildings dating back to the Dutch settlement of the 17th century that make this area particularly charming for those interested in architecture and the history of early New York. Unlike the Mid-Town and Uptown areas of New York where the streets more or less run in an orderly fashion and perpendicular to one another, one of the special charms of lower Manhattan is that the streets are narrow and winding and it's not difficult to imagine the life, the times, and the people of a much earlier century in the city's history. What's particularly fascinating is the contrast between the towering skyscrapers and the quaint old buildings tucked in amongst them.

Within the Financial District, below Chambers Drive and between West Street and FDR Drive, there are many sights to see, among them:

New York Stock Exchange: The site of trading shares in the world's corporations. Free tickets for same-day visits at the visitors' center at 20 Broad Street. (8–18 Broad Street, 212-656-3000.)

Trinity Church: Built in the 19th century in the Gothic Revival style with a towering spire and massive bronze doors. 45-minute guided tour available. (Broadway at Wall Street, 74 Trinity Place, 212-602-0800.)

South Street Seaport: Site of many of the early buildings in the seaport of the 19th century, including the Seaport Museum and the Fulton Fish Market (viewing the latter is a very early-morning experience, usually before dawn). (12 Fulton Street.)

Fraunces Tavern: The site of George Washington's farewell address to his troops, now a tavern and a museum. (54 Pearl Street, 212-425-1778.)

New York, New York!

Civic Center: The civic center, the site of the city's government, is located just north of the financial district. Within the area are many interesting and historical buildings.

City Hall: An early-19th-century building of magnificence. (City Hall Park.)

Woolworth Building: Built in 1913 and the world's tallest building at 792 feet, until the completion of the Chrysler Building in 1930, this is a monumental design of architecture. (233 Broadway at Barclay Street, between Park Place and Barclay Streets.)

Brooklyn Bridge

St. Paul's Chapel: An 18th-century Georgian building of great design. 40-minute guided tours available. (Broadway between Fulton and Vesey Streets, 212-602-0874.)

Brooklyn Bridge: Built in the 19th century, the Brooklyn Bridge is one of the most wonderful architectural statements in all of New York's history. Walking across this bridge is one of the real treats of a visit to New York.

OTHER AREAS OF INTEREST IN THE DOWNTOWN AREA INCLUDE:

Chinatown: The neighborhood of Canal, Mott, Bayard, and Pell Streets—the home of many of the Asians resident in New York and a colorful and fun place to visit.

Little Italy: North of Chinatown, between Canal and Houston Streets. A lively area of neighborhood shops and cafés.

Soho and Greenwich Village: An area south of Houston Street of great charm, great streets, shops to explore, artists, clothing, cafés, and coffee houses. Be sure to visit Washington Square, one of New York's special parks and places to absorb the atmosphere around you.

THE BOROUGHS

Outside the usual tourist areas of interest, there are additional sights well worth time if that is available or if your interest is so sparked. These would include in the **Bronx**, the **Bronx Zoo**, the largest urban wildlife park in the United States (Bronx River Parkway at Fordham Road, 718-367-1010), and the **New York Botanical Garden** (200th Street and Southern Boulevard, 718-817-8700).

In the borough of **Brooklyn**, most easily reached by subway from any location in Manhattan, is **Brooklyn Heights**. This is now a very popular residential area for those who work in Manhattan. Along the harbor the views of lower Manhattan are absolutely breathtaking. Brooklyn is also home to the **Brooklyn Museum** with its outstanding collection of Egyptian artifacts (200 Eastern Parkway at Washington Avenue, 718-638-5000) and the **Brooklyn Botanic Garden** (1000 Washington Avenue, 718-623-7200).

The borough of **Staten Island** is reached by taking the Staten Island Ferry (718-815-2628), from which you have spectacular views of the **Statue of Liberty** and the Manhattan skyline.

From the Statue of Liberty, hop on the next ferry to **Ellis Island**. Ellis Island is one of the highlights of New York—a *must see* for all visitors to New York. More than 12 million immigrants between 1892 and 1954 came to the United States in search of freedom and economic opportunity. It is mind boggling to comprehend that 40% of Americans can trace their heritage to someone (often a child) that waited in line in the great Registry Room for their chance to clear customs and be accepted into the land of their dreams. How brave these people were to sacrifice so much to come to the land of freedom in hopes of building a better life for their family.

Allow many hours to see this museum which has 200,000 square feet of exhibit space. There are two theaters and the best way to get oriented is to begin your tour by seeing the documentary film, "Island of Hope, Island of Tears." Rent an audio headset before beginning your tour so that you will understand what you are seeing. Along with explanations of some of the history of the immigration, there are poignant immigrants' narratives giving first-hand stories (often in very broken English) of their experience entering America.

As you walk through the museum, you frequently see people standing in front of a display with tears quietly running down their cheeks—it is quite obvious they are identifying the photographs of some of their ancestors who made the arduous, all too frequently dangerous, journey from their homeland to America. However, even if you are not directly associated with any of these courageous immigrants, you cannot help but be moved by what you see and very proud to be an American.

Both Ellis Island and the Statue of Liberty (which is on a nearby island) are part of the National Park Service and, as usual, the park service does a brilliant presentation. The official agent for the tours to Ellis Island and the Statue of Liberty is the Circle Line–Statue of Liberty Ferry, Inc. The ferries depart from Battery Park, which is located at the southern tip of Manhattan Island. Because parking is expensive, it is best to go to the dock by public transportation or a taxi.

To enter the monument you need to have a time pass. Some are issued at the ferry ticket office on a first come, first served basis, but it is best to reserve in advance both for time passes and ferry tickets by calling the ferry company at 855-782-8834 or 212-269-5755. No matter whether you have tickets or not, the boarding of the ferry is on a first-come first-served basis. We highly recommend taking the first ferry of the day, which leaves

Battery Park at 8:30 am. It is recommended that you be at the ferry dock a minimum of 45 minutes prior to the departure. You will have to wait in line for the ticket office to open, but as the day progresses the line gets longer and longer. (If you take a later tour, it is recommended that you be at the dock two hours in advance.) There is very tight security. When you pick up your ferry tickets, you will need a credit card and photo ID; then before boarding the ferry, you need to go through a security check similar to that at an airport.

Buy the ferry ticket that includes both the Statue of Liberty and Ellis Island. The parks are open daily except December 25. The parks are open from 8:45 am to 6 pm. The first stop is at the Statue of Liberty, which is perched on a 12-acre piece of land. Not surprisingly, the security here is exceptionally tight. After September 11, the statue was closed and didn't reopen until December 2001. You cannot climb up to the top of the statue (again due to security concerns) but you can view inside the statue through a glass ceiling. There are park rangers there to give tours that are about 30 minutes long.

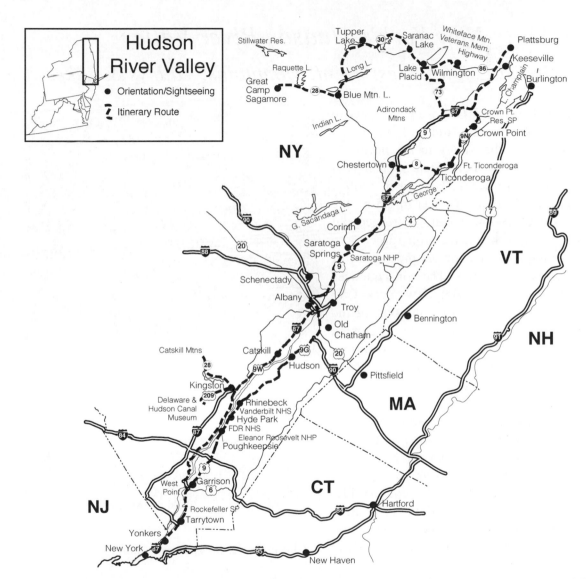

Hudson
River Valley

● Orientation/Sightseeing

⌇ Itinerary Route

Stillwater Res.

Raquette L.

Tupper Lake

30

Saranac Lake

Whiteface Mtn. Veterans Mem. Highway

Plattsburg

Keeseville

Great Camp Sagamore

28

Blue Mtn. L.

Lake Placid

Wilmington

86

Burlington

L. Champlain

Indian L.

Adirondack Mtns

73

87

Crown Pt. Res. SP

Crown Point

NY

9

9N

Chestertown

8

Ft. Ticonderoga

Ticonderoga

87

L. George

4

7

89

90

G. Sacandaga L.

Corinth

VT

20

88

20

Saratoga Springs

9

Saratoga NHP

Schenectady

Albany

Troy

87

Old Chatham

Bennington

91

NH

Catskill Mtns

28

Catskill

9G

20

90

9W

Hudson

Pittsfield

Kingston

209

MA

Delaware & Hudson Canal Museum

84

87

Rhinebeck
Vanderbilt NHS
Hyde Park
FDR NHS
Eleanor Roosevelt NHP
Poughkeepsie

9

Garrison

West Point

6

CT

Rockefeller SP

Tarrytown

Hartford

84

NJ

Yonkers

New York

87

95

New Haven

25

New York's Hudson River Valley
Grand Estates, West Point, Mountains, Valleys & Lakes

Just as New York City is the gateway to the country, so the Hudson River is the gateway up the valley to the northeast sector of New York State. When first discovered by Henry Hudson in 1609 it was thought that this river might be the way to China but when that turned out to be a false hope, the river turned into a strategic means for the movement of supplies and armies. The consequences of this were twofold: New York City became the foremost trading port of the nation and the Hudson Valley became a vital part of the Industrial Revolution. One of the loveliest itineraries in New York State follows this river north from the city of New York or from any of the airports that serve the greater New York metropolis. Wherever you start from, the pace and the frenzy of New York City quickly evaporates as you begin to feel the tranquility of the countryside, see the green trees, and visit the bedroom communities where the commuting executives of the great city sleep

Looking across the Hudson to Storm King Mountain

between their mega-transactions. The attractions along both banks of the Hudson reflect many of the significant events and people in America's history—visiting them will give you insight into their lives and their many accomplishments as leading statesmen. Many of the more interesting historical places to pause at along the way are south of Albany, the state capital, while much of the state's natural beauty is found in its mountainous regions—the Catskills and the Adirondacks.

Recommended Pacing: The routing for this itinerary is outlined on Map 3 at the front of the book. The itinerary's pace could be leisurely, with probably two days of driving interrupted by a further two to four days of seeing the sights along the way, depending on your particular interests. When you reach the Adirondacks, you can then continue north into Canada and the city of Montreal; travel west along the St. Lawrence Seaway; and return by the fastest route, the New York State Thruway, to New York City and its airports. If your interest in antiquing is passionate, you can wander to the east just over the borders into Massachusetts and Connecticut and follow Route 7 from town to town and shop to shop (with *The Green Guide to Antiquing in New England* in hand, of course). If you elect to follow the latter path, you should add another day to your itinerary.

There are many routes northward and your choice depends on the time you have available and your destination. The New York State Thruway (I-87) most quickly moves you upward toward Albany; the Palisades Interstate Parkway and Route 9W follow the west side of the Hudson River; the Henry Hudson Parkway and Route 9 lead you along the eastern bank of the Hudson; and the Saw Mill River and Taconic State Parkways provide you the most scenic and winding route on the east side. The Saw Mill River and Taconic State Parkways were designed years ago when cars did not go so fast, when travel was more to be enjoyed than to be completed quickly, and when there was great appreciation for the plantings of trees and shrubs which in and of themselves made a trip on these parkways so pleasurable.

Whichever route you choose to follow, you'll find rolling countryside with farms, charming towns, and great inns for an overnight stay. To the west are the Catskill Mountains with their resorts attracting honeymooners into heart-shaped spa tubs, and to the east lie the Taconic Mountains with their beauty most especially striking in the autumn when trees color and leaves fall to the ground.

A good start to this adventure on the Hudson would be to follow the signs for the Saw Mill River Parkway north from New York City. (For sightseeing suggestions in New York City, see the section beginning on page 13.) In no time at all you will arrive in **Yonkers** and **Sunnyside**, the home of author **Washington Irving**, whose contributions to American writing include the stories of Rip van Winkle and Ichabod Crane. The tales he wove of life in Sleepy Hollow country and the home he built here are part of the history of this area. His home contains elements of Scottish, Dutch, and Spanish influence, reflecting his travels around the world. (Sunnyside: 914-591-8763.) Nearby in **Tarrytown** (take the I-87 exit from the Saw Mill River Parkway to Route 9) is a Gothic Revival castle with turrets and towers called **Lyndhurst**, designed by architect Alexander Jackson Davis whose reputation for design of this style made him famous in his time. This home, run by the National Trust for Historic Preservation, is worth a visit to see the several Tiffany windows, elaborately decorated rooms, art, and landscaped gardens. (914-631-4481)

An hour north of the city and not far from Lyndhurst is yet another National Trust property, **Kykuit**, the most famous of several homes built by the Rockefeller family along the Hudson. It too is located on Route 9, north of I-87 by 2 miles. The original house, built for John D. Rockefeller, has been modified into the grand home that exists today. Nelson Rockefeller was its resident at a time when his interest in art, particularly modern art, came to the fore and the house has famous paintings by the most important of the modern artists. The collection of outdoor sculpture on the grounds of the estate enhances the landscaping and the views across the Hudson River. (914-631-9491)

Another of the attractions of Route 9, just north of Kykuit, is the **Union Church of Pocantico Hills**, which contains the only set of stained-glass windows created by Mark Chagall for an American church. The rose window was designed and created by Henry Matisse. (914-332-6659)

Farther north, in **Garrison-on-Hudson** there is an example of the finest of American Federal architecture, interiors, and furniture—**Boscobel**, whose contents have been meticulously assembled to show the influence of the period of the Adam style. Of particular note is the freestanding stairway in the front hall—the grace of this architectural detail sets the tone for the rest of this lovely home. (845-265-3638)

Continuing north on Route 9, in **Hyde Park** you come to the **home** of **Franklin Roosevelt** and the **FDR Library**, which contains the papers and mementos of his presidency and his collection of books on naval history (800-337-8474). Here also is **Valkill Cottage**, the home to which **Eleanor Roosevelt** moved after the death of her husband (845-229-9422).

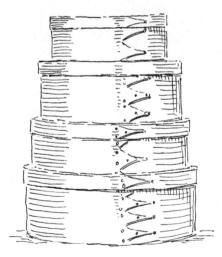

In Hyde Park you also find the **Vanderbilt National Historical Site**, a 50-room Beaux-Arts mansion displaying the wealth and elegance of life at the end of the 19th century. This is a mansion of incredible opulence and reflects the lifestyle of the times when the privileged classes entertained in a grand way. (845-229-7770)

On Route 9G in **Hudson** you come to the **Olana State Historical Site**. This mansion bears much of the style and feeling of Sunnyside and has within its walls many paintings by Frederic Edwin Church, the original owner, who in its construction was influenced by the places he and his wife had visited in their worldwide travels. (518-828-0135)

Farther north, on I-90 east of the river in **Old Chatham** (exit B2), is the **Shaker Museum and Library**, an exceptional museum reflecting a way of life and a style of living. This museum houses the largest collection of all things Shaker displayed in several different buildings. After the days of Victoriana the Shaker lifestyle was much simpler, as is reflected in the design of furniture, working tools, and textiles. (518-794-9100)

On Route 9W on the west bank of the Hudson River you find yet another series of interesting historical places to visit. If you have started your journey up the east side of the river, you can join up with Route 9W by crossing over to the west bank on the Bear Mountain Bridge, 5 miles north of Peekskill. Traveling north, you come to **West Point Military Academy** on its spectacular site with views of and across the Hudson. West Point was established as a fort in 1778 and not until 1802 did it become a training academy for the army. (For tours, call: 845-446-4724.) A **visitors' center** explains the history of West Point and offers tours of the Cadet Chapel (845-938-2638), Fort Putnam, the military museum, and various monuments, all of which are worth seeing.

The **Catskill Mountains** are one of the diversions to which many are attracted while following the Hudson River Valley. The Catskills are easily reached from New York City and since 1900 this has been the area to which New Yorkers have come to escape the heat of the city. The heyday of the Catskills was in the period from 1920 to 1970. Many of the major resorts that were so popular then have closed in favor of smaller hotels but some still carry on with traditions established decades ago. Among the things to do in the area is to climb to the site of the **Catskill Mountain House**, long since gone, from where you can enjoy incredible vistas made famous by artists of the 19th century. This is an area of many vacation homes and much recreational activity of every form including swimming, boating, rafting, skiing, golfing, bicycling, fishing, horseback riding, and snowmobiling. This is also a great area for climbing and many of the trails have been in use for more than 150 years. A visit to the Catskills can be just a few hours' diversion on the way north or you can make it into an overnight stay.

Entrance to the Catskills, an area of great beauty, is through the town of **Kingston**, which sits on the west bank at the edge of the Hudson River and the Catskills. With the town dating back to the 17th century, there is much to be enjoyed in strolling through the historic district—many of the old houses built of stone can still be seen. From Route 9W in Kingston take Route 28 into these mountains and explore the winding roads and beautiful scenery.

While in the area, consider taking the time to travel south and west of Kingston to visit the **Delaware and Hudson Canal Museum**, 17 miles away via Route 209 south and Route 213 east. This small museum recounts the history of the canal and its role in hauling coal from Pennsylvania. There is a walking path along the now dried-up canal and locks. (845-687-9311)

Albany, the state capital, sits on the Hudson River in central New York and was in its earliest years the gateway to western New York, traveling the Erie Canal to the Great Lakes. The **Capitol Building** looks for all the world like a château and the grand and large plazas in front of it serve all the more to reinforce its grand image. (518-474-2418)

North of Albany and easily accessible from I-87 (the New York State Thruway) is the town of **Saratoga Springs**, a town of Victorian homes with wide wraparound front porches and great character. Between 1865 and 1900 Saratoga Springs was the summer resort to which all the "right" people made journeys. With its large hotels and a race track, this was a place of great entertaining and sport but perhaps it was best known for its healing mineral-water baths. The old casino closed in 1907 and with it a change took place in life in Saratoga Springs. Now this is a place to come to enjoy its shops, antique stores, and the numerous bed and breakfasts that have replaced of many of the large hotels. There are 900 buildings on the National Register of Historic Places here and you can obtain information on locations and self-guided walking tours at the **Saratoga Springs Visitor's Center & Heritage Area** (518-587-3241).

The **National Museum of Racing and Hall of Fame** with its collections of the highlights of the world of horses is a mecca for those interested in thoroughbred horse racing. Information about the town is available at 518-584-0400.

Other attractions in Saratoga Springs include the **National Museum of Dance**, the country's only museum devoted to dance (518-584-2225); the **Saratoga National Historical Park**, which focuses on the battles in the late 18th century between the French and the Americans (518-664-9821); and the **Hyde Collection** with its exquisite collection of paintings by such well-known artists as Botticelli, da Vinci, Rubens, Rembrandt, El Greco, Renoir, Van Gogh, and Picasso (518-792-1761).

The collection of paintings is housed in an Italian Renaissance villa built in 1912 where a central courtyard of sculpture and plants is particularly attractive. If you are an opera buff, you may want to visit the **Marcella Sembrich Memorial Studio** where mementos of her coloratura soprano career in Europe and the United States are displayed. (518-644-9839)

The **Adirondacks**, only a little north of Saratoga Springs and accessed easily from I-87, are without doubt a very special part of New York State. Located in the northeast corner of the state and covering more than 6 million acres, the Adirondacks offer travelers the opportunity to enjoy the mountainous terrain and to participate in all the sports that mountain and water alike make possible. About the size of New Hampshire, they are larger than the national parks of Yellowstone, Grand Canyon, and Yosemite combined, encompassing more than 4,000 lakes, ponds, swamps and bogs, 2,000 mountainous peaks, and 21,000 miles of rivers, streams, and brooks. This is an area of great scenic beauty—there is nothing like having a day to quietly explore the winding ways of this part of the Mid-Atlantic. Much can be enjoyed as you drive within the Adirondacks but there is also much more to be experienced if you can take the time to hike the mountains, follow a trail through the woods, or enjoy water sports on the lovely clear lakes.

In the early 1930s the Adirondacks became famous when **Lake Placid**, reached by taking Route 73 from I-87 north (the New York State Thruway), hosted the Winter Olympics, as it did again in 1980. The **Olympic Stadium**, with its four ice-skating rinks, is available for touring by appointment (518-523-1655 or 800-462-6236). As well as offering a variety of sports activities, the village of Lake Placid (actually on Mirror Lake) is today a very upscale place for shopping and eating in great restaurants.

Among the various things you might do while visiting in the area would be to drive the **Whiteface Mountain Veterans Memorial Highway**, open sometime between mid-May and June depending on the melting of the winter snow. To reach this highway take Route 86 in Lake Placid to Route 431 at Wilmington—follow the signs for 3 miles to the tollbooth.

Whiteface Mountain Veterans Memorial Highway is a two-lane highway leading to one of the peaks, from which on a clear day you can see for 110 miles from Lake Placid itself to Lake Champlain. (518-946-2223)

In the village of **Blue Mountain Lake**, at the junction of Routes 28 and 30, is the **Adirondacks Museum**, a compound of buildings, galleries, and exhibit halls, which is thought of as the Smithsonian Museum of the Adirondacks. It is unfortunately open only from Memorial Day to mid-October but it is well worth a visit to see the boat museum, homes built in the finest Adirondack style of architecture, the 1907 schoolhouse, exhibits on logging and mining, and the art museum. The Road and Transportation Building is especially impressive with its 45,000 square feet of exhibit space displaying sleighs, buggies, wagons, and a private Pullman car. Outside, you can tour a 1900 steam engine and passenger car. (518-352-7311)

Seasonally available for the visitor is **Great Camp Sagamore**, summer home of the Vanderbilt family, which was once able to provide accommodations for more than 100 guests. Today it is a National Historic Site and guided tours are provided. The camp is located 4 miles south of the town of Raquette Lake, off Route 28 and west of Blue Mountain Lake. (315-354-5311)

On the eastern edge of the Adirondacks, east of I-87, is the **Champlain Valley**, which slopes down from the mountainous terrain to the lake itself. The "must-see" site in this area is **Fort Ticonderoga**. To reach the town of Ticonderoga, take Route 8 east from I-87 to Route 9N and then drive north into town. The fort was an important military post in the 18th century and known as "the key to a continent" because of its strategic position on the waterway connecting New York and Canada. It was held at different times by France, England and the USA but was abandoned after the Revolution. It was not until the early 20th century that the fort was purchased by a wealthy merchant, which led to its preservation. (518-585-2821)

Other interesting things to see north of Ticonderoga on Route 9N include the **Crown Point State Historic Site** (518-597-4666), the ruins of **Fort Frederic,** which was built in 1737 by the French, and the **Kent-Delord House Museum** in Plattsburgh, with its vast collections of art, furniture, and accessories (518-561-1035). Also worthy of a visit in Plattsburgh is the **Alice T. Miner Museum**, whose collections are wider and more eclectic that one can possibly imagine. (518-846-7336)

This itinerary ends in the Champlain Valley. Options are to continue north into Canada to visit Montreal (less than two hours away); to drive east into Vermont and to connect with one of the itineraries outlined in our New England guide; to travel along the Saint Lawrence Seaway; or to return swiftly on the New York State Thruway back to New York City. If your point of origin was the New York area and you need to return there to fly home, the most interesting and varied route south would be to travel down Route 7 through Vermont, Massachusetts, and Connecticut.

Cadets at West Point Academy

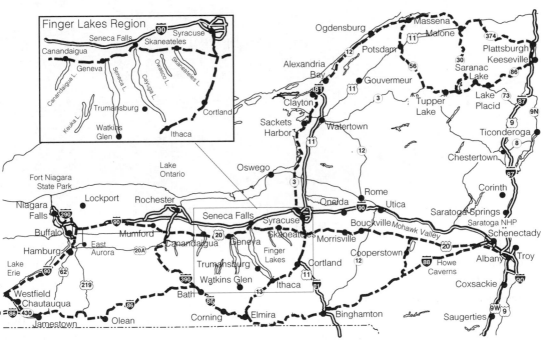

The Water's Edge

- Orientation/Sightseeing
- Itinerary Route

Canada

PA

The Water's Edge
The Seaway, the Lakes & Islands Galore

The Water's Edge

The northern edge of New York State stretches from its most eastern point at Lake Champlain, along the St. Lawrence River into Lake Ontario, and across to the southern coast of Lake Erie. The spectacularly beautiful St. Lawrence separates the United States from Canada, flowing eastward for some 700 miles from the eastern end of Lake Ontario to the sea. This river has historically provided the means for the westward expansion into the interior of the country and has been used as the major shipping route of goods both into and out of the Great Lakes. The St. Lawrence, its tributaries, and the more than 1,700 islands comprise what is known as the Thousand Islands region of New York State. Whether your journey begins in the Lake Champlain Valley and goes west, or begins at the state's most western point on Lake Erie and goes east matters not—you need only to determine the best point at which to begin and which of the many things to do are of greatest interest to you.

Recommended Pacing: The routing for this itinerary is outlined on Map 3 at the front of the book. This itinerary begins in Plattsburgh, New York, winds west to the St. Lawrence River at Rooseveltown and then follows the river along its path to Lake Ontario. You may choose to visit part of the Thousand Islands region before reaching Rooseveltown or at one of the other river towns along Route 37. After a visit to Alexandria Bay, the itinerary turns south to Syracuse and the Finger Lakes where among other things you visit the state's wineries. Skimming along the top of the Finger Lakes on Route 20 then connects you to I-90 where you will continue west to Buffalo and then north to Niagara Falls. Traveling south from Buffalo to Westfield and then to Jamestown puts you on the route back east through Corning where a visit to the Corning Glass Museum is a must. At this point you can travel north to Ithaca and the southern part of the Finger Lakes or continue east on to Binghamton. From Binghamton travel east on I-88 toward Albany, perhaps with a side trip to Cooperstown. This routing will take more or less five days, depending on the number of stops along the way.

To begin this journey westward along the water's edge, take Route 374 west from Plattsburgh (just north of the end of our Hudson River Valley itinerary—see page 25), to Route 24 west to Malone. Here you pick up Route 37 traveling initially northwest then turning southwest to follow the scenic path of the **St. Lawrence River**. (An alternative to proceeding directly to the St. Lawrence is to leave Plattsburgh going south on I-87 to Routes 9N and 86 to Lake Placid and some of the lakes in this **Thousand Lakes** region. Route 3 west from Saranac Lake to Tupper Lake is wonderfully scenic. From this area you can drive north on Route 30 to Malone or take Route 56 north to the river.)

The **Frederic Remington Art Museum** is located in the town of **Ogdensburg** on Route 37. Remington spent his childhood years here and summers here thereafter. In this house where he lived, and where his widow lived after his death, is the largest single collection of his paintings, watercolors, and sculptures. (315-393-2425)

Continuing along on Route 37, follow Route 12 to **Alexandria Bay**, a town built out onto a promontory into the bay, which is now the center of much of the area's tourism. Boat tours depart from the town and while cruising the bay one can see many of the homes built by wealthy vacationers in an earlier era. Eleven miles farther on in the town of **Clayton** is the **Antique Boat Museum**, in which are displayed some 150 of the freshwater boats that plied the waters of the area (315-686-4104). From Clayton proceed south to **Sackets Harbor**, now a commercial center for local tourism. The positioning of Sackets Harbor is such that it played a historical role as the center of naval activity in the early 1800s.

As you drive south either on the picturesque Route 3 along Lake Ontario or more speedily on I-81, you arrive in **Syracuse.** Here you find the **Erie Canal Museum**, which depicts the history of the development of the Erie Canal and its role in the growth of trade in the areas it served. On display is a 65-foot replica of a canal boat, which gives the visitor a great sense of what traveling on a canal was all about. (315-471-0593)

Syracuse marks the eastern edge of the **Finger Lakes** region of New York. This region is one of the most beautiful parts of the state and has within its boundaries a series of long, slender lakes with miles of shoreline unencumbered with towns or homes. The Finger Lakes have become one of the state's major wine producing regions, with the vineyards being concentrated in the **Seneca**, **Cayuga**, **Keuka,** and **Canandaigua Lakes** area. Staying at a nearby country inn and exploring and tasting the wine produced here is one of the major reasons for visiting the area. There is a series of towns at the northern tips of the lakes along Route 20 that are interesting to visit, including **Canandaigua** with the **Sonnenburg Gardens and Museum** (585-394-4922 weekdays, 585-393-9404 weekends) and the **Granger Homestead and Carriage Museum**, a showcase of the history of this region (585-394-1472). In **Geneva** you can visit **Rosa Hill Mansion**, a Greek Revival mansion built in 1839 (315-789-3848).

Halfway between Buffalo and Syracuse just north of I-90 lies the city of **Rochester**, the state's third-largest city. This is a city of learning institutions, including the **University of Rochester** with the **Eastman School of Music**. The city is also the home of the **Rochester Symphony** and the **Strong Museum**. This museum is an eclectic one, with over 300,000 objects including a collection of 27,000 dolls, dollhouses, pattern glass, folk art, Tiffany glass, toy trains, and miniatures of a large and varied lot (585-263-2700). Be sure to explore East Street, beyond the inner ring, a wide boulevard that is graced with the city's grandest estates—one of which belonged to George Eastman. The **George Eastman House and Museum of Photography** is the home of the father of photography and on display are the furnishings of his home and all things related to the industry of which he was the leader—cameras, photographs, and films (585-271-3361).

(While this itinerary continues west from here, if your time is short, you could join our routing back towards Albany by driving south on the I-390 to connect to I-86 east.)

So very different from the eastern part of the state is its rural western fringe with its important farming industry. There are many small towns in this area, interconnecting with one another on winding roads that force the traveler to slow down and enjoy the region. Most of the visitors coming here include a visit to **Niagara Falls**, where the Niagara River plunges into the boiling cauldron below (716-278-1796). The falls are located north of Buffalo off I-190. On this New York side of the falls, the land banding the pounding expanse of water is owned by the State Park. Look across the churning of water to Canada where, by dramatic contrast, high-rise hotels and casinos line the edge of the cliffs. Niagara Falls State Park offers a luxurious expanse of lawn and trails and a spectacular overlook of waterfalls, rapids and gorge: Niagara Falls, Bridal Veil Falls and Horseshoe Falls (which stretches across to the Canadian border). There are three principal parking areas. P1 is near the visitor center on the tip of the Prospect Point peninsula. P2 and P3 are located across the small bridge on Goat Island. One can walk everywhere or take advantage of the scenic trolley. The Observation Tower and the departure point for the boats (Maids of the Mist) are located near the visitor Center/Festival Theater. Privately operated, the boats travel (May to October) to the edge of the thundering water (716-284-4233). Take the trolley or cross the pedestrian bridge to Goat Island and you can view the water surge over the brink from Terrapon Point or take the elevator down to the Cave of the Winds—where unbelievably, wearing protective raingear, you can actually walk under and in the spray of the falls.

From Niagara Falls take the Robert Morris Parkway, a beautiful drive that hugs the edge of the gorge and then past the Power Authority to **Old Fort Niagara**. Located 15 miles north of Niagara Falls, this 18th-century fort at the confluence of the Niagara River and Lake Ontario was at various times in its history commanded by the French, British, and American military forces. Its position controlled access from Lake Ontario to the other four Great Lakes and thus played a strategic role in the shipping of goods. The views from the fort are well worth a visit. (716-745-7611)

The city of **Buffalo**, the second-largest city in the state and the center of business and the arts in western New York, is just south of Niagara Falls. Downtown Buffalo has many 19th- and 20th-century buildings built in the then-popular art deco style of architecture. On the 28th floor of the city hall is an **observatory** (716-896-5200). **Delaware Park**, designed by the noted landscape architect Frederick Law Olmsted, is a haven of quiet in the midst of this bustling city—open space and woods are there for the visitor to enjoy, as well as the country's third-oldest zoo. A world-class art museum, the **Albright-Knox Art Gallery**, is located in Buffalo (716-882-8700). Its holdings of contemporary and modern art are extensive but there are also smaller collections of Asian, European, and Greek art and sculpture. Foremost in the collections are the works of American abstract expressionists.

Southeast of Buffalo in **East Aurora** via Route 400 south is the **Roycroft Campus** and the **Elbert Hubbard-Roycroft Museum**, located on the former site of the manufacturers of furniture and accessories in the Arts and Crafts style. The museum, in the home of a leather-craft worker of this era, has carved woodwork, copper fittings, stained glass, and furniture that reflect the best of this time and style. (716-652-4735)

Chautauqua County to the south of Buffalo is largely farm country. What has given it an international reputation is the **Chautauqua Institution**, to which politicians come to learn and to teach, and at which concerts are held each summer for a nine-week period. As many as 7,500 students come to attend courses during the day and more join them in the evenings for lectures or concerts. (716-357-6250 or 800-836-ARTS) The quickest way to reach Chautauqua is to take I-90 (the New York State Thruway) from Buffalo to Westfield and then drive south on Route 394.

From Chautauqua, cross the lake at Stow and travel east to **Jamestown**. Set on the river just inland from the lake's eastern shore, Jamestown was Lucille Ball's childhood home and there is a museum, the **Lucille Ball-Desi Arnaz Center** (716-484-0800) that serves as a tribute to the first couple of comedy. For wildlife enthusiasts follow signs to the outskirts of town to the **Roger Tory Peterson Institute.** Set on 27 acres, the institute has a wonderful exhibit of this century's greatest naturalist. Enjoy the art, the photography and if time allows, take advantage of the extensive wooded trails.

After this visit to the western part of New York State take I-86 east to **Corning**. Be sure to plan a stop and tour of the **Corning Museum of Glass**. The primary reason for visiting the museum is to see the exhibits of glass spanning 3,500 years—these are extraordinary exhibits and one cannot help marveling at the glass utensils and objects of art created before the birth of modern times. (607-937-5371) Besides the museum, within the Corning Glass complex are a hot-glass demonstration area, a hall of science and industry, and a retail store for Corning products. Also in Corning is the **Robert Rockwell Museum** with its collections of American western art, toys, and more than 2,000 pieces of the art glass of Frederick Carder, co-founder of the Steuben Glass Works. (607-937-5386)

From Corning, the quickest way to reach Albany is to travel to Binghamton and pick up the I-88 from there. However, you may want to detour northeast on Route 13 to **Ithaca**, site of **Cornell University**, founded in 1886, which sits high above the town. Cornell has tours of its campus, best done by walking after you have parked at the Plantations headquarters. The tour takes you through the oldest buildings on campus on a walk named Founders Loop. (607-254-4636)

About 24 miles before Ithaca there is an interesting side trip via Route 14 to the **Watkins Glen State Park**, considered to be the finest glen in the Finger Lakes region. With its deep gorge and rushing waters, there are dramatic waterfalls and breathtaking views from the suspension bridge 85 feet above the river. (607-535-4511)

Depending on your route to Albany, retracing your tracks south to the I-88 or continuing north from Ithaca and turning east on Route 20, there are several areas of interest, including the **Mohawk Valley**, an area where settlers and travelers in the 18th and 19th centuries moved along the valley paths and on the Erie Canal to new lands and the promise of a new life on the rich farmlands of the west; **Schenectady**, home of **Union College**; the **Howe Caverns** (518-296-8900); and numerous other historical sites.

Nestled on the south tip of Lake Otsego, **Cooperstown**, equidistant between I-88 and Route 20, is best known as the home of the **National Baseball Hall of Fame**, whose three floors contain the history, memorabilia, data, and records of those who made this sport what it is today. There is a theater with a multimedia presentation, and a library housing records from this great sport, information about baseball reporting, and film clips of the great moments of baseball. (607-547-7200) Other worthwhile things to see in Cooperstown include the **Farmers' Museum**, a collection of 19th-century buildings moved to this site and in which are now displayed the trade buildings of the time (doctor's office, school, church, farmhouse, and a general store) and within them the tools and artifacts of the tradesmen. There are also demonstrations here of the trades that were part of the rural life in an earlier era (607-547-1450). The **Fenimore House Museum**, located on the shores of Otsego Lake, houses a collection of Native American and American folk art. There is a new wing focusing on the crafts of textiles, beadwork, basketry, masks, and costumes of various Indian tribes (607-547-1400). The **Alice Water's Glimmerglass Opera** (607-547-5704), to the north of town on the edge of the lake, affords a spectacular backdrop of lake and mountain for its seasonal concerts.

When you reach Albany you may return south on the New York State Thruway (I-87) to New York City or head north to Saratoga Springs and the Adirondacks.

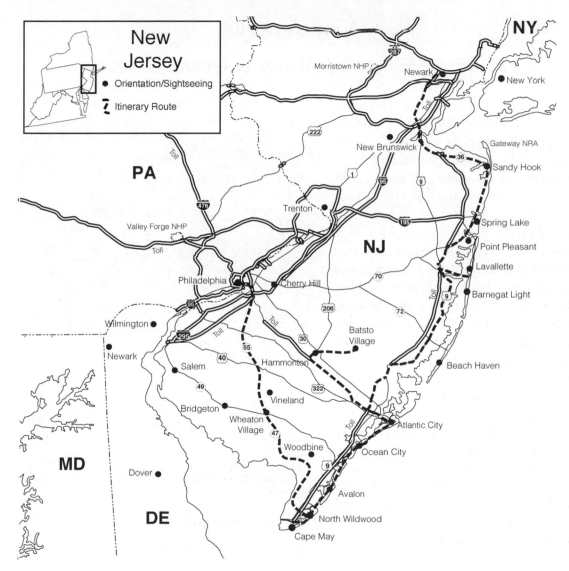

New Jersey

Pearls of Sand, Salt Water & Ocean Breezes

New Jersey, the state that you pass through on the way to somewhere else, rarely stopping to enjoy it, does indeed have some wonderful destinations. It's a state of many contrasts, encompassing lively cities, beautiful ocean seashore and, inland, lovely farms in pastoral settings. New Jersey is the state where George Washington crossed the Delaware and fought many battles so there is much history and you find many historic sites to visit here. This itinerary leads you south from New York City (or its airports), with its fast pace of life and crowded highways, down along the coast to feel the sand between your toes, the water on your feet, and the salt air on your face, enjoying the more relaxed pace of the southerly shore towns. Alternatively, you can follow the same route from south to north and link up easily and effortlessly with other itineraries outlined in this guidebook.

Spring Lake, New Jersey

Recommended Pacing: The routing for this itinerary is outlined on Map 2 at the front of the book. The time needed to travel the coast of New Jersey is but a few hours—most certainly less than eight—but the time spent on enjoying the many attractions may be as little as two days or as long as a week. You can meander between the old Victorian shore communities, highlighted, if you are interested, by some of the action that Atlantic City or those seaside towns with a reputation for the fast life may provide. Your time will depend, as always, on your desire to become more familiar with the towns along the way, to get to know the side streets, and to walk along the ocean.

Find the **Garden State Parkway** by following the signs from the airports and taking either the Holland or Lincoln Tunnels or the Washington Bridge from New York City. Arm yourself with the change to feed the frequent tollbooths, and begin the drive south to the shore. You may want to exit the parkway as quickly as possible and get onto Route 35, closer to the coast. From there you can take the narrow roads to the coastal communities and then drive from village to village, absorbing the local scene as you pass through each one.

The first opportunity to escape the busy highways may be to take Route 36 to **Sandy Hook** and to visit the **Gateway National Recreation Area**. Miles of sandy beach, often windswept and barren, with the bay on the west and the ocean on the east, will greet you. There's a lot to do here—swimming, fishing, picnicking, windsurfing, and great walking along the water's edge, but be aware on summer weekends that you need to allow extra time for traffic and navigating through crowds.

Farther south on the parkway you exit for the first of the wonderful old summer seashore communities, **Spring Lake**. Just shut your eyes and imagine life as it was in the first half of the 19th century when families returned year after year to the same homes, when generations gathered and grew older together, and when little changed over the years and even the decades. Consider spending a night or two in one of the many inns here—walk to the beach with a mug of early-morning coffee to see the sun rise and return after dinner to see the day end.

Continuing south along the coast, you can drive along the spit of land with its string of villages, remain inland following Route 9, or return to the parkway. Your pace will be determined by your self-imposed time schedule and your interest in dawdling along the way, stopping for a mid-morning cup of tea and a cinnamon roll or an afternoon espresso. Eventually the spit of land ends and the villages cease to be as the ocean takes command and you are forced to rejoin Route 9 south at Tom's River. Don't miss the **Barnegat Lighthouse**, a fun choice for some exercise as you climb its 217 steps for the commanding view from the top. Eventually, after crossing the Mullico River, you will arrive in **Atlantic City**. If gambling, casino shows, and a 4-mile boardwalk are of interest, this may be a place to pause; otherwise, you have the option to bypass all this by staying on Route 9. (If you wish to access the coast from Philadelphia, an equally viable starting point, simply take the Atlantic City Expressway.)

Batsto Village, northwest of Atlantic City on Route 542, is a 19th-century rural industrial town with a visitors' center that explains the history of the glass and iron industries that began here in the 18th century. The tour includes a visit to the 36-room Italianate mansion built in 1876.

Batsto Village

South of Atlantic City, Route 52 leads to **Ocean City** where you may resume your coastal travel, visiting the seashore towns of **Avalon**, **North Wildwood**, and **Wildwood**.

Soon you arrive in the granddaddy of all the summer shore communities, **Cape May**, now popular year-round. Difficult as it is to imagine, in the early 1800s holidaymakers came to Cape May to wade in the ocean waters in woolen clothing. By the middle of the 19th century Cape May had become the country's number-one resort and today the historic Victorian town has many inns and guesthouses just a short walk from the beach, the boardwalk, the shops, and the restaurants. Visitors can enjoy trolley and carriage tours of the historic district, and sightseeing and whale-watching cruises. The walking tour of the historic Victorian section of town is especially worthwhile: enjoy the variety of Victorian style and trim—and the imagination of the owners in their choice of paint colors. Information is available at the **Welcome Center** (609-884-9562). The **Cape May Point State Park** and the **Cape May Lighthouse** are also interesting attractions to visit, as is the **Cape May County Historical Society Museum**.

Inland excursions might include a visit to **Wheaton Village**, reached by taking Route 47 west. This is an old glassmaking community that has been re-created on the historic site where there was once a glass factory built in 1888. Within the village you find the **Museum of American Glass** where some 7,500 glass objects are on display, most notably a collection of American paperweights. (800-998-4552)

Cape May connects to the Delaware coast by ferry, which saves many hours of driving and enables you to continue a journey into Delaware, Maryland, and the Eastern Shore.

New Jersey

New Jersey

Philadelphia
City of Independence

Sometimes called the "Cradle of Liberty" and often referred to as the "City of Brotherly Love," Philadelphia is where the United States of America was born on July 4, 1776 with the adoption of the Declaration of Independence. This is also where the Constitution of the United States was drafted in 1787. The city was founded in 1682 by William Penn who, with a group of Quakers, left religious persecution in England to establish a community in the New World based on freedom of conscience. Philadelphia has always carried with it a sense of its own history and its citizens bring to this current time values whose roots go deep into the past.

Independence Hall

As with many American cities, sections of Philadelphia have been developed not only in different centuries but at varying paces, leading in time to its expansion into the surrounding countryside. The visitor to Philadelphia, whether from the USA or from overseas, can partake of what the city offers on many levels: its history, its commercialism, its educational institutions, and, in the areas that surround the city, museums, gardens, and residential areas of great charm with homes made of local stone. Philadelphia is easy to reach although there are fewer non-stop flights from more distant domestic and international cities than you will find into New York or Washington airports. With its location on the Eastern Seaboard, it has good rail service and bus transportation. A subway system provides visitors with convenient access to the most sought-after destinations. The ease of getting into and out of the heart of Philadelphia gives you the choice of staying in a downtown hotel or driving in from the suburbs.

Recommended Pacing: The length of time you spend in Philadelphia depends entirely on the degree of interest you have in the history of the founding of America and your desire to explore not only that history but also the threads that go forth into the surrounding area. To understand the historical significance of all that went on in the 18th century, the visitor should plan to spend two days in the city. To the degree that you want to include shopping and exploration of the suburbs, particularly the areas that include the Valley Forge National Park, you should allow at least another couple of days in the area. For these excursions, see our itineraries to Bucks County and to the Brandywine Valley.

Independence National Historic Park lies at the heart of historic Philadelphia. This area covers approximately 12 blocks and contains all the most important historic sites.

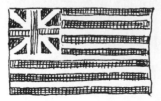 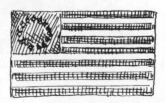 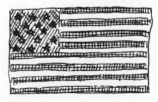

The **visitors' center**, located at 3rd and Chestnut Streets, is the place to begin your visit—don't miss the 28-minute film and interactive computers, which explain much of the history of the founding of the country. There is a bell tower at the center that houses the Bicentennial Bell, a gift from Great Britain. In many of the historic buildings within this area are guides who provide wonderfully educational tours for children and adults alike, guaranteeing a lasting memory of a visit to Philadelphia. (215-965-2305)

There are many buildings within the park that played important roles in our country's history. Some of the ones not to be missed include:

Second Bank of the United States and the National Portrait Gallery: This Greek-Revival building with its marble columns was opened in 1824 as the Second Bank of the United States under a 20-year Act of Congress. Subsequently this structure was the Philadelphia Custom House and now has within its walls the exhibit "Philadelphia, Portraits of the Capital City." Portraits of delegates to the Continental Congress, signers of the Constitution, and the officers of the Revolution and the War of 1812 hang there. One of the galleries has a collection of street scenes and portraits of life in the Federal period in Philadelphia.

Independence Hall: Constructed as the Pennsylvania State House between the period of 1732 and 1756, this is a modest brick structure with a bell tower in which the Liberty Bell hung. Tours of this building should include the large central hall, the Assembly Room, the second-floor Long Room, and the Governor's Council Chamber.

Congress Hall: This was built in 1787 as the home of the Philadelphia County Courthouse but was actually used as the hall where the delegates of the newly founded country met—the Senate in the second-floor courtroom and the House of Representatives in the first-floor chamber.

Old City Hall: The mirror image of the Congress Hall, this building served for a while as the home of the Supreme Court. It has now been restored to show how it looked when it served as the nation's highest court.

Liberty Bell Pavilion: This building was newly constructed for the Bicentennial Celebration in 1976 and now houses the Liberty Bell. There is an especially wonderful talk here by national park rangers on the history of the Liberty Bell, its creation, and it's subsequent recasting.

Franklin Court: This was originally built as the home of Benjamin Franklin and now houses audio presentations of his life and his many accomplishments. The 18th-century printing office and bindery of Benjamin Franklin's grandson has also been re-created in this building.

Beyond Independence Park

Philadelphia is one of those wonderful U.S. cities where, with good walking shoes and a desire for exercise, you can walk to almost everything. Some less centralized attractions worth considering are:

Atwater Kent Museum: This museum is the official museum of Philadelphia's 300-year-old history. (15 S. 7th Street, 215-685-4830.)

Old City: This area, the heart of the original city of Philadelphia, has been extensively restored and includes galleries, restaurants, and various historic buildings. It's located a few blocks north of the Independence National Historical Park, south of Race Street and east of 5th Street—within walking distance except perhaps in the heat and humidity of the summer.

Christ Church: Dating back to 1695, Christ Church is one of the nation's most historic churches. The architecture is magnificent and well worth a visit. (North 2nd and Church Streets, 215-922-1695.)

Elfreth's Alley: Take the time to walk down this street, between North 2nd and Front Streets, lined with 33 narrow brick houses dating back to 1725.

Betsy Ross House

Betsy Ross House: The home of Betsy Ross, the Quaker seamstress who made the first Stars and Stripes flag, is well worth a brief visit for the legends that are now associated with the role of the flag in our country's history. (239 Arch Street, 215-686-1252.)

United States Mint: This is the largest of all the United States mints. There is a self-guided tour of the building showing historical information on the creation of coins and commemorative medals. You can look down through windows onto the floors where coins are being produced today. (5th and Arch Streets, 215-408-0114.)

Society Hill: With a great deal of history dating back to the 18th century, the streets and houses of this part of Philadelphia, bounded on one side by Independence Hall and Lombard Street and on the east and west sides by South Second and South Fifth Streets, have now been restored.

Physick House: Dr. Philip Physick, known as the father of American surgery, lived in this house with his family from 1815 to 1837 and his descendents lived here until 1940. The building has been restored to be a showpiece of the Federal period. (321 South 4th Street, 215-925-7866, Visiting hours: afternoons, Thursday through Sunday.)

Penn's Landing and South Street: This area along the Delaware River, between Chestnut and Spruce Streets, is a recreational area with parks, jogging and walking paths, a skating rink, an amphitheater, and a seaport museum. **The Seaport Museum** displays permanent exhibits, two historic ships, and continually changing traveling exhibits. (211 South Columbus Boulevard, 215-925-5439.)

Center City: Anchored by some of the city's finest architecture, the modern Center City is Philadelphia's vibrant downtown area. Next to old buildings with restaurants, theaters, shopping areas with great boutiques, and grand department stores, there is architecture dating back to the 19th century. **City Hall**, with its 700 rooms, is one of the finest examples of French Renaissance architecture. On the top of the building is a statue of William Penn, designed by Calder, and an observation deck. (Broad and Market Streets, 215-686-2840.) Also in this area is the **Masonic Temple** (1 North Broad Street, 215-988-1917), the **Museum of American Art** of the Pennsylvania Academy of the Fine Arts (Broad and Cherry Streets, 215-972-7600), and the **Rosenbach Museum and Library** (2010 Delancey Street, 215-732-1600), renowned for its collection of rare books and manuscripts.

The **Benjamin Franklin Parkway** leading from the center of the city was modeled after the Champs Elysées in Paris. It stretches from City Hall to the Philadelphia Museum of Art and the beginning of Fairmont Park. Within this area there are many worthwhile places to visit, including:

Cathedral of Saints Peter and Paul: An Italian Renaissance-style cathedral built for the Irish Catholic immigrants who came to settle in Philadelphia. (Benjamin Franklin Parkway and North 18th Street, 215-561-1313.)

Academy of Natural Sciences of Philadelphia: Reputed to be the greatest place to learn about dinosaurs. (1900 Benjamin Franklin Parkway at Logan Circle, 215-299-1000.)

Franklin Institute Science Museum: This museum has a science center with exhibits for children and adults, the Fels Planetarium, a Victorian railroad station with a steam locomotive, a walk-through version of the human heart, and the Tuttleman Omniverse Theater with its Omnimax screen. (North 20th Street and Benjamin Franklin Parkway, 215-448-1200.)

Rodin Museum: Exhibits of the drawings and sculpture of Auguste Rodin—one of the largest exhibits outside France. (North 22nd Street and Benjamin Franklin Parkway, 215-763-8100.)

The Thinker

Philadelphia Museum of Art: One of the major art museums in the United States, this museum also hosts Wednesday evening programs devoted to the arts. (North 26th Street and Benjamin Franklin Parkway, 215-763-8100.)

In the area of **Fairmont Park**, one of the largest city parks in the world, are the **Museum of Art;** historic homes; the **Horticulture Center** (North Horticultural and Montgomery Drive, 215-685-0096); Boathouse Row, off Kelly Drive just north of the Water Works, with its private boating clubs; an azalea garden; the **Fairmont Water Works Interpretive Center** (off

Kelly Drive behind the Museum of Art), which originally supplied the city with its water; and the **Philadelphia Zoo** (3400 W. Girard Avenue, 215-243-1100), the first in the United States and now the home of animals from all over the world.

In **West Philadelphia** you find the **University of Pennsylvania**, between South 34th Street and South 40th Street, with the university's **Institute of Contemporary Art** (215-898-7108) and the **Museum of Archaeology and Anthropology** (33rd and Spruce Streets, 215-898-4000.).

These are some of the highlights of a visit to Philadelphia, but only highlights. There is always more to do and to explore based on your interests and the time you have for your visit.

From Philadelphia easy excursions take you into the Brandywine Valley to visit mansions, museums, and gardens; charming and historic Bucks County; and Lancaster County, home of the Amish and Mennonite people. (See itineraries on pages 59 and 70.)

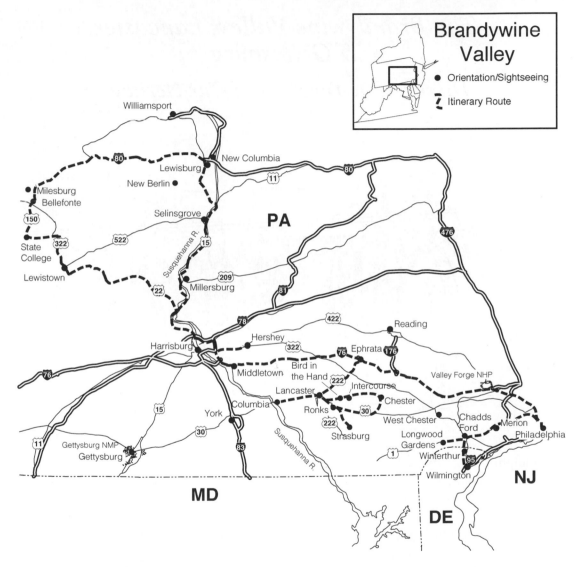

The Brandywine Valley, Lancaster & Gettysburg

Discover the Diversity of Our Heritage

An Amish Family

Philadelphia, the City of Brotherly Love, is an ideal base from which to travel into the surrounding countryside, beautiful in its rolling hills and valleys. The towns of these neighboring suburbs, particularly those in the Brandywine Valley, have some of the best museums and attractions to be found anywhere. Nearby Pennsylvania Dutch Country provides you with the opportunity to see the Amish and the Mennonites as they live their lives according to their long-held customs and beliefs, while Valley Forge and Gettysburg offer a very different kind of experience—that of learning of the conflicts that have shaped our nation's history. Your choice of one or more of these excursions will depend upon the time available to you and the depth of your interest, whether it be as a tourist or as a scholar, but all are worthwhile.

Recommended Pacing: The routing for this itinerary is outlined on Map 4 at the front of the book. The highlights of this itinerary are memories in the making and if you select based on your personal interests, you'll be rewarded many times over. A quick tour of the highlights of the fabulous museums and gardens close to Philadelphia can probably be accomplished in two days—visits that give you an opportunity to study and to linger may take three to five days. Getting a feel for the Amish and Mennonite way of life can be accomplished in a day, unless you go their markets on market day, or tour the farms and homes open to the public. Time spent touring the visitors' center and then driving through the battlefields at Gettysburg will vary with the level of your interest—this can be a day-long trip or if you find this period of history one that fascinates you, you could spend two to three days in the area. For sightseeing in Philadelphia itself see page 51.

Nearby points of interest include **The Barnes Foundation** only 5 miles south of the city center via I-76 to Route 1 in the town of **Merion.** The gallery was built by Dr. Albert Barnes, a wealthy physician and pharmaceutical manufacturer, to house his incredible art collection. This now includes more than 1,100 Impressionist and Post-Impressionist paintings by Renoir, Cézanne, Matisse, Monet, Manet, Picasso, Modigliani, and others of these schools. (610-667-0290) Traveling a little farther, southwest of Philadelphia on Route 1 you will find yourself in the **Brandywine Valley**. This area in the southeast corner of the state abutting Delaware has a rich history, starting with the arrival in 1682 of William Penn, and offers many attractions including lovely mansions, gorgeous gardens, and fascinating museums, as well as beautiful countryside. The **Brandywine River Museum** in **Chadds Ford** is the first of the many attractions. This museum, located in a converted Civil War grist mill, focuses on the artwork of the Wyeth family— probably the most noted of all artistic families in America. The works of N. C. Wyeth, his son Andrew, and in turn his son Jamie are hung here in various galleries. In addition, there are changing exhibits of other area artists. (610-388-2700)

Just over the state line in **Winterthur**, Delaware, on Route 52, you find the outstanding **Winterthur Museum, Garden, and Library**. If you are interested in the decorative arts of America, a half-day visit to this museum is a "must" and will make you crave for more. Originally the home of Henry Francis du Pont, this estate now houses a testimony to the arts and crafts of America. It was assembled through the purchase not only of specific works of art but also of complete rooms with their paneling, wall covering, art, and furnishings. Reservations are required for either the standard tours or for the special tours that focus on specific arts. A taste of this museum is a must: participation in any of their many study programs is a real reward. (302-888-4600)

A little farther along Route 1 from Chadds Ford, you come to **Longwood Gardens**. Pierre du Pont, one of the members of the family that founded the DuPont Company, expressed his interest in horticulture through the purchase of more than 1,000 acres of gardens, conservatories, and fountains in Kennett Square, which have become the world-renowned Longwood Gardens. Throughout the year there are changing gardens that follow the seasons. In the summer the festival of fountains during the day (and on some evenings with fireworks) are wondrous to behold. A visit here will take approximately half a day but if horticulture is of great interest, plan a full day. (610-388-1000)

Also in Delaware, on the outskirts of **Wilmington** on the site of the first DuPont powder works, is the **Hagley Museum**, an outdoor museum on 230 acres. While there is the home of E.I. du Pont, the first du Pont family home, to visit, the outstanding attractions of this museum are the waterworks and black powder works, which stretch along 2 miles of the Brandywine River. From the visitors' center there is a shuttle bus that takes you along the route and stops at various points of interest. (302-658-2400)

Wilmington is also home to **Nemours Mansion and Gardens**. This Louis XVI-style château built in 1909 was the home of Alfred I. du Pont. Its 102 rooms are filled with

European antiques and art and its extensive gardens present one of the best examples of French-style gardens in America. (302-651-6912)

Longwood Gardens

Also on the outskirts of Philadelphia, **Valley Forge National Park** is 20 miles northwest of the city, via I-76 west. For those interested in the War of Independence, this visit is one not to miss. It was in Valley Forge that George Washington's army of 12,000 troops camped in the winter of 1777. The British occupied Philadelphia at that time and the Continental forces were ill, badly trained, and in need of provisions. With assistance from Congress, the army began to rally and by the spring of 1778 had been transformed into a disciplined, spirited, and self-confident force, which went on to defeat the British at Yorktown. The **visitors' center** is the place to begin this visit and to understand the dynamics of the history of this time. Plan to drive into the surrounding areas of the park, where at significant points the National Park Service provides interpreters of the events and the battles. A visit here for the tourist, contrasted with the student, will take two to three hours. (610-783-1077)

The real driving itinerary starts out by taking you a little farther into the rolling hills of Pennsylvania. In **Lancaster County** farming has long been a way of life for the **Amish** and the **Mennonites**. With their unique style of life centered around their deeply felt religious beliefs, these people and the land on which they live have become magnets for visitors for over 300 years. Whether the attraction is the simple way of life they have devised, their quilts for which they are widely known, or their wonderful food products is less clear than the fact that these folk seem to set an example of life that others envy. The Amish and Mennonite people, originally from Germany and Switzerland, speak either English or their own language—a mixture of English and German. They dress simply: women are clothed in black, with either straw hats or bonnets and men are equally simple in style. Even young boys will be seen with hats. Schools are often in just one room but the education the children receive is no less rigorous than that in other American institutions.

To reach Lancaster County from Philadelphia, take I-76 west either to Route 222 and then south to the city of Lancaster or Route 202 west from Philadelphia to Route 30 into Lancaster. (If you are coming from the Brandywine Valley, take Route 322 north then turn west on Routes 202 and 30.) While access by car will afford you views of the scenic farmland and roadside stands with quilts, crafts, and food products, Lancaster can also be reached by flying into either the Lancaster or Harrisburg Airports.

Once there, or in planning your trip in advance, you should contact the **Pennsylvania Dutch Convention and Visitors' Bureau**, 501 Greenfield Road, Lancaster, PA 17601, 800-723-8824. Other information centers include the **Downtown Lancaster Visitors' Center** at S. Queen and Vine Streets (717-397-3531) and the **Mennonite Information Center**, 2209 Millstream Road, off Route 30, 4½ miles east of Lancaster (717-299-0954).

Centers can give you information on buggy rides, one of the most unique ways to see a portion of this countryside, and the opening days and times of the many farmers' markets.

The city of **Lancaster** is the seat of Lancaster County and is worth a visit for its historical buildings and the central market. Guided walking tours lasting 90 minutes are available. Five miles south of downtown Lancaster off Route 222 an interesting visit may be made to the **Hans Herr House** at 1849 Hans Herr Drive. This restored home, the oldest in the county, was the home of Hans Herr who with a small group of Mennonites escaped religious persecution in Germany in the early 18th century. (717-464-4438) Another interesting stop would include **Wheatland**, the home of **President James Buchanan**, located at 1120 Marietta Avenue. This mansion is elegantly decorated with the furniture gathered during his years in Washington. (717-392-8721)

Roads spiral out in every direction from historic downtown Lancaster and weave through the countryside and villages where the Amish have established their homes and communities in and amongst our modern society. If you truly want a glimpse into their way of life and see how it neighbors ours, I would recommend you spend a day exploring the roads that transect the acres upon acres of farmland. Depending on the time of year and the stage of harvest, you will see them plowing their land with the aid of large draft horses or families congregating en masse in the fields to manually pick the crops. Drive through the villages whose shops often sell their handmade products and share the road with canvas, black-topped, horse-drawn buggies and children walking home from school. If you didn't have an opportunity to stop at a visitors' center, ask the locals about the weekly markets and inquire as to which ones are largely attended by the Amish. This is a wonderful way and opportunity to meet the Amish personally as they often man their own stands selling produce, pretzels, boxes, baskets, carvings, and quilts.

The Amish are not a sightseeing attraction, but rather a community that displays a commitment to its religious beliefs, upon which it bases its way of life.

For a better understanding and appreciation of this culture, there are some staged exhibits such as the **Amish Farm and House** on Route 30 east of Lancaster (717-394-6185), the **Amish Village** in **Strasburg** (717-687-8511), and the **Weavertown One-Room Schoolhouse** in **Bird-in-Hand** (717-768-3976). Also, the **Ephrata Cloister**, 632 W. Main Street in **Ephrata** (northeast of Lancaster on Route 222) provides guided tours of several of the religious commune's original Germanic-style buildings. (717-733-6600)

However, after visiting the region and many of the advertised locales, we found the **Amish Country Homestead** by far the best and the most comprehensive and rewarding in terms of a glimpse and understanding of the Amish. Located between the charming towns of Bird-in-Hand and Intercourse on Route 340, the Amish Country Homestead complex includes a nine-room furnished house, where you learn about Amish clothing and living without the benefit of electricity; a wonderful large shop; and the Plain & Fancy Restaurant, which serves, family style at long tables set for twelve, the traditional Amish meal of seven sweets and seven sours. Joining other guests, you sample fare such as baked sausage, chicken pot pie, dried corn, sweet and sour relishes, shoo-fly pie, dumplings, and homemade breads. At the homestead you can also arrange for individual

buggy rides or a more extensive, organized bus tour that visits an Amish farm. The highlight of a visit to the homestead is its remarkable theater and the program entitled "Jacob's Choice." This is the only "experiential" theater on the East Coast and it is truly unique. The audience, sitting on benches as the Amish do in church, feel as if they are observing life on an Amish farm as they watch the story of the Fisher family brought to life through a high-tech, multimedia presentation with remarkable special effects and three-dimensional sound and imagery. (717 768-3600)

While exploring Lancaster County, as well as becoming acquainted with the Amish community, those interested in things that tick will want to visit the **Watch and Clock Museum** located 10 miles west of Lancaster in **Columbia**. Take Route 30 west to Route 441 and then go left on Poplar Street. This museum has a collection of about 8,000 timepieces and clock-related items. (717-684-8261)

In the nearby town of **Strasburg** is the **Railroad Museum of Pennsylvania**. (From Lancaster take Route 896 then turn east on Route 741 for 1 mile.) For those interested in trains—either full-size or model trains—this is the place to visit. (717-687-8629) You can take a 45-minute trip through the Amish countryside on a train with a coal-fired locomotive—call 717-687-7522 for the schedule.

Harrisburg, the state capital, lies west of Lancaster via Route 283. The **capitol building**, an Italian Renaissance structure dedicated in 1906 by President Teddy Roosevelt, is worthy of a visit and a guided tour. (717-787-6810) The **State Museum of Pennsylvania**, 3rd and North Streets, houses and features the arts and artifacts of the state. (717-787-4980)

Leaving Harrisburg to the east on Route 322, you soon come to the town of **Hershey**, the city of chocolate, with the **Milton S. Hershey Museum**, **Hershey's Chocolate World**, and **Hershey Gardens**. If chocolate is a passion of yours, then you will enjoy the tourism that has grown with the success of Milton S. Hershey, the creator of the chocolate kiss. (717-534-3492)

An interesting loop from Harrisburg is to leave town on Route 15 along the Susquehanna River proceeding north to **New Columbia** and then west on I-80 to **Milesburg**. Turn south at this point on Routes 144 to Bellefonte and 322 back into Harrisburg or detour southwest from Bellefonte on 150 and then west on 322 to **State College**. Home to Penn State, the community of State College embraces the university. The little towns and the surrounding farms and countryside are wonderful. Turn off the main roads to visit these smaller settlements and in so doing you will not only see the countryside of farms and quiet villages linked by winding roads of much scenic beauty, but also have the opportunity to feel and experience a part of Pennsylvania into which the Amish way of life has expanded, building on their traditions of faith. Robert Louis Stevenson in 1879 said, "And when I had asked the name of the river from a brakesman and heard it was called the Susquehanna, the beauty of the name seemed to be part and parcel of the beauty of the land—that was the name, as no other could be, for that shining river and desirable valley."

Soldiers at Gettysburg

South of Harrisburg lie the battlefields of **Gettysburg**, reached by taking Route 15. Gettysburg is famous for its place in history and those interested in the Civil War will want to include it in a trip in this part of Pennsylvania.

To visit Gettysburg and to gain an understanding of the **Civil War** you will need to plan a minimum of one day in this area. Gettysburg was the site of the war's worst battle and the greatest loss of men in just three days during the summer of 1863. With Robert E. Lee making a move toward capturing the capital of Harrisburg and Major General Joe Hooker moving north, the two armies, war-worn, tired, and discouraged as they were, met and fought in what history has recorded as the deciding battle of the Civil War. When it was over thousands were dead and more wounded. It was at the consecration of the Gettysburg cemetery for the war dead that President Lincoln made his famous address beginning, "Fourscore and seven years ago our fathers brought forth on this continent a new nation, conceived in liberty and dedicated to the proposition that all men are created equal."

In addition to a quaint and historic town, among the memorable sights here are the **Gettysburg National Military Park** with its **Visitor Center**, the **Soldier's National Cemetery**, **Cyclorama Center** and the **Eisenhower National Historic Site** with the Eisenhower home complete with furnishings.

Incredibly over 6,000 acres have been preserved as the **Gettysburg National Military Park** (open all year from 6 am to 10 pm), securing for all time one of our history's most poignant battles and a war, tragically fought brother against brother, friend against friend, countryman against countryman. A few homes and farms, pastures and cornfields divided by the old split rail fences are scattered across the vast acreage. With the exception of the over 1,400 monuments that adorn the acreage placed by veterans to honor their fallen comrades, it is almost as if time has stood still. An ideal way to tour the park is by car with two well marked Auto Tours (one two-hour and one three-hour itinerary) signed and easy to follow along the predominately one lane roads that spider web through the park.

Begin at the **Visitor Center** (open daily 8 am to 5 pm or 6 pm depending on the season, closed holidays) where you can obtain a complimentary map that details the two routes and explains significant points of interest as signposted and numbered along the routes. At the Visitor Center you can also view the **Electric Map Presentation** that, through the use of color lights superimposed on a large relief map, offers a narrated orientation to the battle and Gettysburg Address. Through a program referred to as the **Licensed Battlefield Guide Service**, it is also possible at the Visitor Center to hire a guide to accompany you in your own vehicle on a two-hour tour of the battlefield. Guides are available on a first-come, first-serve basis. Seasonally, there are also buses with knowledgeable guides that depart from the center. Also available for purchase or rental are Audio Tape Programs. Note: In addition to the programs offered by the park service, there are also a number of commercial tours offered by companies near the park.

Adjacent to the Visitor Center is the **Cyclorama Center** which contains exhibits, paintings and the 360° painting that depicts **Pickett's Charge**—one of the defining moments of Gettysburg with the climatic attack by the Confederates. A sound and light presentation using the painting as a backdrop takes approximately 20 minutes. (Note: The painting is currently being restored and hence, is not available to view, nor will there be a sound and light presentation until the restoration is finished. Also, the painting will then be relocated to a new visitor center which is currently being built and will replace the existing one—all with an estimated completion for sometime in 2007-2008.)

Also, neighboring the Visitor Center is the **Soldier's National Cemetery** open all year from dawn until sunset as is the **Eisenhower National Historic Site**. Purchased in the 1950s, the complex of three farm buildings served as a refuge for the President and Mrs. Eisenhower during his time in Washington and then later became their retirement home. The home and grounds transferred to the National Park Service in 1979. The home and immediate grounds are open to the public by shuttle bus from the Visitor Center.

Information on visiting Gettysburg may be obtained from the Gettysburg National Military Park, *www.nps.gov/gett*, 97 Taneytown Road, Gettysburg, PA 17325, 717-334-1124.

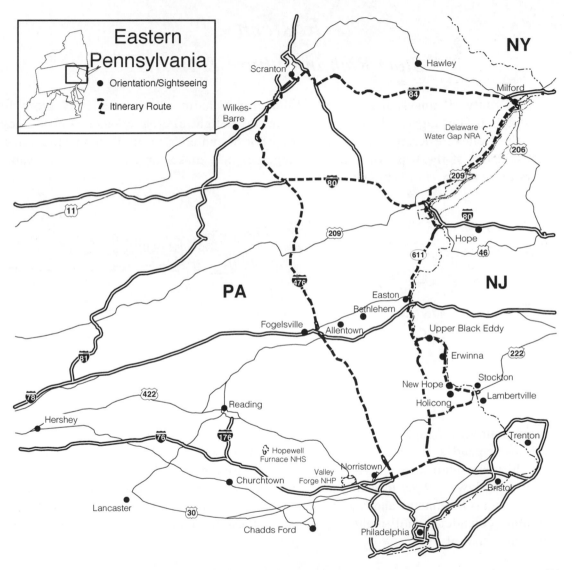

Eastern Pennsylvania

● Orientation/Sightseeing

⌇ Itinerary Route

NY

Scranton

Hawley

Wilkes-Barre

Milford

Delaware Water Gap NRA

206

80

209

11

PA

209

476

Hope

46

611

Easton

Bethlehem

NJ

Fogelsville

Allentown

Upper Black Eddy

222

81

Erwinna

78

422

New Hope

Stockton

Reading

Holicong

Lambertville

Hershey

76

176

Hopewell Furnace NHS

Trenton

Churchtown

Valley Forge NHP

Norristown

Bristol

Lancaster

30

Chadds Ford

Philadelphia

71

Eastern

A State Rich in Culture & Heritage

Bucks County, Pennsylvania, is full of historical charm and conveniently close to Philadelphia. Our suggested routing begins in this delightful area, extends your journey along the Delaware River as it winds its way north, and ends in the Pocono Mountains. Each segment of the trip is different but together they make for a few days' enjoyable excursion in this part of Pennsylvania.

The Upper Delaware

Recommended Pacing: The routing for this itinerary is outlined on Map 4 at the front of the book. Spend a leisurely day exploring the byways of Bucks County, the scene of much historic interest, overnight at one of its charming inns. On the second day drive along the Delaware River traveling north into the Delaware Water Gap. Spend a third day in the Pocono Mountains and return south to your starting point on the fourth. If time is available, consider a multi-night stay in any of these three areas for each is worthy of a vacation in and of itself.

From the city of Philadelphia (for sightseeing suggestions see section beginning on page 51), it is an easy drive into **Bucks County** taking I-276 to Route 611 north into the heart of the county. This is an area where the weekending crowds from the neighboring cities flee to tend their gardens, mow their lawns, and enjoy life in the country. Scattered about are picturesque towns and villages of great charm with old stone-built homes, some dating back into the 18th century. Here and there are great antique shops and restaurants.

Spend a day meandering pleasurably through **Doylestown** and **New Hope** with time for antiquing, for a leisurely lunch, and perhaps for attending a performance at the **Bucks County Playhouse** in New Hope. A short stroll across the bridge in New Hope takes you into **Lambertville**, New Jersey, which provides great browsing opportunities for a delightful afternoon. Doylestown is particularly charming with its Federal houses and proud Victorians. The architect, archaeologist, and ceramist Henry Chapman Mercer built three buildings now open to the public—**Fonthill**, his castle-like home (215-348-9461), the **Mercer Museum**, with its collections of pre-industrial artifacts (215-345-0210), and the **Spruance Library** at the museum with its collection of historical and genealogical records of the county. Also interesting to visit in Doylestown are the **Moravian Pottery and Tile Works** (215-345-6722) and the **James A. Michener Art Museum** (215-340-9800). History buffs can visit the **Washington Crossing National Park**, where **George Washington** was said to have crossed the Delaware River, and other monuments marking events in the Revolutionary War.

There is nothing more charming than the drive on Route 611 alongside the **Delaware Canal** and the **Delaware River**. This is countryside at its best—winding roads force you to take a slower pace, mature trees hang their branches low toward the street and the water, all is green and lush. Opportunities abound to pause to take a photograph, to walk, bike, or run along the old canal, and to stop at one of the many inns for lunch or an overnight stay. From New Hope there is a 2-mile mule-drawn barge trip in the spring, summer, and fall months—a delightful way to relax, to see into the lives of those who live along the river, and to listen to the songs of the history of the canal.

Route 611 winds its way north into **Easton**, a college town and also the home of the **National Canal Museum** and the **Crayola Factory**. For young and not-so-young alike a tour of the Crayola Factory where one can see crayons being made is just plain fun. Exhibits are oriented toward children and are creatively designed to stimulate their imagination in the world of color and design.

From Easton continue north on Route 611 to Stroudsburg and then along Route 209 and the **Delaware Water Gap**. Here you find recreational activity of every available type year round. Whether you enjoy fishing and boating on a lake, skiing on a mountain, whitewater rafting on a fast-running river, hiking, biking, horseback riding, or camping, all these and more are available in the Delaware Water Gap National Recreation Area and nearby **Pocono Mountains**. (Easy access to the Poconos may be had via the I-80 from Stroudsburg.) And if you want none of these activities, there is beautiful scenery at every turn of the road as well as credit-card activities like shopping and antiquing. For specific visitor information, contact **Visitor Services** at the **Pocono Mountains Vacation Bureau**. (800-762-6667)

When you arrive in Milford on Route 209, turn west on I-84 to Scranton and then south on I-476 back to Allentown and Philadelphia. Better yet, take as many back roads like Route 447 into the heart of the Pocono Mountains for as many hours as you can find so as to maximize the pleasure of your visit to this region. Following are some activities in the area that may be of interest to you.

Steamtown National Historic Site: Lackawanna Avenue and Cliff Street, Scranton. A visit here will acquaint you with the history both of steam engines and the coal industry. (888-693-9391)

Eckley Miners' Village: Off Route 940 East, 9 miles east of Hazleton. A model coal-mining town with an interesting visitors' center.

Bushkill Falls: 2 miles west of Route 209 on Bushkill Falls Road. The waters of the Bushkill and Pond River Creeks rush through a rock canyon creating eight falls.

By the time you return to the City of Brotherly Love, you will have had the opportunity to see much of the best of Pennsylvania—its towns, its back roads, its history, and most especially its charm.

An Amish Covered Wagon

Eastern Pennsylvania

Washington, D.C.
The Nation's Capital

The White House

Named for America's first president, Washington is a beautiful city with impressive buildings on wide tree-lined streets, grassy parks, museums, art galleries, and historic monuments. See government at work in Supreme Court sessions and Senate debates. Visit the icons that symbolize the American heritage: the Declaration of Independence and the Lincoln Memorial. Tour the White House, one of the few residences of a head of state open to the public. Retire for respite in trendy Georgetown with its wealth of shops, cafés, and restaurants.

Recommended Pacing: Washington, the nation's capital, is one of those cities where you could spend a lifetime without seeing it all. To skim the highlights would take two or three days; to do it some justice, plan on a week.

Getting around Washington is fairly easy using a combination of walking, the Metro system, and (we recommend) Tourmobile Sightseeing, whose buses connect major landmarks via several interconnecting routes through the city and out to Arlington National Cemetery. Unlike many of the tour companies where you travel with a group and have an allotted time at each sightseeing venue, with Tourmobile, which is affiliated with the National Park Service, your ticket is valid for the entire day (9:30am to 4:30pm) and you hop off to visit the places that interest you, spending as much time as desired and then hop on the next bus that comes along. (Buses are approximately thirty minutes apart.) Tickets may be purchased with credit cards (MC, VS) at certain stops where there are ticket booths, or if you have cash or traveler's checks you can embark at any stop and purchase tickets on board. (For pricing and information, www.tourmobile.com, tel: 888-868-7707. Note: Inquire about their two-day pass and know that they also offer an evening, twilight tour.) Each bus is staffed with a park service representative who provides interesting and informative narrative about Washington's landmarks.

We give you the major sights in a natural order so that you can plot them on a detailed city map. Our selection is just a sampler of all there is to see and we suggest that for exploring Washington in depth, you purchase a comprehensive guidebook on the district.

Sightseeing in Washington focuses on **The Mall**, a vast sweep of lawns that stretches from the Capitol to the Lincoln Memorial. Bordering its eastern end are the magnificent museums that comprise the Smithsonian Institution, while its western section presents a vast area of parkland interspersed with famous memorials.

The Capitol Building is home to the Senate and the House of Representatives. It distinguishes a district of Washington D.C. referred to as Capital Hill. When the houses are in session you can see democracy in action either by making your own way round or taking a guided tour. Either way requires a ticket to enter, which can be obtained on the east side near the Supreme Court. Contact your senator or congressman for a special gallery pass. (1st Street NW between Independence and Constitution Avenues, 202-225-6827.) Interesting to note, standing proud in the middle of Capital Hill, located at the corner of 7th and D Streets, is a popular Washington restaurant, **Monocles**, still owned by the same family who 50 years ago stubbornly refused to relocate. A pretty, soft, yellow clapboard building, it is easy to spot as it contrasts dramatically with the regal architecture of the government buildings that surround it!

Behind the Capitol you can watch the justices of the **Supreme Court** in action in this gleaming white building by sitting through an hour of oral argument. If time is pressing, opt instead for a three-minute slot amidst a throng of rotating visitors. Lines for tickets are often long. When the court is not in session the building is still open. (1st and E. Capitol Streets NW, 202-479-3030.)

The adjacent **Library of Congress**, the largest library in the world, is located in what was D.C.'s first public school. The collection started with 5,000 books and has grown to millions of volumes housed in three buildings of which the Jefferson Building, modeled after the Paris Opera House, is the most interesting. (1st Street and Independence Avenue SE, 202-707-5000.)

The museums collectively called **The Smithsonian** are named after James Smithson, an Englishman who never visited the United States but left a $500,000 bequest to "found an establishment for the increase and diffusion of knowledge among men." Your first stop should be the **visitors' center** in the turreted **Smithsonian Castle** to collect a comprehensive map and a daily calendar of events. (202-357-2700) Depending on your interest, you can easily spend a day in each of the institution's museums. There are also four gardens that neighbor the castle, which, depending on the season, offer a serene respite from the rigors of sightseeing. In the spring, the rose garden is breath taking.

Freer Gallery of Art (The Smithsonian): The Freer has an outstanding collection of Asian art as well as one of American art including works by John Singer Sargent and James MacNeil Whistler.

Arthur M. Sackler Gallery (The Smithsonian): Magnificent ancient Chinese paintings, bronzes, and jade carvings collected by Arthur Sackler and generously given to the nation. An underground corridor connects to the adjacent museum of African Art.

National Museum of African Art (The Smithsonian): As you might expect, this delightful little museum contains thousands of masks and carvings alongside everyday pieces such as stools and headrests.

Hirshhorn Museum and Sculpture Garden (The Smithsonian): The Hirshhorn looks rather like a stone donut and houses Joseph Hirshhorn's extensive collection of modern art. Statues by Rodin, Calder, Moore, Matisse, and others line the circular hallways overlooking the central courtyard. In front of the museum, a sunken sculpture garden displays some exquisite stone and marble masterpieces.

National Air and Space Museum (The Smithsonian): This most popular museum chronicles the history of aviation from early flight through modern rockets. Planes and rocketry hang from every rafter as you stand and marvel at the *Wright Flyer*, the *Spirit of St. Louis*, the *Apollo 11* command module, Amelia Earhart's *Vega*, and much more. Sensuround movies in the IMAX theater take you on a virtual-reality tour of flight.

National Museum of the American Indian (The Smithsonian): Tells the stories of the diverse tribes and provides the most intriguing piece of architecture on the mall—rough-hewn and curvilinear the building resembles the walls of a canyon.

National Gallery (The Smithsonian): The east building houses a portion of the nation's collection of 20th-century art. The west houses European and American paintings and sculpture from the 13th to 19th centuries including three Vermeers, Whistler's *White Girl*, and Botticelli's *Adoration of the Magi*. Beside the National Gallery is a **Sculpture Garden** full of large pieces of the most fanciful creations.

National Archives (The Smithsonian): Behind the Sculpture Garden you find the National Archives, built, as Herbert Hoover said, to "house the most sacred documents of our history." It's home to the original Declaration of Independence, the Constitution, and the Bill of Rights, all encased in bronze-and-glass containers sealed with helium. Every night these charters of freedom are lowered 23 feet below ground into a vault!

Natural History Museum (The Smithsonian): Anything and everything—fossils, minerals, and more. View the 45-carat Hope Diamond, once owned by Louis XIV. Marvel at the length of Diplodocus in the Dinosaur Hall and relax in the IMAX theater to enjoy a really big nature film.

American History Museum (The Smithsonian): Everything you ever wanted to know about America's past seems to be displayed here. Objects range from the original Star Spangled Banner to Archie Bunker's chair. It's a fabulous collection with some highlights being the first ladies' ball gowns, a Conestoga wagon, the reconstructed *Titanic* radio room, and a reconstructed portion of the White House. You could spend days studying the exhibits. Please note: This museum closed September 2006 in order to replace and reposition artifacts and is scheduled to reopen in 2008.

A self-guided tour of the **White House**, home of the nation's President, gives you a chance to view the Green, Blue, and Red Rooms, the State Dining Room, and the East Room. The West Wing containing the Oval Office is not part of the tour nor are the family quarters. Visit by timed ticket mid-March to Labor Day and in December (available at White House Visitors' Center). At other times of the year no tickets are needed. Avoid the lines and write to your senator or congressman for VIP tickets. (1600 Pennsylvania Avenue NW, 202-208-1631.)

Just steps away from the Washington Monument, the **Holocaust Memorial Museum** serves as a national memorial to the many millions who were persecuted by the Nazis from 1933 to 1945. The Museum seconds as a research center with a library, archives, an interactive learning center and any one can enter, take advantage of the resources as well as view the special exhibits. To visit the permanent exhibit, *The Holocaust*, requires a reservation. A limited number of same-day tickets are given out at the museum daily starting at 10 am. These are for use during a specific time period; for use that same day. However, it is possible and well worth the small handling fee to get tickets in advance—

call 800-400-9373. The exhibit is incredible, stirs emotions and will take approximately three hours. To personalize the experience, upon entry, you are issued an identification card with the wrenching story of a Holocaust victim. Follow the history of the holocaust from the rise of the Nazis to power, through the chilling reconstruction of life in the concentration camps, past photographs of victims, through the stories of resistance, and finally to the liberation of the camps. Extremely moving are the recorded narratives of actual survivors. (14th Street and Independence Avenue, 202-488-0400.)

A magnificent view of the district presents itself from atop the 550-feet-tall marble obelisk of the **Washington Monument**—the world's largest building with no internal structure that is held together by the earth's gravitational pull. It is no longer possible to walk up the structure, one must take the elevator, but there are times when one is permitted to walk down! A limited number of same day tickets are given out first thing each morning. Avoid the lines by paying a small service charge to obtain advance tickets from Ticketmaster (see your local listing).

Practically in the shadow of the Washington Monument is the incredible **World War II Memorial** that opened in 2004. Honoring the over 16 million who served, the over 400,000 who died and the millions who supported the war effort from home, symbolic and dramatic columns ring a magnificent pool and fountain. Four thousand imbedded gold stars represent the 400,000 lost lives. Quite beautiful, the memorial has quickly become a popular and favorite place to gather and settle for a rest or picnic!

A short walk paralleling the reflecting pools from the World War II Memorial through the park, finds you at the **Vietnam Veterans Memorial**, a curve of polished black granite etched with the names of those who died (or are missing in action) in the Vietnam War. Visitors stare at the row upon row of names, trace with their fingers looking for a loved one or comrade, and leave notes, flowers, and mementos. Just across the reflecting pool is the **Korean War Veterans Memorial** depicting 19 soldiers on patrol.

Standing guard at the western end of The Mall, the **Lincoln Memorial** honors the memory of Abraham Lincoln who led the country through the Civil War. The statue of Lincoln at its center is 19 feet tall. Interesting to note, it was sculpted by Daniel Ford who opened the first school for the death and he sentimentally positioned Abraham Lincoln's hands to "sign" A and L. Ford also carved on the back of Lincoln's head the name of his opponent in battle, R.E. Lee. The 36 columns represent the states in the Union at the time of Lincoln's death. Murals depict scenes from his life and inscriptions from the Gettysburg Address and Lincoln's second inaugural address are etched in marble. Challenge your kids or friends to find the typo—"Future" was wrongly carved as "Euture", but, after-the-fact, too costly to redo!

Banded by park and water and located along the famous Cherry Tree Walk near the National Mall is the stunning memorial to Franklin D. Roosevelt. Be sure to stroll through the over 7 acres and the sequence of four outdoor rooms depicting the achievements of this president and his time in office. The **Franklin D. Roosevelt Memorial** has many wonderful sculptures and a ten-foot sculpture depicting our 32nd President.

With a sweep of the Potomac at its back is the 19-foot-high statue of President Jefferson housed in the **Jefferson Memorial.** This striking and beautifully positioned memorial is a fitting tribute to a man who should be recognized for a multitude of achievements. Thomas Jefferson was a political philosopher, architect, musician, book collector, scientist, horticulturist, diplomat, inventor, in addition to being the third President of the United States.

The **John F. Kennedy Center for the Performing Arts** is one of the country's most splendid performing spaces. Overlooking the Potomac River, six theaters offer everything from opera to dance. The best way to tour is to attend a performance (free performances are offered daily in the Millennium Theater at 6 pm) or you can wander around on your own. Next door is the **Watergate Building**, the site of the 1972 break-in that led to the resignation of President Nixon.

Home to Georgetown University, exploration of **Georgetown** with its picturesque residential streets, fabulous shops, and plethora of inviting restaurants is a must. Enchanting and charming, Georgetown has a character all its own—it is almost like a village within the big city. Walk along M Street, the heart of the shopping area. Stroll down the Chesapeake and Ohio Canal towpath or hop aboard a canal boat for a one-hour trip. From Wisconsin Avenue (also a shopping street) turn down any of the streets between N and Q to elegant side streets (there are mansions at Q and 31st).

Take the Tourmobile to the Virginia side of Memorial Bridge to **Arlington National Cemetery**. The most stirring sight, apart from the graves of President John F. Kennedy and his family, is the Tomb of the Unknown Soldier, watched over by guards who change on the hour (and half hour April to September) with great ceremony and military precision.

A splendid day trip from Washington is a visit to **Mount Vernon**, the home of George Washington. Sitting in an 8,000-acre estate overlooking the Potomac River, it is located 16 miles south of Washington (about half an hour's drive or reached by the Tourmobile April to October). George Washington inherited Mount Vernon from his grandfather in 1754 and lived there from 1783 until his death in 1799. Much of Martha and George's original furniture is in the home. Outbuildings contain the kitchen, smokehouse, and wash house, and there's a splendid 35-acre garden. (703-780-2000)

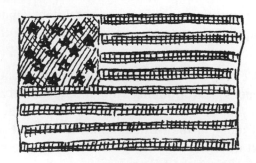

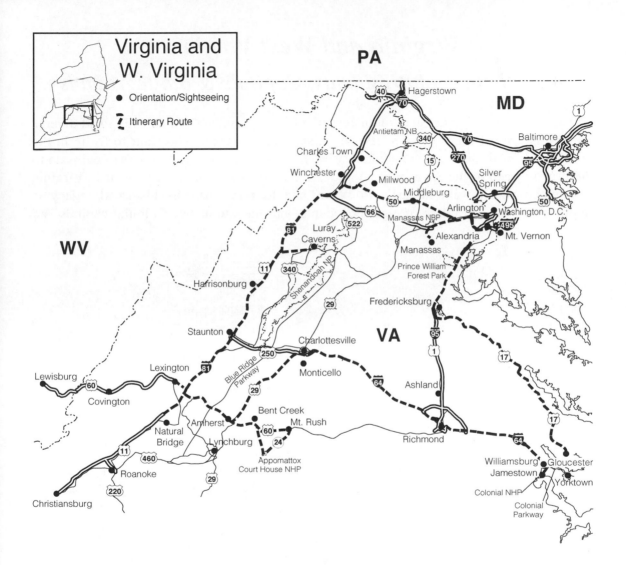

Virginia and West Virginia
A Birthplace of Presidents, Capitals & Battlegrounds

The state of Virginia is steeped in history and offers a banquet of interesting and diverse attractions for all kinds of travelers—for historians, for those who want to frolic in the ocean, and for those love the mountains. From the seashore of the Delmarva Peninsula to the broad sweep of the Shenandoah Valley, to the mountains of the Alleghenies, Virginia is a place you'll want to taste, to savor, and to remember. Its historical legacy is impressive—the birthplace of eight presidents, and the site of two Colonial capitals and

Monticello

more Civil War battlegrounds than any other state in our nation. Take that history and add the state's natural beauty and handsome, fascinating old towns, and you have a bounty of attractions and memories in the making.

The first permanent settlement in America was established at Jamestown in 1607, with the state's capital being moved from Jamestown to Williamsburg and then to Richmond in 1779. In 1775, when the war between England and the Colonies broke out, Virginian Patrick Henry made his now famous "Give me liberty or give me death" speech. Thomas Jefferson, Benjamin Franklin, and John Adams, native sons of Virginia, were all instrumental in the creation of the Declaration of Independence, which was signed on the Fourth of July, 1776. In 1781 the British surrendered to George Washington at Yorktown, ending the Revolutionary War, and 80 years later the Civil War came to an end with the surrender of General Robert E. Lee to General Ulysses S. Grant at Appomattox. Much of the history of the battlefields has been memorialized in Manassas, Appomattox, Fredericksburg, Petersburg, Yorktown, Richmond, and Lexington.

Recommended Pacing: The routing for this itinerary is outlined on Map 5 at the front of the book. Leaving Washington, D.C., a visit to Arlington and Alexandria can take a day of leisurely meandering—this day can be added on to your visit to the nation's capital or can be the first day of your Virginia itinerary. A second day is delightfully spent traveling west through the Virginia hunt country and beginning a drive down the Blue Ridge Mountains. Plan to spend the night in the Staunton, Lexington, or Charlottesville areas. On the following day extend your drive farther down the Blue Ridge Parkway to Roanoke and Christiansburg or visit the historic treasures in and around Charlottesville. On day four travel on to Richmond and Williamsburg. Plan on spending two nights here so that you will have an entire day for exploring this Colonial town before returning to Washington, D.C.

Cross the Potomac for the short drive to the neighboring town of **Alexandria.** The boyhood home of Robert E. Lee is steeped in history and many of its 18th-century homes have been preserved. A walking tour of the town provides a glimpse into that earlier time and visiting Alexandria's many boutiques, antique shops, galleries, and restaurants can make for a delightful diversion. **Christ Church**, where George Washington attended services and where Lee himself was a member almost a century later; **Lee's boyhood home**; the **Old Presbyterian Meeting House**; **Woodlawn Plantation** with its formal gardens; and **Mount Vernon** are all worthy of your time. Most impressive of all is Mount Vernon, made all the more so if you approach this home of **George Washington** by boat as he did in his day (Driving the George Washington Memorial Parkway to Mount Vernon is a lovely alternative way of getting there.) This ancestral home dating back to 1738 has been restored as it was in Washington's later years. The main house, the outbuildings, and the gardens set on a rise up from the Potomac River are lovely as well as historic. (703-780-2000)

Just north of I-66 and off Route 234 is one of the most famous of all Civil War battlefields—**Manassas**, where the armies of the North and the South engaged in the most bloody and deadly battles of the Civil War. For those interested in this period of history, the battlefields of Manassas are marked so as to give the visitor an understanding of the troop movements and the strategies that were employed. (703-361-1339)

To the west of the suburbs of Washington on Route 50 is **Middleburg**, a town whose surrounding countryside is known as "horse country." Mile upon mile of white fences separate green pastures smelling of freshly mown grass where horses graze, and one can only imagine the gracious farmhouses very sophisticatedly but comfortably decorated for those privileged enough to live in this area.

The drive west on Route 50 is particularly lovely since the countryside is so beautiful—there are no fast-food establishments or other highway detractions from your enjoyment of this part of northern Virginia. Of particular note for lovers of antiques is the town of **Millwood** where there are several shops.

Just to the west of these historical suburbs and countryside of northern Virginia you come to the beginning of the mountainous region of this state (I-66 west or Route 50 west to I-81 south or the more leisurely Route 11 south). The ridge that lies along the western edge of Virginia and the eastern borders of West Virginia includes the Shenandoah,

Appalachian, Blue Ridge, and Allegheny Mountains. Along the top of this mountain ridge runs the **Blue Ridge Parkway**, 569 miles of road winding amid spectacularly beautiful scenery unspoiled by any of the commercialism of most of our nation's byways. These mountains are known for their spring-flowering dogwoods and rhododendrons, and in the fall the changing color of the deciduous trees is magnificent. Whether you drive the entire length of the parkway is unimportant—what is important is that you drive at least a portion of this road to appreciate the beauty of this state. In a time when most freeways are driven at 65 miles an hour or more, the Blue Ridge Parkway gives you an opportunity to slow the pace and to relish your surroundings.

Blue Ridge Parkway

Halfway down the state, detour west into the mountains on I-64. A scenic loop takes you up Route 42 to Millboro Springs and west on Route 39 to Warm Springs, returning south to I-64 at Covington. The medicinal springs in this region have made the area a health resort for generations. Once back in Covington you can travel west to White Sulfur

Springs and Lewisburg in West Virginia or return eastward to rejoin the Blue Ridge Parkway. The road through the mountains is an especially beautiful one—but do be sure to check weather conditions if you are considering traveling it during those months when ice and snow may restrict access.

An alternative drive south is along Route 11, which parallels I-81, passing through many historical towns with lots of buildings on the National Register of Historic Places. All the commercial activity in each of the towns is on this route, including a large number of antique shops. Among the towns and historical sites worth visiting are **Staunton**, birthplace of Woodward Wilson; **Lexington**, where you find **Washington and Lee University**, the **Virginia Military Institute**, the **George C. Marshall Museum**, and the **home of Stonewall Jackson**; and **Roanoke**, the commercial center of this area. South of Roanoke is the **Booker T. Washington National Monument**.

Among other attractions of this portion of the state are the **Natural Bridge**, a 23-story arch located south of Lexington, and the **Luray Caverns** on Route 211 just outside Luray. These caverns, enormous in size, have thousands of unusual stone formations.

The area bordered by the Blue Ridge Mountains to the west, Charlottesville and Richmond to the north, and the North Carolina border to the south is called the **Piedmont** and is known as the heartland of Virginia. It's an area of beautiful valleys and rolling hills, as might be expected in a valley between the mountains and the coastal plain. Within this Piedmont region is **Appomattox**, reached from the Blue Ridge Parkway by taking I-81 or Route 11 then Route 60 east to Route 24 south. Appomattox is the site of the famous Civil War battle where **General Robert E. Lee** became surrounded by the armies of the North and surrendered on behalf of the South.

Charlottesville, located just north of I-64, is where **Thomas Jefferson** built his home, **Monticello**. Touring Monticello is an opportunity to glimpse into Jefferson's life and to understand the life and times of this American patriot (434-984-9800). Charlottesville is also the home of the **University of Virginia**, founded in 1817, many of whose buildings were designed by Jefferson.

Heading east on I-64, you come to **Richmond**, which was for a time the capital of the Confederacy and is now the capital of the state. It's a city of much historical interest while at the same time having a thriving modern business economy. Information on guided tours of the city may be found at the **Metro Richmond Convention and Visitors' Bureau**, 550 East Marshall Street, 888-742-4666. Visitors' centers are also located at 1710 Robin Hood Drive (exit 78 off I-95), Bell Tower on Capitol Square (off I-95 at exit 75), 101 Ninth Street, and at the Richmond International Airport.

Of interest in the city are the **Museum of the Confederacy** with its collections of more than 15,000 articles associated with the Confederacy (1201 E. Clay Street, 804-649-1861); the **Virginia Museum of Fine Arts** (2800 Grove Avenue at N. Boulevard, 804-340-1400); the **Virginia State Capitol** on Capitol Square (804-698-1788); **The Valentine**, the museum of the life and history of Richmond (1015 East Clay Street, 804-649-0711); and the Virginia Historical Society's **Center for Virginia History** (428 North Boulevard, 804-358-4901).

Referred to as Virginia's Historic Triangle are the colonial towns of Yorktown, Williamsburg and Jamestown. An interesting way to begin to understand the history of this area is to visit these three significant towns, all part of the **Colonial National Historical Park,** located on a peninsula between the James and York Rivers, and connected by the beautiful and scenic **Colonial Parkway**.

Straddling the banks of the York River, the historic seaport of **Yorktown** was the site where Lord Cornwallis surrendered to General George Washington, which proved to be the last major battle of the American Revolutionary War. Tour the battlefield and then enhance the experience with a visit to the **visitors' center** where the battle on land and at sea is presented through a series of multi-media exhibits. Founded as a tobacco port and seat of the county government since 1634, Yorktown's picturesque streets are home to antique shops, galleries and some historic homes. The waterfront development, Riverwalk Landing, was designed in keeping with the colonial character of town and features a variety of shops and restaurants. Yorktown's Visitor Center provides information on narrative cruises and the candlelight walking tour complete with tales of resident ghosts that are said to haunt the town as well as the historical events that have made this area so famous. (800-447-8679)

Predating Plymouth in Massachusetts by 13 years, **Jamestown** became the original settlement in North America when three merchant ships carrying 104 men and boys landed on what are now Virginia shores in 1607. Board life-size replicas of the three ships for a full appreciation of what these early colonists endured to reach the new land. The year 2006 marked the 400th anniversary of the Jamestown settlement and numerous activities and festivities are planned through 2008 to commemorate this special occasion.

While very little of the original Jamestown remains, other than the **Old Church Tower,** there has been much excavation in this area and there are many monuments and statues of those prominent in Jamestown's history. Much of the history of the War of Independence has been recorded here and those interested in the history of our nation will find much to study and see. Visit historic Jamestowne, site of the original English Settlement, which brings history to life as a living museum; visit the fort and the Powhatan Indian Village.

Colonial Williamsburg is one of our nation's treasures and certainly one of the highlights of a visit to the Mid-Atlantic States. After you have toured Richmond, it is but a short drive to reach Williamsburg, first on I-64 and then south on Route 199. First settled in 1633 and known as Middle Plantation, it was the capital of the state and the social and cultural center for over 80 years. Thereafter, Thomas Jefferson moved the capital to Richmond, where it remains today.

Williamsburg, whose **visitors' center** is near the Governor's Palace (757-220-7645), has been restored to closely resemble the 18th-century town as it originally existed. There are more than 80 buildings on this 301 acre living museum, from the 18th and 19th centuries

Raleigh Tavern, Colonial Williamsburg

while others have been rebuilt on original sites. Among these are public buildings and numerous shops, taverns, homes, and gardens, all now open to visitors. Trades are demonstrated as they were originally practiced and interpreters of the history of Williamsburg are dressed in period costume, making the past come alive with their interesting dialogue on life in the 18th century.

The village has numerous events, both during the day and into the evening, which are suitable for young and old alike. In addition to touring the historic area, especially the **Capitol**, the **Governor's Palace**, the **DeWitt Wallace Gallery**, and the **Bruton Parish Church**, you should visit the **Abby Aldrich Rockefeller Folk Art Center**. (757-220-7645)

At the heart of the town of Williamsburg is the **College of William & Mary**, one of America's finest academic institutions since it was founded more than three hundred years. Many of the students who attend this college get involved in the reenactment of history as staged throughout Williamsburg.

From Williamsburg travel back to Yorktown. From there bridge to Gloucester on Route 17 north, connecting just south of Fredericksburg to I-95 north, which will speedily transport you back to Alexandria and Washington, D.C.

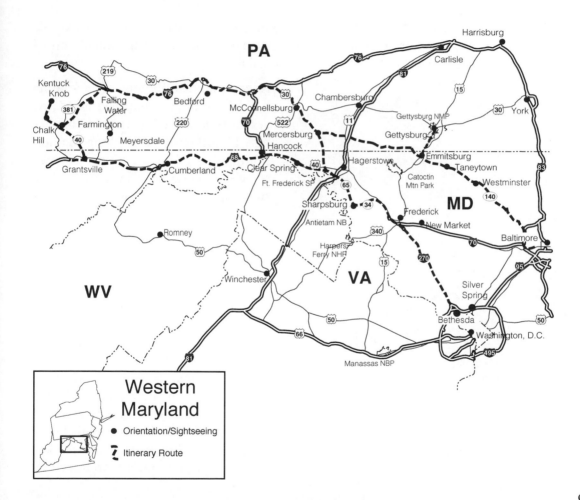

PA

Harrisburg

Carlisle

Kentuck
Knob

Falling
Water

Bedford

McConnellsburg

Chambersburg

Gettysburg NMP

Gettysburg

York

Chalk
Hill

Farmington

Meyersdale

Mercersburg

Hancock

Hagerstown

Emmitsburg

Taneytown

Westminster

Grantsville

Cumberland

Clear Spring

Ft. Frederick SP

Catoctin
Mtn Park

MD

Sharpsburg

Antietam NB

Frederick

New Market

Baltimore

Romney

Harpers
Ferry NHP

WV

Winchester

VA

Silver
Spring

Bethesda

Washington, D.C.

Manassas NBP

Western
Maryland

● Orientation/Sightseeing

Ƨ Itinerary Route

Western Maryland
Experience History, Cities & Mountains

This itinerary departs from Washington, D.C., taking you northwest into battlegrounds that shaped our nation's history then through the Cumberland Pass into the mountains of Northwestern Maryland and Southwestern Pennsylvania.

Frank Lloyd Wright's Fallingwater

Recommended Pacing: The routing for this itinerary is outlined on Map 1 at the front of the book. This itinerary may be followed as one long loop or, if time is at a premium, as two separate itineraries. The shorter of the two routes begins from the city of Washington, D.C. and travels northwest into the battlefields just north of the Maryland state line in Pennsylvania before returning. It's a trip that, assuming an interest but not a consuming passion in the history of the nation, could be traveled in two or three days. The longer route passes through the mountainous western areas of Maryland and southern Pennsylvania including not only the beautiful scenery of mountains and lakes but also a visit to Frank Lloyd Wright's Fallingwater, his most famous contribution to architecture.

This extended westerly loop could easily add three days to your travel for the distances are great and you won't want to spend all the time in the car gazing at the passing scenery.

From **Washington, D.C.** drive northwest on I-270 into the area where much of our country's history was told on bloody battlefields and over long winters. Plan to stop in **Frederick** (from the 270 take I-70 east for 3 miles), an historic town with lovely old stone structures and then, if antiquing is a passion, visit **New Market**, a few miles farther east, generally considered to be the capital for antiquing in Maryland. Keep an eye out for the numerous vineyards that lie in this area and the tasting rooms where you can stop and taste the latest creations of the local winemakers. Back on I-70 heading northwest toward Hagerstown you'll have the opportunity to visit many small historic towns—a great way for you to get a feel for the area and its history. This is also the beginning of the foothills of the Allegheny Mountains whose slopes are covered with orchards.

A side trip worth taking is that to **Sharpsburg** and the **Antietam National Battlefield Site** (Route 34 west from I-70 or Route 65 south from Hagerstown). It is here that the Union forces under the command of General George McClellan met those of General Robert E. Lee and turned back their attempt to move into northern territory.

Continuing on I-70, at Clear Spring take Route 56 south to **Fort Frederick State Park** and visit the museum there. This fort figured in the French and Indian Wars, the American Revolution, and the Civil War. Back on the 70 traveling west, there are several scenic overlooks with grand views into the surrounding mountains.

If time does not permit you to travel farther west, turn north on Route 57 to Mercersburg, where you turn east onto Route 16 for Gettysburg (described later in this itinerary). After visiting this historic area you continue eastwards, picking up Route 140 in Emmitsburg and following it into Baltimore.

The extended loop of this itinerary lets you see more of a very different part of Maryland—one of small towns in rural settings—as you travel west into its mountainous region. The I-70 connects to I-68 as you leave Hancock to travel into the **Cumberland**

Pass and the **Allegheny Mountains**. Once you have climbed the Cumberland Pass and are traveling into the western part of Maryland on I-68, you have the opportunity to visit lovely lakes, and to ski, hike, and camp.

The industrial city of **Cumberland** on the Potomac River, also dating back to the time of the French and Indian Wars, is home to many historic sites and the headquarters of the **Western Maryland Scenic Railroad**. In the town of **Grantsville** as you wend your way west on I-68, you will notice the descendants of the Amish and the Mennonite farmers who today live their lives as their ancestors did for the last century or more. Of special beauty is the area not far to the south around **Deep Creek Lake**.

From the I-68 west of Grantsville, take Route 40 west to Farmington, Pennsylvania and then drive north on Route 381 towards your goal of Frank Lloyd Wright's masterpiece, Fallingwater. However, before you get there, you might want to stop at **Kentuck Knob**, another **Frank Lloyd Wright** home, located 6 miles north of Route 40 and 2½ miles south of Ohiopyle on Chalk Hill-Ohiopyle Road. Opened to the public in 1996, this home embodies many of Wright's architectural principles and philosophies and the owners have filled it with furniture and accessories designed by Wright. Panoramic views from the house overlook the Youghiogheny River Gorge and the mountains. Reservations are suggested for the 1½-hour guided tour. (724-329-1901)

A little farther north you come to **Fallingwater**, acknowledged as one of the greatest 20th-century architectural achievements in America and designed by Frank Lloyd Wright when he was 68 years old. What inspired Wright was the opportunity to merge one of the most beautiful of all sites—a waterfall and stream running through rocky terrain—and a structure designed to harmonize with the majesty of the setting. If you have ever built a house and if you are fascinated by design, you must travel to visit this Frank Lloyd Wright creation—it will provide you with a lifelong memory. Visiting Fallingwater is by 45-minute guided tour only. Opening times vary by season, so call 412-329-8501 to be sure that you will be able to see this masterpiece. The **Western Pennsylvania Conservancy**, dedicated to preserving habitats for a diversity of life and uses, is responsible for the conservation efforts here at Fallingwater. (724 329-8501)

Continue north to connect with I-70, and travel east to Mercersburg on Route 16 then Route 140, which will take you eventually to Baltimore and the end of the journey. As you drive through the Pennsylvania countryside you see the historic markers and sites of the battles fought here. Of special note is Gettysburg, reached by detouring north on Route 15 at Emmitsburg.

To visit **Gettysburg** and to gain an understanding of the **Civil War** you will need to plan a minimum of one day in this area. Gettysburg was the site of the war's worst battle and greatest loss of men in the summer of 1863. With Robert E. Lee making a move toward capturing the capital of Harrisburg and Major General Joe Hooker moving north, the two armies, war-worn, tired, and discouraged as they were, met and fought in what history has recorded as the deciding battle of the Civil War. When it was over thousands were dead and more wounded. It was at the consecration of the Gettysburg cemetery for the war dead that **President Lincoln** made his famous address beginning, "Fourscore and seven years ago our fathers brought forth on this continent a new nation, conceived in liberty and dedicated to the proposition that all men are created equal." Among the sights here are the **Gettysburg National Military Park** with its visitors' center, the **National Cemetery**, and the **Eisenhower National Historic Site** with the Eisenhower home complete with furnishings. Information on visiting Gettysburg may be obtained from the Gettysburg National Military Park, 97 Taneytown Road, Gettysburg, PA 17325, 717-334-1124, or the Gettysburg Convention and Visitors' Bureau, 35 Carlisle Street, Gettysburg, PA 17325, 717-334-6274. (Note: Additional information is also referenced in the *Brandywine Valley, Lancaster & Gettysburg* itinerary.)

Your trip ends in **Baltimore** and you'll want to allow time for a visit. This is a city whose resurgence is remarkable, with a downtown area and a waterfront that is nothing short of exciting. You should not miss a tour of the **harbor** (410-727-3113) and among other sights to see are the **B&O Railroad Museum**, the **Baltimore Museum of Art**, and the **Evergreen House**. The **Baltimore Visitors' Center** can assist you with information on the many tours (especially walking tours) available. (300 W. Pratt Street, 410-837-4636 or 800-282-6632.)

Western Maryland

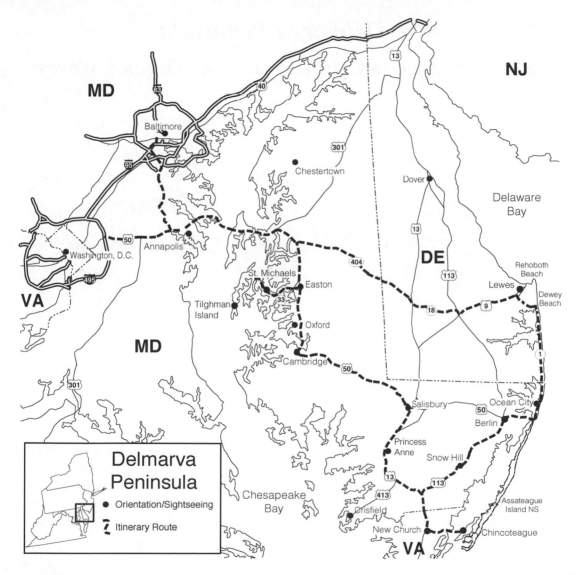

MD

NJ

Baltimore

Chestertown

Dover

Delaware
Bay

DE

Rehoboth
Beach

Lewes

Dewey
Beach

Annapolis

St. Michaels

Easton

Tilghman
Island

Oxford

Washington, D.C.

VA

MD

Cambridge

Salisbury

Ocean City

Berlin

Princess
Anne

Snow Hill

Chesapeake
Bay

Crisfield

New Church

VA

Assateague
Island NS

Chincoteague

Delmarva
Peninsula

● Orientation/Sightseeing

Itinerary Route

101

The Delmarva Peninsula

Travel with the Oyster, the Crab & the Ocean's Waves

Chesapeake Bay divides the state of Maryland neatly into two parts—to the west you find the state capital of Annapolis, the city of Baltimore, and the suburbs of Washington, D.C. To the east lies the Delmarva Peninsula, whose eastern coast is bounded by the Atlantic Ocean. "Delmarva" is an acronym for Delaware, Maryland, and Virginia, the three states that share this peninsula, sometimes also called the Tidewater Peninsula or the Eastern Shore.

Recommended Pacing: The routing for this itinerary is outlined on Map 1 at the front of the book. Starting either from Baltimore or Washington, travel to Annapolis and on to the Delmarva Peninsula. Visiting the peninsula can take as little as two days with an overnight in one of the charming towns. Do not rush—you could easily spend a week moseying around and it will be all the more pleasurable if you plan your trip to avoid the hot and humid summer months.

Begin your trip in **Salisbury**, reached by driving east over the Chesapeake Bay Bridge then south and southeast on Route 50. The art of decoy carving has now been recognized as American folk art and from their humble beginnings as functional objects used by hunters to attract waterfowl, decoys have now become sought-after and expensive treasures for serious antique collectors. To see some of the best decoys carved by Maryland's renowned carvers, visit the **Ward Museum of Wildfowl Art** located at 909 S. Schumaker Drive. (410-742-4988)

Turning east from Salisbury, travel toward the Atlantic-coast beaches on Route 50 and to the major Maryland beach resort of **Ocean City**. Once upon a time Ocean City was known for its boardwalk, tourist attractions, and hotels whose residents were escaping from the sweltering heat and humidity inland to the coolness of the ocean. This once-charming town has now become a bustling city of wall-to-wall condominiums, hotels, homes, and even a convention center, losing much that once made it so special. But there's still a boardwalk, now 3 miles long, lined by shops, restaurants, and arcades, and there's still plenty of saltwater taffy. Don't miss the carousel (circa 1802) with its hand-carved animal mounts. There are also still miles upon miles of white sandy beaches and some of the best ocean around in which to dodge the incoming breaking waves on a hot summer's afternoon. From Ocean City there is good deep-water fishing for blue marlin, tuna, wahoo, and bull dolphin. On the bay beneath the bridge that connects Ocean City to the mainland, you find good windsurfing, jet-skiing, and para-sailing.

An interesting side trip from Ocean City is to drive 30 miles north on Routes 528 and 1, bringing you into Delaware and the towns of **Dewey Beach**, **Rehoboth Beach**, and **Lewes**—Lewes with its shops and restaurants is particularly charming. A car ferry connects Lewes with the lowest tip of New Jersey and the picturesque Victorian village of Cape May, where you could join our itinerary along the New Jersey shore, which begins on page 45. If your time is limited, return west to Annapolis on Route 9.

Eight miles south of Ocean City on Route 611 is the northern end of **Assateague Island National Seashore**. This 37-mile-long narrow spit of land is a wildlife refuge and also the home of the Chincoteague ponies. The National Park Service has a visitors' center where you may obtain information on the seashore activities here like fishing, crabbing, swimming, and camping.

From Ocean City take Route 50 west and then turn south on Route 113, stopping first in **Berlin**, a town that has been restored and provides the opportunity for some antiquing. Farther south, just outside Snow Hill, you come to **Furnace Town**, the site of Maryland's only bog-ore furnace.

Continue southwest on Route 113 then south on 13, crossing the border of Maryland into Virginia and turning east onto Route 175 for the **Chincoteague National Wildlife Refuge**. From the refuge parking lot, where there are National Park Service and Wildlife Refuge centers, you can take a tram into the southern end of Assateague Island National Seashore. Walk along the shore in this peaceful and often isolated park watching the shorebirds dodge the waves and listening to their cries. This is an area for serious birdwatching and a checklist is available at any of the visitors' centers.

On Assateague back country, camping is available on either the bay or ocean sides of the island—though the "ocean" camping is still 4 miles from the ocean itself. The island is well known for its wild ponies. If you have children, share with them the book *Misty of Chincoteague* and the delights of pony-penning. This event is held on the last Wednesday and Thursday in July when the young foals are rounded up to swim across the strait between Assateague and Chincoteague before being auctioned off to eager buyers.

Continuing south on Route 13 will take you to the famous **Chesapeake Bay Bridge-Tunnel**, a 17.6-mile-long bridge and tunnel—undoubtedly one of man's greatest engineering feats—which connects to Virginia Beach, a convenient way to join our Virginia itinerary, which begins on page 83.)

If visiting the wildlife refuge or the Assateague seashore is not in your itinerary, after passing through Snow Hill, leave Route 113 at Pocomoke City and drive north on Route 13 towards **Princess Anne**. A short side trip to **Crisfield** (via Route 413) at the southwestern tip of Maryland brings you to a village of fishermen, their boats, and the ever-present seagulls. The primary activity here is fishing for oysters and crabs, both softshell (in the summer only) and hardshell—all three are great delicacies and eating them in their varied ways of preparation is part of the true experience of visiting the Eastern Shore.

Joining Route 50 north in Salisbury, travel northwest. Take Route 333 west to **Oxford** and allow time to walk the streets of this town, located at the tip of a peninsula between the Tred Avon and Choptank Rivers. See the fishing and the boat-building industry that flourishes here. For an interesting change of pace take the Oxford-Bellevue ferry to shortcut the trip to **St. Michaels**, using Route 33 to reach this resort town, sailing, and boating center. This is an especially attractive area in which to spend a day or two.

If you have not taken the ferry, return to Route 50 north and the town of **Easton**, the commercial center for this part of Maryland. This is an attractive town and a good place to do some antiquing—while consuming more of the seafood of the Eastern Shore. From

Easton travel Route 33 west to St. Michaels and on to **Tilghman Island** at the end of a spit of land curling west into the Chesapeake Bay.

There are many historic structures here on the Delmarva Peninsula and they deserve to be enjoyed at a leisurely pace, so plan to spend a night or two at one of the inns recommended in this guide. Each of these towns has its own special charm and you also need to allow some time to walk the main streets and to explore the antique shops where treasures abound.

Route 50 leads north from Easton to the Chesapeake Bay Bridge and west over to **Annapolis**, the state capital, also known as the site of the United States Naval Academy and as a major yachting center. Congress assembled here in 1783 and 1784, making it the first capital of the United States. Annapolis is one of the oldest cities in Maryland and touring the historic buildings and walking the streets will charm you and at the same time give you insight into the importance of this city as a commercial center and state capital.

While you are here take a boat tour of the harbor and its bustling activity. Be sure to take a guided tour of the **State House** on State Circle, the oldest capitol in continuous legislative use and the only one where Congress has met (410-974-3400). If you tour the **Naval Academy**, try to time your visit to coincide with the noon formation in front of Bancroft Hall or in the spring, fall, or at commencement with one of the formal dress parades. Information on Academy tours is available at the Armel-Leftwich Visitors' Center. (410-263-6933) To ensure that you don't miss a thing in and around this fascinating city, drop by the **Annapolis and Anne Arundel County Conference and Visitors' Bureau** at 26 West Street. (410-280-0445)

Places to Stay
Delaware

We arrived on the ferry from Cape May and found the little historic town of Lewes and the Inn at Canal Square sitting just off the town's short Main Street—the only waterfront inn in Lewes. The inn's handsome, contemporary, appearance looks fresh and clean among all the historic structures. Inside there are 22 large guestrooms and two suites, many with a balcony overlooking the working harbor, where fishing boats (as well as pleasure craft) provide great entertainment. Rooms 401, 402 and 403 boast some of the best views. The two suites are located in the neighboring Waterview and Courtyard Buildings with their wonderful wrap-around deck; enjoy two bedrooms, two baths, living room, kitchenette and wonderful views. The Admiral's Suite is the more spectacular of the two! Every corner of this inn has been carefully decorated. Just inside the entrance you find a small but exquisitely furnished guest area with a fireplace where you can relax and there is a nice dining area where an expanded Continental breakfast is served. Settle in this oldest town in Delaware just before or after taking the Cape May–Lewes ferry. A great walking town you will enjoy its antique shops and the boutiques, and it is no distance at all to the ocean and bay beaches. A conference center is available for meetings or receptions. *Directions:* From the ferry landing turn right on Cape Henlopen Drive, left on Savannah Road, and right on Front Street to Market Street to the inn.

INN AT CANAL SQUARE
Manager: Stacey Wiles
122 Market Street
Lewes, DE 19958, USA
Tel: (302) 644-3377, Fax: (302) 644-3565
Toll Free: (888) 644-1911
24 Rooms, Double: $230–$600
Open: all year, Credit cards: all major
www.karenbrown.com/deinnatcanalsquare.html

Inns like this whose reputation spreads far and wide, where a planned stay is greeted with envy by your friends, and whose brochure speaks quality before you've even booked your reservation are the inns around which you want to plan your trip. You'll not be disappointed in this one. Fortunately there's so much to do in the area with Winterthur, Longwood Gardens, the Brandywine River Museum, Hagley, Nemours, etc., that you just have to stay for several nights. Montchanin makes up a village, with many buildings surrounded by profusely blooming flower gardens providing accommodations, all displaying class and great taste whether they are luxurious or more simple. The bed sheets alone would be worth a visit and you will love the marble bathrooms, the living rooms, the TVs, the air conditioning, and the mini-kitchens. The great room in the barn reception building has been reconstructed with hand-hewn beams, a large fireplace, and several sitting areas and is a great place for an aperitif before dinner in the inn's restaurant, Krazy Kat's, with its whimsical cat décor and memorable food. Paintings of cats in every kind of attire—one frolicking with a maiden in a meadow, others in Oriental dress—create a delightful background for an outstanding food experience. This inn has it all: location, accommodations, and food—you must not miss it! *Directions:* From Route 1 or I-95 take Route 52 to Kirk Road or Route 100 and turn east to the inn.

INN AT MONTCHANIN VILLAGE
General Manager: Jacques Amblard
Route 100 & Kirk Road
P.O. Box 130, Montchanin, DE 19710, USA
Tel: (302) 888-2133, Fax: (302) 888-0389
Toll Free: (800) 269-2473
28 Rooms, Double: $179–$399*
*Breakfast not included: $12-$18
Open: all year, Credit cards: all major
Select Registry
www.karenbrown.com/deinnatmontchanin.html

Located in one of Delaware's most popular beach towns, the interior ambiance of this inn is surprisingly sophisticated. When I walked through the front door I felt as if I was transported across the Atlantic to a countryside hotel in England. Although, larger than most properties we consider for our guide, the Bellmoor is family owned and the Moores are personally involved with the operation, guest attention, and welcome. As a larger hotel, the Bellmoor is able to offer services not always possible in a smaller property such as a concierge, two pools, a full-service spa, and business center. Public areas are regal and impressive, yet cozy and inviting. Rich woods, beautiful hardwood floors, large open wood-burning fireplaces, shuttered windows, Oriental rugs, and soft leather seating entice one to settle in. Opening onto the central garden, The Garden Room with its paned windows and enclosed terrace is where a hearty country breakfast is set out each morning. For a little more exclusivity, ask for the Concierge floor (the 4th floor specially accessed by the elevator) or the Garden annex, an attractive green-shuttered brick building whose rooms are more quaint with quilts and knotty pines. Just two blocks to the beach or one might just decide to simply enjoy The Bellmoor. *Directions:* Traveling Route 1 from north, take Rehoboth Beach Exit 1A. Follow Rehoboth Avenue towards the town center. Turn right at an angle onto Christian Street. The Hotel is on your right.

❄ ☕ ⚒ 💳 📷 🏠 🐕 ⛲ 🏋 ☕ P ⊘ ☘ 🏊 📺 🏄 ♿ ✝ 🎾 ⚓ 🚣

THE BELLMOOR
Innkeeper: Chad Moore
6 Christian Street
Rehoboth Beach, DE 19971, USA
Tel: (302) 227-5800, Fax: (302) 227-0323
Toll Free: (800) 425-2355
78 Rooms, Double: $110–$495
Open: all year, Credit cards: all major
Select Registry
www.karenbrown.com/bellmoor.html

Places to Stay
District of Columbia

The Capitol Building

DuPont Circle is a great area of Washington to stay in—it's got that old-neighborhood feeling and from this inn you can easily get to excellent restaurants with all types of international cuisine. This is also a great part of Washington for walking, with art galleries and embassies galore close by. Celebrating ten years, the DuPont at The Circle is an inn (formerly two side-by-side Victorian townhouses) with an eclectic atmosphere; for example, an antique cherry corner cabinet and traditional long mahogany dining table are surrounded by contemporary art. While the Cuban Room in which I stayed was small, it had a desk and a good chair, the queen bed was very comfortable, and the bathroom had a wonderful shower/Jacuzzi tub (a feature in four of the rooms). Other rooms are larger. The Canopy Room has a four-poster bed, a sunny eastern exposure, and a good reading chair in the bay window, while the Lincoln Room has the same furniture as the room of that name at the White House. The English Basement is a studio apartment with a kitchen nook and a private entrance. The Plum Suite is luxurious, with a chaise lounge, large desk, entertainment center, spacious marble bathroom with Jacuzzi, and a working fireplace. There's a patio out front where you can sit and watch the passersby. *Directions:* From the Beltway (I-495) take Connecticut Avenue, Route 185 south. Turn left onto Q Street and immediately left onto 19th Street. The inn is the first townhouse on your left.

❋ ▬ CREDIT ☎ P 🚭

DUPONT AT THE CIRCLE
Owners: Alan & Anexora Skvirsky
Innkeeper: Inés de Azcárate
1604-1606 19th Street N.W.
Washington, DC 20009, USA
Tel: (202) 332-5251, Fax: (202) 332-3244
Toll Free: (888) 412-0100
7 Rooms, Double: $170–$375
1 studio apartment
Open: all year, Credit cards: all major
www.karenbrown.com/dcdupont.html

In a city of tradition and polished mahogany, the bright and colorful Hotel George, on Capitol Hill, stands out with its refreshingly contemporary, upbeat design. The two-story lobby, decorated in black and white with touches of red in the carpet, has a grand piano near the reception desk and huge windows that flood the area with sunlight. You may also hear the clunk of pool balls from the guests' billiards room upstairs. As the hotel's brochure says, here you'll find no chintz, no overstuffed chairs, no clutter—and this is very true in the 139 sleekly styled bedrooms and suites. What you will find are touches of marble in the bathrooms, all the amenities like robes, irons, and ironing boards, and all the extra services like complimentary shoe shine. The Zinc Bar will serve your favorite cocktail and the Bis restaurant will present you with a dinner complementing "French cuisine with an American sensibility." The George also has a fitness center and a steam room. Everything about this hotel says "boutique" and it's absolutely great. *Directions:* From Dulles Airport, follow the sign toward Washington then take the I-66 east exit. I-66 will go across the Theodore Roosevelt Bridge. Take the exit for Constitution Avenue. Following Constitution Avenue eastbound, turn left on 6th Street. Take 6th Street to E Street and turn right. The Hotel George is on the left after New Jersey Avenue.

HOTEL GEORGE
Manager: Dixie Eng
15 E Street N.W.
Washington, DC 20001, USA
Tel: (202) 347-4200, Fax: (202) 347-4213
Toll Free: (800) 576-8331
139 Rooms, Double: $240–$875*
*Breakfast not included
Open: all year, Credit cards: all major
www.karenbrown.com/dchotelgeorge.html

Located on Lafayette Square, across from the White House, The Hay-Adams is a hotel of luxury and tradition, and is one of the choice hotels for both business and leisure travelers. Those who consider it their "home away from home" will be pleased to learn that the hotel has spent a fortune renovating the property to bring back the polish and grandeur it had when it first opened its doors in 1928. This is a great hotel with a caring staff anticipating and meeting your every need, a wonderful restaurant, The Lafayette, and Off the Record bar, Washington's place to be seen and not heard. Bedrooms are spacious and grand, with comfortable seating and reading chairs and a convenient desk with complimentary high-speed Internet access. My room looked out through large windows at the White House; other rooms overlook historic St. John's Church. The bathrooms are adorned with marble and brass and provide all the amenities you could possibly want. But after all the trimmings, the great things about this hotel are its pedigree and the people who make it what it is. The Hay-Adams is an institution, offering the best of everything. *Directions:* From New York and Baltimore take I-95 south to I-495 west. Exit onto Connecticut Ave South towards Chevy Chase and drive for about 7 miles. Continue under Dupont Circle for about 7 blocks then turn left on H Street. Proceed to 16th Street and turn left: the hotel is on the left at 16th and H Streets.

❄ ⚓ 🅲🆁🅴🅳🅸🆃 ☎ 🐕 🏨 ☗ ⅄ P ⑁ ♿

THE HAY-ADAMS
Manager: Hans Bruland
One Lafayette Square
16th & H Streets N.W.
Washington, DC 20006, USA
Tel: (202) 638-6600, Fax: (202) 638-2716
Toll Free: (800) 424-5054
145 Rooms, Double: $359–$6,500*
*Breakfast not included: $30
Open: all year, Credit cards: all major
www.karenbrown.com/dchayadams.html

Swann House, built in 1883, is located on New Hampshire Avenue just a few blocks from DuPont Circle and within easy access of many fine restaurants and museums. The inn sits diagonal to the street, providing a limited number of off-street parking places for guests, a feature of great value in this city where parking is hard to find. You enter through Swann House's great arched front porch and find yourself in parlors with 12-foot ceilings, crown moldings, inlaid wood floors, crystal chandeliers, and elaborate fireplace mantels. At the back guests enjoy a sunroom with wet bar, a private garden, and a small pool. A couple of the bedrooms have private decks including the Regent Room, which has a king bed, fireplace, Jacuzzi, and double marble shower. The romantic Blue Sky Suite has a luxurious queen bedroom with fireplace and a charming sitting room decorated in blue toile. Il Duomo is a king-size room with cathedral ceilings, Gothic windows, a fireplace, and wet bar. The bathroom in the turret features an oversized claw-foot tub and a wonderful rain bath shower. An expanded, very satisfying Continental breakfast including the inn's own granola is served each day. The inn is available for private parties, weddings, conferences, luncheons, dinners, and teas. *Directions:* From the Beltway (I-495) take Route 185 south to DuPont Circle to New Hampshire Avenue. The inn is on the left a few blocks north of DuPont Circle.

SWANN HOUSE
Innkeepers: Mary Lotto Ross & Rick Verkler
1808 New Hampshire Avenue N.W.
Washington, DC 20009, USA
Tel: (202) 265-4414, Fax: (202) 265-6755
9 Rooms, Double: $150–$365
Open: all year, Credit cards: all major
Select Registry
www.karenbrown.com/dcswannhouse.html

Georgetown is that lively part of the District of Columbia where Georgetown University is located, just minutes from downtown Washington. As in any such setting, there are many young people and lots of little shops, coffee bars, restaurants, and fun things to do including people watching and walking along the historic streets and the canal. There are several places to stay in this historic and charming community, but I favor one that is only a few years old—the Hotel Monticello. It's one of those newer suite hotels where the rooms, though fairly predictable, are bright and cheery and spacious enough to be comfortable either for a business stay or for sightseeing around Washington. Each suite has a two-line telephone with data port and voice mail, TV, microwave, coffee maker, and wet bar. The hotel has meeting space, secretarial services, and free membership to a nearby fitness center with pool and steam sauna. The National Airport is just ten minutes away and the Metro rail can easily be reached for transportation within the greater Washington area. *Directions:* Take the Beltway (I-495) south to signs for Tysons Corner then follow The George Washington Memorial Parkway east. Exit for Key Bridge and cross the bridge. Turn right on M Street for three lights to Wisconsin Avenue, then turn right for one block onto K Street. Turn left for two blocks and then left on Thomas Jefferson to the hotel on the right.

HOTEL MONTICELLO
Director: Fletcher Stark
1075 Thomas Jefferson Street N.W.
Washington–Georgetown, DC 20007, USA
Tel: (202) 337-0900, Fax: (202) 333-6526
Toll Free: (800) 388-2410
47 Rooms, Double: $269–$350
Open: all year, Credit cards: all major
www.karenbrown.com/dcmonticello.html

Places to Stay
Maryland

Intimate European-style hotels are special finds here in America and such is the Admiral Fell with its 80 rooms divided among eight adjoining buildings, some dating back to the 18th century. As you enter the graciously comfortable reception area you note the fireplace and the sofas and chairs that beckon you to relax for a few moments with the daily newspaper or a magazine. Guestrooms are decorated with Federal-period reproduction mahogany furniture. Our large, exceptionally quiet back room had two double beds, a writing desk, and comfortable chairs in which to relax. The bathroom, while not large, had everything we could have wanted, including quality toiletries. There's a first-class restaurant in the inn and our dinner there was exceptional—as was the service and the accommodation of the chef to a variance from the menu. Seafood always rates highly in this part of the country, and here it was excellent. With advance notice, the inn provides complimentary shuttle service to nearby Inner Harbor attractions, the Johns Hopkins Hospital, and other locations, while you can take a water taxi to the various Inner Harbor activities. The inn is superbly located, with access to all of the activities and shopping of one of the most widely acclaimed renewal projects of any city in the country. *Directions:* In the revitalized historic section of Baltimore overlooking the harbor at the foot of Broadway.

ADMIRAL FELL INN
Innkeeper: Dominik Eckenstein
888 South Broadway
Baltimore, MD 21231, USA
Tel: (410) 522-7377, Fax: (410) 522-0707
Toll Free: (800) 292-4667
80 Rooms, Double: $215–$395
Open: all year, Credit cards: all major
www.karenbrown.com/mdadmiralfell.html

Inns located among the hustle and bustle of major cities provide travelers with an alternative to the facelessness of many hotels. While Celie's Waterfront B&B is not fancy or pretentious, its location in the historic Fell's Point waterfront renewal area of downtown Baltimore makes it an attractive in-town inn for visitors to the city. Water taxis provide a delightful means of transportation to shopping, the sports stadiums, the convention center, the world-renowned Johns Hopkins Medical Center, and cultural events. The inn's seven bedrooms and two suites either provide limited views of the harbor itself or look inward into the city of Baltimore. Guestrooms are comfortably but simply furnished and two large rooms have wood-burning fireplaces. Four rooms offer single whirlpool tubs and two have their own private balconies. Guests enjoy a small common room with wood-burning fireplace on the first floor, a dining room with a rectangular table for breakfast (Continental), and a garden, which in summer is a delightful place to relax and have breakfast. Whether you're in Baltimore for business or pleasure, robes, TV/VCRs, telephones with answering machines, modems, desks, fax machines, refrigerators, and coffee makers are all there to make your visit a pleasurable one. There's a spectacular rooftop deck with wonderful views of the harbor. *Directions:* Contact the inn or check the website for easy-to-follow directions.

CELIE'S WATERFRONT B&B
Innkeepers: Nancy & Kevin Kupec
1714 Thames Street
Baltimore, MD 21231, USA
Tel: (410) 522-2323, Toll Free: (800) 432-0184
9 Rooms, Double: $129–$349
Open: all year, Credit cards: all major
www.karenbrown.com/mdcelieswaterfront.html

In the countryside a little northwest of Baltimore at the end of a long, winding drive you find the Tudor-style Gramercy Mansion, set high on a hill in 45 acres, including a certified organic garden featuring herbs. There are many separate buildings on the property. As you would expect, the spacious front hall of the main home has a lovely staircase that winds upwards to the guestrooms. With the addition of two new bedrooms there are now a total of ten guestrooms. The rooms have king beds and many enjoy fireplaces with interesting period tiles, art deco or art nouveau, and mantles of walnut or oak. Bathrooms are generous, if not huge, and many have two-person spa tubs set in marble surrounds. Guests here experience a moment from an earlier time and whether you eat in the formal dining room at tables for two or on the terrace, the style of gracious living surrounds you everywhere. Amenities include an Olympic-size pool, a tennis court, and walking trails through the woods. The Carriage House and The Mansion are reserved for weddings, parties, and seminars. *Directions:* Located five minutes north of Route 695 in Greenspring Valley. Take Route 695 to the Falls Road exit, 23B, and go left at the second light to Greenspring Valley Road. Drive for 1 mile, crossing the light at Greenspring Avenue to the first driveway on the right.

GRAMERCY MANSION
Owner: Anne Pomykala
Manager: Cristin Kline
1400 Greenspring Valley Road
Baltimore, MD 21153, USA
Tel: (410) 486-2405, Fax: (410) 486-1765
Toll Free: (800) 553-3404
10 Rooms, Double: $100–$375
Open: all year, Credit cards: all major
www.karenbrown.com/mdgramercymansion.html

Just outside one of the Eastern Shore's most charming towns, Chestertown, which dates back to 1706, you find an inn with charming innkeepers—Danielle and Mike Hanscom. Set on 35 acres, the Brampton Inn was originally built as a plantation house in 1860 and the gracious style of both the house and its furnishings will make you wish you could stay longer. Wonderful old boxwood bushes decorate the entrance to the inn and inside you find elegant, traditional décor that has been tastefully executed with antiques, reproductions, and beautiful fabrics, always with guests' comfort in mind. High ceilings add to the ambiance and to the sense of grandeur—and grand is the perfect way to describe this inn. Buildings on the National Register of Historic Places are often difficult to transform into wonderful accommodations but this has been accomplished here with class and style. The bedrooms in the original building welcome you and create an easy, relaxing atmosphere. In an old horse barn there are two large rooms with sitting rooms and double-Jacuzzi bathrooms. Whichever room you choose, you cannot go wrong at this inn. Chestertown is a lovely town bordering the river—the homes that line the riverbank are particularly attractive and the historic town itself could easily consume an afternoon of sightseeing. *Directions:* Follow Route 50 to Route 301 north to Route 213 north, then take 291 west to Route 20. The inn is 1 mile from Chestertown on Route 20 west.

❄ ☕ 🏌 💳 P ♿ 🚶 👫

BRAMPTON INN
Innkeepers: Danielle & Michael Hanscom
25227 Chestertown Road
Route 20
Chestertown, MD 21620, USA
Tel: (410) 778-1860, Fax: none
Toll Free: (866) 305-1860
10 Rooms, Double: $165–$375
Open: all year, Credit cards: all major
Select Registry
www.karenbrown.com/mdbramptoninn.html

One of the distinguishing characteristics of old homes on the Eastern Shore of Maryland is the high ceilings with which most of them have been designed, keeping them cooler in the summer but also providing a grandeur of architecture. These are homes of large rooms and high style, yet ones where you can relax and be comfortable. Special to inns on Chesapeake Bay like the Great Oak Manor are the sweeping patio and lawns that slope away from the buildings toward the nearby water's edge and chairs from which to view it all. This inn is gracious in every sense. There are 12 particularly large bedrooms with queen or king beds, sitting areas, desks or dressing tables, and private bathrooms. My favorite was on the second floor, the former master suite named Marmaduke, which takes up the whole of one end of this grand old home: its soft colors seem to promise a relaxed stay. The inn is also ready for your special occasion—business conference, family gathering, or wedding. The innkeepers in this region provide a hospitality that is truly Southern in style and expanse. Great Oak Manor has all these features and great innkeepers and invites you to become part of its life for a multi-night visit. You will enjoy every moment. *Directions:* Take Route 50 to Route 213 to Chestertown. Drive through town to Route 291 west, to Route 20 west and then Route 514 to the bay and follow signs for Great Oak Manor.

GREAT OAK MANOR BED & BREAKFAST
Innkeepers: John & Cassandra Fedas
10568 Cliff Road
Chestertown, MD 21620, USA
Tel: (410) 778-5943, Fax: (410) 810-2517
Toll Free: (800) 504-3098
12 Rooms, Double: $160–$275
Open: all year, Credit cards: all major
Select Registry
www.karenbrown.com/greatoakmanor.html

In the center of the town of Chestertown the White Swan Tavern stands proudly on the broad street that goes from the river into the heart of town with its shops, restaurants, and local businesses. There are several antique shops here to entice you with their merchandise. The inn, with its columned front entrance, dates back as a building to pre-Revolutionary times and its current owners have restored it with recognition and appreciation of that earlier time. Hand-hewn beams, paneling, low ceilings, and Colonial furnishings make this a cozy overnight stop in your travels on the Eastern Shore. There is something especially warm and welcoming about dark wood paneling, low ceilings, and hand-hewn beams, and in the dining room these make your meal all the more delightful. The bedrooms, all with private baths, have been furnished with period and reproduction furniture in the style of the era in which the tavern was built. Several rooms have romantic, canopied beds. The T.W. Eliason Suite on the second floor has two bedrooms—one king and one twin—and a comfortable sitting room. Guests are served a Continental breakfast in the dining room. Complimentary morning newspaper, beverages throughout the day, a fruit basket, and afternoon tea are available. The owners have established a small museum containing Colonial artifacts found during an archaeological dig on the site. *Directions:* Take Route 50 to Route 213 to Chestertown to the inn.

WHITE SWAN TAVERN
Innkeepers: Mary Susan Maisel & Wayne McGuire
231 High Street
Chestertown, MD 21620, USA
Tel: (410) 778-2300, Fax: (410) 778-4543
6 Rooms, Double: $140–$240
Open: all year, Credit cards: MC, VS
Select Registry
www.karenbrown.com/mdwhiteswan.html

Indeed, there is something magical about Lake Pointe Inn. The setting, at the edge of a lake with distant views, is romantic; there's a long porch with green rockers where you could spend hours just daydreaming; there are canoes waiting to be used; trails expectantly waiting for footsteps; and there's a ski slope just out the front. The living room of Lake Pointe is decorated in the Arts and Crafts style of the house itself and this makes for an exceptionally warm and welcoming greeting as you stand with your back to the large stone fireplace. There are two dining rooms set for breakfast, with views of the lake and pine trees blowing in the wind. The inn has a total of ten bedrooms, of which two are suites. Each guestroom has a private bathroom and six are equipped with two-person jetted tubs, some with steam showers. Seven bedrooms have gas fireplaces. To enjoy the beauty of the setting, ask for one of the three rooms with a balcony overlooking the lake. The Lake Pointe Inn serves a full breakfast and buttermilk pancakes are a specialty. We arrived to the smell of spiced cider and chocolate chip cookies in the oven—touches that make this inn speak softly but with a loud message. *Directions:* Take I-68 to Route 219 south for 12½ miles. Turn right onto Sang Run Road for two blocks, left on Marsh Hill Road for ¼ mile to Lake Pointe Drive to the inn.

LAKE POINTE INN
Innkeeper: Caroline McNiece
174 Lake Pointe Drive
Deep Creek Lake, MD 21541, USA
Tel: (301) 387-0111, Fax: (301) 387-0190
Toll Free: (800) 523-5253
10 Rooms, Double: $168–$269
Closed: Christmas, Credit cards: MC, VS
Select Registry
www.karenbrown.com/mdlakepointe.html

Gems of little inns are like rare jewels—they are hard to find and once found most surely are to be enjoyed for what they offer the traveler in terms of rest and comfort. This one not only has all that going for it but it also boasts a restaurant of uncommon quality—small and intimately decorated, painted in warm and invigorating colors, a room in which the artwork (for sale) is spectacularly beautiful. A patio with fountain for outside dining is also available. The menus are wonderful and the growing acclaim of the restaurant is surely well deserved. The seven bedrooms boast 406-count, Italian linens that are not only a visual feast but also of a quality that one seldom experiences. There's nothing here that has escaped the attention of the owners. The décor of the bedrooms is as carefully planned and executed as that in the common rooms and dining room—it's fresh and warm and visually exciting. I loved the spacious Town Room, painted yellow, overlooking the second floor porch and front street, and at back, The Hamilton whose king iron bed is set against soft violet walls and on old pine floors. The artwork throughout the bedrooms complements the rooms. The formula here works wonderfully, from the 1790 Federal mansion, the inn, the restaurant to the owners. The town of Easton with all its attractions is within a few minutes' walk. *Directions:* Approaching Easton on Route 50, take Dover Street into town and turn left onto Harrison Street.

❄ ☕ 🛒 💳 ☎ P 🍴 🧍 🐎 ⛷

THE INN AT EASTON
Innkeepers: Andrew & Liz Evans
28 South Harrison Street
Easton, MD 21601, USA
Tel: (410) 822-4910, Fax: (410) 822-6961
Toll Free: (888) 800-8091
7 Rooms, Double: $175–$395
Restaurant: open Wed through Sun
Open: all year, Credit cards: all major
www.karenbrown.com/mdinnateaston.html

Combsberry 1730 is an English country manor on the eastern shore of Maryland that exudes the country charm of an old home where history and architecture come together to provide some unique accommodations. This inn is out in the countryside and its very location makes you pause and relax in the beauty of your surroundings. The seven large bedrooms, each with its own bath, are sumptuously decorated with floral wallpapers and fabrics, making spring and summer ever present. The two-story Oxford Cottage has a queen-size white and brass bed, a fireplace in the living room, French doors leading to a brick terrace, and a luxurious bathroom with a double sink and a Jacuzzi. Views of the water are everywhere in this inn, especially from the kitchen and dining area where a wide expanse of windows floods the room with sunlight and brightness. A full breakfast is served either here or in the formal dining room. Other rooms have steep stairs to second-floor bedrooms and baths, making ingenious use of the space available in an historic building. This inn has formal and informal gardens, with lovely old box hedges and masses of flowers during the summer in the annual and perennial gardens. Nearby Oxford, an interesting and very old town on the river, is a great place for sightseeing and walking the streets. *Directions:* Take Route 50 to Route 322 south to Route 333 south for almost 7 miles. Turn left on Evergreen Road then second left at the brick entranceway.

❄ ☕ ⚞ 💳 🐾 P ♿ 🎿 👫 ⛵

COMBSBERRY 1730
Innkeepers: Dr. & Ms. Shariff
4837 Evergreeen Road
Oxford, MD 21654, USA
Tel: (410) 226-5353, Fax: (410) 228-1453
7 Rooms, Double: $250–$395
Open: all year, Credit cards: all major
www.karenbrown.com/mdcombsberry.html

Oxford is one of those exquisite old towns on a tributary of the Chesapeake Bay where history and charm come together to provide the traveler with a lifelong memory of his visit there. The Robert Morris Inn's history dates back to before the Revolutionary War and it has figured prominently in the history of the town, of the state, and of the nation. The inn carries with it many of the traditions that its owners have long believed in and travelers come today to enjoy these traditions as they did in the past. The common rooms are steeped in history and their character is displayed in the furnishings and the décor that has been in place for many years. Bedrooms are either located up the creaking stair of this historic home or, a block away, in the Sandaway Lodge, another old home with its front screened-in porch that is set on an expanse of lawn that distances it from the water's edge. Very romantic, settle in lawn chairs at sunset on summer Fridays to enjoy the local Yacht Club races. Furnishings are comfortable and in keeping with the historical character of the building and the town. The inn has a restaurant whose crab cakes are famous. (They ship crab cakes overnight!) There's a lot to do right here in Oxford and it is also fun to cross the short span of water by car ferry to explore the charming towns of St. Michaels and Tilghman Island. *Directions:* Take Rte 50 to Rte 322, then turn right, driving for almost 3½ miles to Route 333, then just over 9½ miles to the inn.

ROBERT MORRIS INN
Owners: Wendy & Ken Gibson, Innkeeper: Jay Gibson
314 North Morris Street
P.O. Box 70, Oxford, MD 21654, USA
Tel: (410) 226-5111, Fax: (410) 226-5744
Toll Free: (888) 823-4012
35 Rooms, Double: $110–$350, Breakfast not included: $10
Open: Apr to Nov, winter schedule varies
Credit cards: all major, Select Registry
For crabcakes: BestCrabCakes.com
www.karenbrown.com/mdrobertmorris.html

Run away to our home, the brochure for the Five Gables Inn & Spa says, and in a life of too much of everything, doing just that would be rewarded many times over. With a focus on the spa, public areas are limited, nothing is overly fancy, but the inn's special appeal is that a stay here will enable you to take time for yourself, to let others soothe away your tiredness and stress with an array of spa treatments, and to luxuriate in the use of a pool, sauna, and steam room. The inn is located next to the Chesapeake Maritime Museum, in the town of Saint Michaels, in a charming area of Maryland called the Eastern Shore, at the end of the main street. The town itself, with its pretty setting along the river and its bustling harbor, is reason enough for visiting, but add a group of carefully restored historic homes and boutiques and antique shops where memories of your visit await you, and you've even more reasons to plan for a stay at Five Gables. Rooms are located in two buildings, essentially across the street from each another, and they are bright and cheery in painted colors that make my heart sing. The furnishings are painted pine with some cute details. Bathrooms have everything that you could desire plus a spa tub for two. Breakfast is offered in a charming room at the top of the stair in the main house. *Directions:* Take Route 50 to Easton by-pass Route 322. Turn right at the light to Route 33 for 9 miles to Saint Michaels. The Five Gables is on the right.

FIVE GABLES INN & SPA
Innkeeper: Marianne Lesher
209 North Talbot Street
Saint Michaels, MD 21663, USA
Tel: (410) 745-0100, Fax: (410) 745-2903
Toll Free: (877) 466-0100
14 Rooms, Double: $150–$405
Open: all year, Credit cards: all major
www.karenbrown.com/mdfivegables.html

Out of curiosity we went to see The Inn at Perry Cabin which had been described in superlatives but is larger than properties we normally recommend. From the moment we passed through the awning-covered garden entry, there were only statements of welcome rather than the pretentious or corporate feeling I had anticipated. The public rooms resemble an intimate, private estate with English and American antiques and beautiful fabrics. The reception is warmed by an open fire and I could envision myself settled in the front library hoping never to be found. Originally built in 1812, the home was transformed to a charming small hotel by Sir Bernard Ashley of Laura Ashley fame. It was recently acquired by Orient Express Hotels and enlarged using the colonial home as the architectural influence. A large complex of white buildings, the main building is just one room in depth. Passing down the corridor from room to room a never-ending sequence of windows frame the restful, scenic expanse of waterways. To dine here is to experience the region's most highly acclaimed cuisine in a charming restaurant with a coastal feel and theme. Chef Mark Salter creates a menu influenced by both Chesapeake and international specialties. The Parsons Pub is a great place for a lighter fare. *Directions:* Take Route 33 west from Easton. Pass through the heart of town. Just past the relocated Tilghman Drawbridge and the Chesapeake Maritime Museum, turn right to the inn.

THE INN AT PERRY CABIN
Owner: Orient Express Hotels
308 Watkins Lane
Saint Michaels, MD, USA
Tel: (410) 745-2200, Fax: (410) 745-3348
Toll Free: (800) 722-2949
78 Rooms, Double: $295–$550*
*Breakfast not included
Open: all year, Credit cards: all major
www.karenbrown.com/perrycabin.html

The Wade's Point Inn is an enchanting waterfront complex with an 1819 Main House, a century-old Eastern Shore Farmhouse, and a 1990 Mildred T. Kemp Annex; all facing the Eastern Bay where it joins the Chesapeake Bay. Sloping green lawns dotted with Adirondack chairs and hammocks swaying in the summer breeze border the bay. Screened porches off the public rooms and bedrooms allow one to savor the gorgeous setting. This is a summer inn, and it looks and feels just like one—a place to come to for several days on end; to read and relax. Originally, the inn was built in 1819 by Thomas Kemp, the designer and builder of the fast sailing ships called Baltimore Clippers, and the famous "Pride of Baltimore." The living room, dining room, and the large front hall of the main house are spacious and filled with handsome antique furniture. Climb the 1819 stair to rooms that span a hallway just one room deep and benefit from wonderful cross breezes. Rooms are decorated to match the charming character of the home and it is important to note that not all have bathrooms en suite. Turn of the last century country farm buildings also offer delightful, more "modern" accommodation. Breakfast is served at white wicker tables and chairs in a room created in 1890 with a full surround of floor to ceiling windows overlooking the water. *Directions:* Rte 50 to Easton MD, exit to Rte 322 to Rte 33 to Saint Michaels and 5 miles beyond Saint Michaels to Wades Point Rd.

WADE'S POINT INN ON THE BAY
Innkeeper: The Feiler Family
Route 33
P.O. Box 7
Saint Michaels, MD 21663, USA
Tel: (410) 745-2500, Fax: (410) 745-3443
Toll Free: (888) 923-3466
26 Rooms, Double: $150–$260
Open: Mar 15 to Dec 15, Credit cards: MC, VS
www.karenbrown.com/wades.html

Chanceford Hall is a gracious 230-year-old lady with the heart and soul of a member of generation X with nary a glance backward toward the Revolutionary War. Take a charming old town and add a spectacularly large and commanding home set back from the street with beautiful boxwood hedges in an "allee" leading to the front door, and you're in for a treat. Alice Kesterson and architect Randy Ifft have restored a 1759 Greek Revival home with Georgian and Federal details, choosing furniture and accessories of that earlier period and of today with taste and great discrimination. The result is an inn with tremendous character, an inn where guests will want to linger, both in the public rooms and in the four bedrooms with queen four-poster beds, which are uncommonly large and comfortably decorated. Breakfasts of fresh fruit, individual fruit pies, red-pepper stratas, multigrain pancakes, fresh juice, and bountiful mugs of coffee are a great way to begin the morning and are served either in the formal dining room or, when there are only a few guests, at the kitchen table. This inn works so well because of its blend of great age, contemporary touches, architectural style, and the owners' hospitality. There is a large backyard where gatherings and weddings may be hosted. *Directions:* Take Route 12 south from Salisbury to Snow Hill. Follow Route 12 through town to Federal Street and turn right on Federal Street to Chanceford Hall on the left.

CHANCEFORD HALL
Innkeepers: Randy Ifft & Alice Kesterson
209 West Federal Street
Snow Hill, MD 21863, USA
Tel: (410) 632-2900, Fax: (410) 632-2479
5 Rooms, Double: $130–$160
Open: all year, Credit cards: MC, VS
www.karenbrown.com/mdchancefordhall.html

Snow Hill is one of many charming towns on the Eastern Shore of the Delmarva Peninsula. The Knudsens raised their children here and now offer guests delightful accommodation in private cottages behind their main house, set on an expanse of lawn shaded by trees that travels down to the Pocomo River's edge. (Canoes can be rented nearby.) Guests are afforded much privacy with each cottage having its own entrance. Previously the Knudsens opened up their home to guests (even rented a few rooms in the house) but now they have set up an outdoor sitting area under the gazebo at the lovely new pool, equipped with beverages (and even a TV) for guests to enjoy! In the cottage referred to as The Hideaway, the Colonial occupies the first floor and the Garden is found at the top of the outside stair. The other two units have fireplaces and share a screened front porch that overlooks the river view. I especially liked the Colonial with its four-poster bed and in-room Jacuzzi tub. The Garden has an attractive iron bed and upstairs porch. Once the owner's quarters, the Carousel House is a two-story cottage with a dining room, living room, kitchen, two separate bedrooms and a bathroom with a large soaking tub. Breakfast picnic baskets are delivered to the doorstep for guests. *Directions:* From the north or south take Route 13 to Business Route 113 to Snow Hill to Route 12. Turn right on Market Street and the inn is on your left.

RIVER HOUSE INN
Innkeepers: Larry & Susanne Knudsen
201 E. Market
Snow Hill, MD 21863, USA
Tel: (410) 632-2722, Fax: (410) 632-2866
4 Rooms, Double: $160–$300
Open: all year, Credit cards: all major
www.karenbrown.com/mdriverhouse.html

Superb and memorable would be two words for the experience of staying at the Antrim 1844 Country Inn. Dorothy and Richard Mollett and their team have taken a 19th-century home of great historical importance and created one of the truly great country inns of the United States. The rooms, beautifully decorated with guests' comfort in mind, are elegant, warm and inviting, with places to sit and read, wonderful beds topped with blissful, feather comforters, crackling fires, bathrooms with spa tubs for two and every amenity the traveler could imagine. The dining room is yet another fabulous experience. Guests gather for drinks and hors d'oeuvres during the pre-dinner hour, then dinner is served in one of many intimate dining rooms. Especially cozy are tables set on the old brick floors of the original kitchen or smoke house. The table set for two under a skylight and with the moon glowing is particularly romantic. Tablecloths to the floor, soft candlelight, polished crystal and silver, and fresh flowers create an extraordinary atmosphere, which is only exceeded by the six-course dinner that follows. Add a great bottle of wine from the inn's extensive wine cellar and your evening becomes almost idyllic. Too rare are these opportunities and these experiences, for these are what make for lifelong memories. *Directions:* From Baltimore take Route 695 to Route 795 north to Route 140 west to Taneytown. Turn left at Trevanion Road.

ANTRIM 1844 COUNTRY INN
Innkeepers: Dorothy & Richard Mollett
30 Trevanion Road
Taneytown, MD 21787, USA
Tel: (410) 756-6812, Fax: (410) 756-2744
Toll Free: (800) 858-1844
29 Rooms, Double: $160–$400
5 cottages
Closed: Christmas, Credit cards: all major
Select Registry
www.karenbrown.com/mdantrim.html

Charming is the village; charming is the inn; and most charming of all are the owners. Tilghman Island is a working watermen's hamlet at the end of the long spit of land accessed through Easton, and its appeal is that it pretends to be nothing else. It's a place to go when you want to do nothing but wander to the harbor and watch the activity of fishermen at work; to relax on a screened porch with a glass of wine and a good book; to sit on a deck and get some sun. The Wood Duck Inn is a simple place to stay—it has no pretensions of being anything more than a comfortable inn with simply decorated rooms which are immaculately neat and tidy, with nice linens and quality towels. Views from all but one of the rooms include the water and the harbor. This inn is owned by a chef and his wife, she managing the inn and he the kitchen on some evenings. When we visited he was cooking dinner (four courses with a set menu) but it was clear that both guests and locals would like him to be available every day. The breakfast menu is as fine as any I have ever seen—a trio of crepes (maple-braised sausage and apple, sun-dried tomato, and mushroom rice) and white-truffle whipped eggs with asiago cheese are a couple of the nine entrées on the menu, one of which is served daily. *Directions:* Take Route 50 to the Route 322 by-pass in Easton to Route 33 through St. Michaels to Tilghman Island. Cross the bridge and turn left on Gibsontown Road to the inn on the right.

❄ ☕ 💳 P 🍴 ⚡ 🚶 🏇 ⛵

CHESAPEAKE WOOD DUCK INN
Innkeepers: Jeffrey & Kimberly Bushey
Gibsontown Road
P.O. Box 202
Tilghman Island, MD 21671, USA
Tel: (410) 886-2070, Fax: (413) 677-7256
Toll Free: (800) 956-2070
6 Rooms, Double: $129–$259
Dinner some evenings
Open: all year, Credit cards: MC, VS
www.karenbrown.com/mdchesapeakewd.html

Places to Stay
New Jersey

Set on 10 acres and tucked off a country road that weaves through lush landscape is a wonderful inn, the Wooden Duck. Although it looks like an old wooden farmhouse, it was constructed in 1978 and guests will appreciate the luxury of all the modern appointments. Off the entry of the main home is a lovely dining room, which opens onto a side porch and overlooks the swimming pool. In the kitchen there is a coffee maker and a small refrigerator containing complimentary snacks. Step beyond the entry into a lovely common room whose seating area faces a two-sided fireplace, which warms a cozy room with games, puzzles, and a complimentary video library. Two deluxe, spacious guestrooms, the Harlequin and Golden-Eye, enjoying side porches, large soaking tubs, separate showers, and gas fireplaces, are found off the game room. Climb the entry stairs to three very attractive rooms; the Ruddy Duck and Mallard are standard, and the Canvasback has a soaking tub and fireplace. Next door in the carriage house are three more units, Old Squaw, an attractive loft bedroom; Pintail, an entry-level bedroom; and Wooden Duck, designed for guests requiring a wheelchair on the ground level. This is an exceptionally lovely country inn with gorgeous accommodation and attentive service. *Directions:* From I-80 take exit 25, following Route 206 north 7-8/10 miles to Goodale Road. Turn right and drive 1½ miles to the inn.

WOODEN DUCK
Innkeepers: Beth & Karl Krummel
140 Goodale Road
Andover Township (Newton), NJ 07860, USA
Tel & Fax: (973) 300-0395
10 Rooms, Double: $120–$210
Open: all year, Credit cards: all major
Select Registry
www.karenbrown.com/njduck.html

Famous for its lighthouse and sitting at the end of the spit of land off the New Jersey coast well away from the shore's tourist activity, the village of Barnegat Light, where houses are separated from one another with yards and beds of summer annuals, enjoys a delightfully slow pace. The Sand Castle is a newly built inn wrapped around a heated outdoor pool. Amenities abound here, with a grand piano, an exercise room, a sun porch, rooftop observation deck, outdoor Jacuzzi, poolside cabana, shower, and changing room. There are complimentary bikes, beach badges, towels, umbrellas and beach chairs. Each of the five bedrooms and two suites has an outside private entrance. The Lighthouse Vista Suite is on two levels, one with a living area, gas fireplace, king bed, and a loft with a two-person Jacuzzi, balcony, and daybed. A full breakfast is offered buffet style in the formal dining room located on the second floor. Many guests climb to the rooftop and enjoy picnic dinners and panoramic views. Once in the commercial fishing business, Nancy built the property as an inn on the site of her original store. With fishing still the principal industry, Barnegat Light is more commercial that the towns that focus more on the summer tourists along the island's southern tip. *Directions:* From northern New Jersey or New York take the Garden State Parkway to exit 63 to Route 72 east to the end. Turn left onto Long Beach Boulevard for 8 miles to Barnegat Light and go left on 8th Street to the inn.

THE SAND CASTLE
Innkeeper: Nancy Gallimore
710 Bayview Avenue
P.O. Box 607
Barnegat Light, NJ 08006, USA
Tel: (609) 494-6555, Fax: (609) 494-8655
Toll Free: (800) 253-0353
5 Rooms, 2 Suites, Double: $275–$415
Closed: Dec to Apr, Credit cards: MC, VS
Select Registry
www.karenbrown.com/sandcastle.html

Long Beach Island is a narrow spit of land that parallels the Jersey shore. At its northernmost point are Barnegat Light with its lighthouse and many commercial fishing operations. On the southern tip are beach towns whose populations soar with the summer heat. For those without their own summer homes the Amber Street Inn is very convenient to the gorgeous stretch of beach and the heart of town, and is located directly across from Bicentennial Park. Enter from the front wrap-around porch into this attractive 1885 home to enjoy the comfortable public areas. A full breakfast is served each morning consisting of fruit and beverages and followed by a hot entrée. Afternoon refreshments include a baked goodie and a beverage which varies according to the season, sometimes sherry or port is set out to warm the coldest of days. The guestrooms are located up the stairs. Four are on the second floor and two are on the third floor along with a thoughtfully stocked self-service snack area. All the rooms have their own special charm, but I especially liked Number 2—a spectacular front corner room in a décor of blue and white with a shaker four-poster bed in front of an electric stove. Number 3 is a back corner room with a king bed and enjoys its own private terrace. *Directions:* Take exit 63 off the garden state parkway and travel 72 east to its end. At Long Beach Boulevard travel south to the town of Beach Haven. Turn left on Amber towards the dunes.

AMBER STREET INN
Innkeepers: Joan & Michael Fitzsimmons
118 Amber Street
Beach Haven, NJ 08008, USA
Tel: (609) 492-1611
6 Rooms, Double: $150–$285
Open: mid-Feb to mid-Oct
Credit cards: MC, VS
www.karenbrown.com/amberstreetinn.html

Built in 1892 by a whaling captain, the Fairthorne repeats the award-winning formula of the historic properties of the picturesque summer seashore resort of Cape May. It too has broad wraparound porches and, of course, those rockers in which you can relax and lose an hour or two. This inn is built in the Colonial Revival style of architecture: when you enter its wide front hall, you see a parlor on the left and a staircase that climbs to the bedrooms on the second floor. Each of the nine comfortably furnished rooms, some with fireplaces, is named for a woman with historic ties to the house. The Emma Kate suite has a king bed, an adjoining sitting room with a queen sofa bed, and a bathroom with a two-person marble shower. Bridget's Room, overlooking the gardens, has a queen bed with an antique armoire and a bathroom with a shower. Next door, The Cottage has three guestrooms named for the Hutchinson's granddaughters. A gourmet breakfast is served each morning with juice, fruit, freshly baked breads and muffins, and a hot entrée. In the afternoon guests can enjoy tea and light refreshments and before retiring, enjoy a glass of sherry by the parlor's fireplace. The inn provides complimentary beach towels, chairs, bicycles, and on-site or free nearby parking. Restaurants and shopping are as near as the wonderful beach. *Directions:* Take Garden State Parkway to the end, cross two bridges onto Lafayette Street, go to the second light, and then turn left on Ocean Street.

❄ ☕ ✍ ▭ Ⴤ P ⯭ 🍴 🚶

FAIRTHORNE BED & BREAKFAST
Innkeepers: Ed & Diane Hutchinson
111 Ocean Street
Cape May, NJ 08204, USA
Tel: (609) 884-8791, Fax: (609) 898-6129
Toll Free: (800) 438-8742
12 Rooms, Double: $214–$280
Open: all year, Credit cards: all major
Select Registry
www.karenbrown.com/njthefairthorne.html

This is another of Cape May's Victorian inns that has been lovingly restored by its owners to reflect the style of living of an earlier era. Victorian furnishings are used throughout the inn while flowered wallpapers in the parlors and the bedrooms, chandeliers, and furniture of the period all create that Victorian lifestyle. This is an inn where guests come to the formal dining room for breakfast at 9 am and where breakfast is relaxed with good conversation around the large mahogany table. In late afternoon when you return from the beach, shopping, or more active pursuits, you may sit on the porch and have tea—such a civilized way to relax. The Humphrey Hughes House's brochure declares that it is "for ladies and gentlemen on a seaside holiday" and that's exactly why you would come to Cape May and stay in one of these grand old Victorians. The enclave in which it and the others are located will take you back to the time when ladies and gentlemen brought their families to the shore for the cooler temperatures during the summer, when the beach and the ocean created enduring memories for parents and children alike. *Directions:* Take Garden State Parkway to the end, crossing over several bridges onto Lafayette Street. Turn left at the second light onto Ocean Street and the inn is on the corner of Ocean and Columbia Streets.

HUMPHREY HUGHES HOUSE
Innkeepers: Lorraine & Terry Schmidt
29 Ocean Street
Cape May, NJ 08204, USA
Tel: (609) 884-4428, Fax: none
Toll Free: (800) 582-3634
10 Rooms, Double: $165–$425
Open: all year, Credit cards: all major
Select Registry
www.karenbrown.com/njhumphreyhughes.html

Historic homes whose rooms are grand in proportion and whose ceilings are uncommonly high create a glorious welcome for those who cross their thresholds, and Italianate architecture adds an extra touch of grandeur. The Mainstay Inn offers accommodation in three neighboring buildings. The principal building dates back to 1872 when it was built as a club for gentlemen for gambling and other gentlemanly activities, and the use of furniture and accessories from the period and the attention to detail make this inn exceptional. The porch with its rockers beckons and is an ideal spot to settle for tea and cookies served here on a summer afternoon. Once you're inside the large front hall, you're drawn in several directions at once. The tall mirror, the staircase, the small parlor to the left and the dining room just beyond—both with magnificent Victorian chandeliers—and the large parlor on the right are all magnificent. Joined by a brick, garden path, the Cottage is equally lovely. Bedrooms in both buildings enjoy high ceilings and are beautifully proportioned with great beds and bathrooms. Across the street, the four suites of the Officer's Quarters, are spacious, enjoy verandahs, kitchenettes and are charmingly country in their décor. *Directions:* Take Garden State Parkway to the end, continuing straight over several bridges onto Lafayette Street. Turn left at the light onto Madison Avenue and go right after three blocks onto Columbia Ave.

❋ ☕ P ♿ ☂ 🏄 👥 🐎

MAINSTAY INN
Innkeeper: Diane Clark
635 Columbia Avenue
Cape May, NJ 08204, USA
Tel: (609) 884-8690, Fax: (609) 884-1498
16 Rooms, Double: $290–$390
Open: all year, Credit cards: MC, VS
Select Registry
www.karenbrown.com/njmainstayinn.html

Anna Marie and Doug McMain epitomize the best of innkeeping. Their personal attention ensures that anyone who steps across their threshold will be gloriously received and pampered. The Queen Victoria is housed in two handsomely restored Victorian homes, The Queen Victoria and Prince Albert Hall, and tradition carries through to the service and amenities offered. The inn serves afternoon tea with sweets and savories in the finest English tradition. Breakfasts are bountiful and always include a hot entrée. Spacious, immaculately clean, some bedrooms have whirlpool tubs, some have fireplaces, but all have wonderful bathroom amenities, in-room refrigerators and air conditioning and guest pantries are stocked with drinks and popcorn. With its own private entrance and parking (gold in Cape May!), the Carriage House is the most luxurious guest suite with a charming first floor salon, termed the library, and at the top of the stair, under angled eaves, is a bedroom warmed by firestove whose bath has a large Jacuzzi tub. Located at the heart of the historic district, complimentary bikes make it easy to ride to the ocean promenade which shares the sights of a charming old beach community of yesteryear. Note: Just a block away, termed a "hotel", they also own the charming Queen's Hotel. *Directions:* Take Garden State Parkway to the end and continue over two bridges onto Lafayette St. At the second light turn left onto Ocean St.

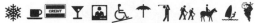

THE QUEEN VICTORIA
Innkeepers: Doug & Anna Marie McMain
102 Ocean Street
Cape May, NJ 08204, USA
Tel: (609) 884-8702, Fax: none
32 Rooms, Double: $100–$485
Open: all year, Credit cards: MC, VS
Select Registry
www.karenbrown.com/njqueenvictoria.html

In all seasons The Inn at Millrace Pond offers hospitality, gracious service, fine food, spirits, and elegant lodging—so says their brochure and so is their custom. Under the guidance of great innkeepers, the inn is a complex of buildings, three providing accommodation and one being used as a corporate conference center. In the main building there's a dining room upstairs and a tavern downstairs, both with exposed beams, which lend great character to the space and make for a cozy dining experience. Mills make for such great spaces and this one takes all possible advantage of its natural charm—wine, for example, is stored by the old mill wheel. Bedrooms in the main building and in two detached buildings are attractively decorated without fussy detail. All are comfortable and have private baths, and there are several rooms with canopy beds. This inn also offers a number of handsome rooms to accommodate offsite meetings. Off the main building there is a patio where you could get fresh air in the middle of a meeting and is also suitable as the setting for a meal or a cocktail party. There's a tennis court on the property and more than enough to do while exploring the countryside. *Directions:* Leave I-80 at exit 12, driving 1¼ miles south on Route 521 to the blinking light. Turn left and the inn is a little way down on the left.

INN AT MILLRACE POND
Innkeepers: Cordie & Charles Puttkammer
Route 519 North, P.O. Box 359
Hope, NJ 07844, USA
Tel: (908) 459-4884, Fax: (908) 459-5276
Toll Free: (800) 746-6467
17 Rooms, Double: $140–$180
Dinner every day except Christmas
Open: all year, Credit cards: all major
Select Registry
www.karenbrown.com/njinnatmillrace.html

Lambertville is a charming village nestled on the banks of the Delaware River, straddling the border of New Jersey and Pennsylvania. A destination in its own right with galleries, antique and boutique shops, and restaurants; the village is in a region of culture and history, a few miles distant from where Washington made his historic crossing and Princeton University. The Lambertville House is an elegant boutique hotèl built by Captain John Lambert in 1812; it has hosted many prestigious dignitaries in its past. A wrought-iron terrace set with café tables off the town's main street is the entry to the four-star, handsome stone and stucco building. Reception is at the end of a long, wide hallway where you pass an enticing gift shop to one side and an intimate side bar, Left Bank Libations, emitting soft, melodious jazz music, on the other. Guestrooms vary in size and whether they have sitting rooms, fireplaces or decks (most have gas fireplaces, all have whirlpool tubs). The romantics will love the Stage House Suite whose space is divided by a dramatic two-sided gas fireplace into a cozy bedroom and bathroom with two-person Jacuzzi, that opens onto its own private deck. There are two similarly appointed guestrooms in a separate carriage house. A European-style continental breakfast is served every morning in the main building. *Directions:* From Philadelphia travel I-95 north to exit 1, then Rte 29 north to Lambertville. Turn left on Bridge Street.

LAMBERTVILLE HOUSE
Innkeepers: Edric & Mary Ellen Mason
32 Bridge Street
Lambertville, NJ 08530, USA
Tel: (609) 397-0200, Fax: (609) 397-0511
Toll Free: (888) 867-8859
26 Rooms, Double: $200–$350
Credit cards: all major
www.karenbrown.com/lambertville.html

South of Atlantic City and north of Cape May are the Wildwoods and in the village of North Wildwood is the Candlelight Inn. The Candlelight Inn offers ten simply but comfortably furnished bedrooms and suites of varying sizes. Seven rooms and one suite are found on three floors in the original Victorian building with its wraparound porch. All rooms and suites in the main house are wallpapered and each has a private bath; some also have double whirlpool tubs or fireplaces. The main parlor contains antiques and features one of the three public fireplaces and an Eastlake period piano. There are also two luxury suites located in the Carriage House offering fireplaces, double whirlpool tubs, and full baths. Out on the deck behind the Carriage House is a hot tub for the use of all the inn's guests. Breakfast is served in the dining room around a large table and you're sure to be satisfied when you finish a full breakfast accompanied by lots of conversation with your fellow guests. The inn is just a short walk to North Wildwood's boardwalk and beach where the wide expanse of fine sand makes for a lazy afternoon of sun and swimming. *Directions:* Take Garden State Pkwy to exit 6, then Rte 147 east into North Wildwood to 2nd Ave (Anglesea Volunteer Fire Co). Turn left onto 2nd, then right onto Central Ave, driving to 24th Ave. The inn is on the right at 24th and Central. Turn onto 24th, pull into the drive, and park in the rear.

CANDLELIGHT INN
Owner: Eileen Burchsted
Innkeepers: Bill & Nancy Moncrief
2310 Central Avenue
North Wildwood, NJ 08260, USA
Tel: (609) 522-6200, Fax: (609) 522-6125
Toll Free: (800) 992-2632
10 Rooms, Double: $130–$245
Open: all year, Credit cards: all major
Select Registry
www.karenbrown.com/njcandlelightinn.html

Romance is in the air when you drive up to a Victorian inn after dark and lights glow softly through the windows, spilling shadows onto a wide front porch with wicker furniture. The Normandy Inn has very traditional Victorian furniture and several sitting areas and the large front hall seems especially welcoming. There's a closed-in porch with a gas pot-bellied stove, a selection of books, and early-morning coffee. On the second and third floors the bedrooms continue the Victorian theme, with flowered wallpaper and touches of Victoriana everywhere. One has a queen bed with imposing Victorian headboard and a marble-topped suite of bureaus and bedside tables, while the queen-bedded suite one floor up has a separate sitting room with fireplace, sofa, and chairs. The inn serves a wonderful full breakfast. The Normandy is just half a block from the ocean, so there's plenty of refreshing salt air. Spring Lake is one of those old shore towns with a boardwalk, wide streets, and houses that tell tales of families growing up by the ocean. Grab a bike and get the benefit of both exercise and the charm of this seaside village. This would make a nice stop away from the cities to the north on an itinerary down the coast. *Directions:* Take Garden State Parkway to exit 98, follow Route 35 south to the traffic circle, and drive round to Route 524, heading east to Ocean. Turn right onto Ocean Avenue and then first right onto Tuttle—the inn is on the left.

NORMANDY INN
Innkeeper: The Valori Family
21 Tuttle Avenue
Spring Lake, NJ 07762, USA
Tel: (732) 449-7172, Fax: (732) 449-1070
Toll Free: (800) 449-1888
18 Rooms, Double: $131–$369
Open: all year, Credit cards: all major
Select Registry
www.karenbrown.com/njnormandyinn.html

Sea Crest is a luxurious inn for romantics. Whether you are strolling on the nearby boardwalk, bicycling past the grand Victorian homes or just lounging in your spacious suite, you will be reminded of your most precious romantic moments. Charm runs high here, in the living room with its fireplace, the breakfast rooms with their bright and cheery décor, and the bedrooms with the extension of this Victorian theme. From the Queen Victoria suite with its four-poster canopy bed, to the nautically-themed Captain's Quarters with its indoor hammock for two with an ocean view, or from the Keys-inspired decor of the new Hemingway suite, to the wow-inspiring Norwegian Wood Suite, you will be taken to other worlds and times. In addition to the luxurious accommodation, the gourmet, candlelit breakfasts, the afternoon teas and the homemade evening cordials are all mount-watering, culinary delights. With the ocean just half a block away, the sound of the sea lulls you to sleep, the salt smell of the air invigorates you—this is the perfect ocean refuge. You can be as active or as relaxed as you want here in Spring Lake while living the charm of a time when grandparents summered on the Jersey shore. *Directions:* Take Garden State Parkway to exit 98, follow Route 34 south to the traffic circle, and drive three-quarters of the way round to Route 524, driving east to Ocean Avenue. Turn right on Ocean Ave., travel one block to Tuttle, then turn right to the inn on the left.

SEA CREST BY THE SEA
Innkeepers: Fred & Barbara Vogel
19 Tuttle Avenue
Spring Lake, NJ 07762, USA
Tel: (732) 449-9031, Fax: (732) 974-0403
Toll Free: (800) 803-9031
13 Rooms, Double: $190–$345
Open: all year, Credit cards: all major
Select Registry
www.karenbrown.com/njseacrest.html

This comfortable Victorian by the seashore beckons with its generous wraparound veranda and colorful, warm interior. Magnificent Tiffany stained-glass windows shower the entryway, parlor, and dining rooms with bursts of light adding to the rich wallpapers and fabrics found throughout the home. Guestrooms are individually decorated and very comfortable. The Rose Rendezvous room offers a sitting area in the turret, a king bed in Laura Ashley fabrics, and private bathroom with shower. The Manor Suite is elegant and spacious and decorated with Ralph Lauren fabrics. Its bedroom features a mahogany king bed and the adjoining parlor has a fireplace with an antique mantle. Queen Anne chairs are wonderful to relax in while you enjoy the fireplace. The bathroom has a double Jacuzzi and a shower. The inn serves a full breakfast of fresh fruit, juice, homemade muffins, cake or bread, the entrée of the day, and plenty of freshly brewed coffee or tea. You can enjoy the breakfast on the porch or in the dining room. Also enjoy the afternoon tea and treat, as well as the evening cordials and chocolate. The inn has on-site parking, bikes, TV/VCRs, beach badges, and health club passes. *Directions:* Take Garden State Parkway to exit 98. Take 138 east to the end, bear right onto Route 35 south, go to the third light, and turn left on Warren Ave, which becomes Lake Ave. Turn right onto Third Ave, go two blocks, and turn left on Monmouth Ave.

VICTORIA HOUSE BED & BREAKFAST INN
Innkeepers: Lynne & Alan Kaplan
214 Monmouth Avenue
Spring Lake, NJ 07762, USA
Tel: (732) 974-1882, Fax: (732) 974-2132
Toll Free: (888) 249-6252
10 Rooms, Double: $189–$335
Open: all year, Credit cards: all major
Select Registry
www.karenbrown.com/njvictoriahouse.html

The Whistling Swan Inn's former existence as a private home began in 1905 but now it enjoys a new life as a country inn. On the first floor there are adjoining parlors—one more formal with seating in front of the fireplace and the other called the hospitality center, with complimentary beverages, a well-stocked cookie jar, and a large video library, which provide that welcoming, considerate, homey touch. There's a formal dining room where a full breakfast is offered buffet style to guests each morning. The gourmet repast includes fresh fruit, yogurts, cereals, and a hot main dish accompanied by homemade breads. Climb the creaking stair to the guestrooms on the two upper floors. The rooms on the top floor tucked under the eaves, all with claw-foot tubs, are especially charming. The High Point Suite has a queen-size feather bed and is located dramatically under the high wooden ceiling of the turret round. Especially appealing are back corner rooms, Waterloo Village and Walnut Valley, that look out to the greenery of the garden. Two new suites have a fireplace and Jacuzzi; one has a steam shower. Liz is definitely making improvements and I loved her artistic stenciling that is now found in many of the guestrooms. *Directions:* Take I-80 to exit 27B, drive north on Route 183 for 1 mile to the Hess Gas Station then turn left on Main Street to the inn.

WHISTLING SWAN INN
Innkeeper: Liz Armstrong
110 Main Street
Stanhope, NJ 07874, USA
Tel: (973) 347-6369, Fax: (973) 347-6379
9 Rooms, Double: $115–$219
Open: all year, Credit cards: all major
Select Registry
www.karenbrown.com/njwhistlingswan.html

Memorable, unique, and wonderful are ways to describe the Woolverton Inn, a 1792 stone manor, but there is something more—perhaps it is its setting in the countryside surrounded by conservation land, perhaps it is the sheep that graze close by and greet you with their melodious "baa", perhaps it is the innkeepers and their warm and friendly welcome—whatever it is we definitely want to return to it soon. On the ground floor of the inn you find the formal living room, the dining room, and a great porch just created for either that early morning cup of coffee or for an afternoon cup of tea. Each of these spaces provides a most gracious feeling. Pulling up a chair to the fire in the living room with one of the chocolate-chip cookies that you've been smelling baking in the kitchen, chatting with fellow guests about the day's activities, talking about dinner plans or how great breakfast was that morning—all these are part of that special experience. Rooms in the manor house are wonderfully romantic, and there are five new luxury cottages complete with all the comforts and then some—private entrances, king beds, fireplaces, sitting areas, porches or decks, and expansive bathrooms with two-person or steam showers and whirlpool tubs for two. A Bose CD player adds the frosting, or the music, to these rooms. *Directions:* Take Route 29 north from New Hope or Lambertville for 3 miles to Stockton. Turn right onto Route 523 for 2/10 mile then left at Woolverton Road.

WOOLVERTON INN
Innkeepers: Carolyn McGavin & Robert Haas
6 Woolverton Road
Stockton, NJ 08559, USA
Tel: (609) 397-0802, Fax: (609) 397-0987
Toll Free: (888) 264-6648
8 Rooms, Double: $125–$425
5 cottages
Open: all year, Credit cards: all major
Select Registry
www.karenbrown.com/njwoolverton.html

Places to Stay
New York

Inns in cities are rare to find and once you find them, you often discover they're not always conveniently located. An exception is the Mansion Hill Inn and Restaurant in central Albany, which is very handy for much of the downtown area and gives you the opportunity to walk to work or to the town's attractions. Albany is a city born 300 years ago and there's a lot of history for visitors to enjoy. Many corporate business travelers stay at Mansion Hill Inn during the week while leisure travelers find their way to Albany and this inn on the weekends. There are eight bedrooms, four with one queen bed and four with two queen beds, which provides great flexibility for the traveler. Each room has a private bathroom—not large but with everything you'll need while staying here—as well as a telephone, data port, TV, and individual heating and air-conditioning controls. In the inn's restaurant, a bright and cheery room on the first floor with a bar at one end, a full breakfast is served each morning, so you'll be off to whatever you need to do well fortified for the day. Between the three buildings that comprise the inn a nice patio and garden provide a great place to relax on a sunny morning with an extra cup of coffee. The inn provides a private parking lot across the street—a nice feature in an in-town property. *Directions:* Take I-87 to I-787 to Route 20, going west on Madison Avenue to Phillip Street. Turn left; the inn is on the right at the second light.

❄ ☕ 🛎 ▭ ☎ 🐕 Ⴤ P 🍴 🖼 🚶 👫

MANSION HILL INN AND RESTAURANT
Innkeepers: Steve & Mary Ellen Stofelano
115 Philip Street at Park Avenue
Albany, NY 12202, USA
Tel: (518) 465-2038, Fax: (518) 434-2313
Toll Free: (888) 299-0455
8 Rooms, Double: $145–$175
Open: all year, Credit cards: all major
www.karenbrown.com/nymansionhill.html

The State House is a small inn in a large city, a soothing place to stay away from the city's busyness and conveniently located to all that a visitor to the state capital might need and want to enjoy. When you climb the stairs to the entrance hall and the reception parlors with their high ceilings, you cannot help feeling that you have stepped into another era and for some small moment in time you can be part of and enjoy the amenities of an earlier year. The bedrooms in this inn have painted walls, which serve to contrast with the dark wood furniture to create a sense of comfort and spaciousness. Some of the rooms have spa tubs. The inn has a wonderful large kitchen with tables where you can eat breakfast. An alternative to eating inside is the courtyard garden with plantings and flowers and places to sit and enjoy all that surrounds you. That's where I would take breakfast and where I would spend any time that I could make available. The owner has another property, just a few doors away, offering ten condos with complete kitchens or kitchenettes, dining areas, living rooms, and bedrooms for those who want or need to be in the Albany area for a longer period (these rent for $135 to $150 with corporate rates for long-term stays). *Directions:* From New York, take I-87 north to I-787 to the Empire Plaza exit. Stay in the right lane onto South Swan Street and go left on Washington Avenue, left on Henry Johnson Blvd, then left onto State Street.

THE STATE HOUSE
Owner: Charles Kuhtic
Innkeeper: Janine Baird
393 State Street
Albany, NY 12210, USA
Tel: (518) 427-6063, Fax: (518) 463-1316
5 Rooms, Double: $135–$200
Open: all year, Credit cards: all major
www.karenbrown.com/thestatehouse.html

A 600-acre estate where in the 1920s the literati and the liberals gathered, Troutbeck has now become a conference center for executive meetings during the week and a country inn to which you can escape on the weekends (or during the week if there are no meetings booked). This is a grand property, very reminiscent of an English country estate, with facilities both large and surprisingly intimate. There are small libraries with fireplaces where you can curl up with a book and there is a ballroom capable of seating almost 250 for that special wedding. The inn has several dining rooms suitable for various sorts of occasions and a first-rate wine list for your enjoyment. Guestrooms are wonderfully large and beautifully furnished, warm, and welcoming, and many have fireplaces. Guests have the use of a covered, heated swimming pool, a summer outdoor pool, a fitness center, tennis courts, and a golf course is in the planning stage. There are plenty of walks through the woods and gardens to enjoy and there are also ventures out into the countryside to visit wineries and taste the locally produced wine. Troutbeck is either a place to stay very busy with all that there is to do on the property or a place to do nothing. *Directions:* From New York, take Route 684 to and through Brewster to Route 22. Continue on Route 22 through Wingdale and Dover Plains to Amenia then turn right at the light onto Route 343 for almost 2½ miles to the inn on the right.

❄ ☕ ⚖ 💳 🏋 P ⑂ ≈ 🚶 🐾 ♿ 👫 🏇 🍇

TROUTBECK
Manager: Garret Corcoran
Leedsville Road
Amenia, NY 12501, USA
Tel: (845) 373-9681, Fax: (645) 373-7080
Toll Free: (800) 978-7688
42 Rooms, Double: $375–$600*
*Includes all meals
Minimum Nights Required: 2 (May to mid-Nov)
Open: all year, Credit cards: all major
www.karenbrown.com/nytroutbeck.html

Bullis Hall, in the tiny village of Bangall, was built as a Greek Revival hall in 1830 and was home for 140 years to generations of the Bullis family. Now it has a new life, a splendid one, as a superb country inn. Under the careful and well-organized direction of Lauren and Addison Berkey, this building has been reclaimed, restored, and polished so cleverly that the renovation looks totally authentic and in keeping with the age of the hall. Guests really feel like cosseted visitors staying at the home of friends, an ambiance enhanced by the display of family photos in lovely frames. The large living room with its glazed red walls beams warmth, as do the sofas, the chairs, and the gas fireplace, which beckon you to relax. The bedrooms, some of which have separate sitting rooms, are tailored in their simplicity but extraordinarily luxurious in their fabrics, from the window treatments to the fabulous sheets and blankets. Within all this luxurious comfort, it's hard to decide whether to squirrel away in your room or to lounge for hours in the common rooms. A Continental breakfast sets you up for a day of exploring local antique shops, historical sites, or the winding roads of this beautiful part of the Hudson River Valley. The dining room, under the direction of a four-star French chef, caters to in-house guests and private parties only. *Directions:* Take Taconic State Parkway north to Route 44. Go right then take Route 82 north to Stanfordville. Go right on Route 65.

BULLIS HALL
Innkeepers: Addison & Lauren Berkey
P.O. Box 630
Bangall, NY 12506, USA
Tel: (845) 868-1665, Fax: (845) 868-1441
5 Rooms, Double: $325–$525
Dinner Tues-Sat for inn guests & private parties only
Open: all year, Credit cards: all major
Relais & Châteaux
www.karenbrown.com/nybullishall.html

As we drove through a town boasting an incredible concentration of antique dealers, I jokingly threatened my husband (I love antiques!) that if I saw an appealing inn, we were staying the night. Later, he thought I was kidding when I asked him to turn back after passing what appeared to be a very promising inn. A handsome, two-story cobblestone building topped by an octagonal roof and chimney stacks, Ye Olde Landmark Tavern hugs the contours of the street corner. The front entry delivers you into the inviting bar and presents glimpses into numerous, intimate dining rooms. Wood tables, soft lighting, and country stenciling create a charming ambiance. With just five guest rooms at the top of a narrow stairway, in Europe this would be termed a Restaurant with Rooms. Befitting an antique town, the rooms are decorated with lovely antiques and enjoy private baths. The rooms were already reserved, but we were fortunate to view a suite spanning the front of the inn that enjoys a sitting room and separate bedroom. A continental breakfast is offered in the downstairs dining room. The tavern has hosted travelers for over 150 years. Today, a warm welcome, assurance of good food, and comfortable lodging are extended by a team of two brothers—Andrew, a Culinary Institute graduate, oversees the kitchen and Will mans the reception. *Directions:* The inn is located on the US 20, approximately 34 miles east of Syracuse.

YE OLDE LANDMARK TAVERN
Owner: Stephen Hengst
Innkeepers: Will Shoemaker & Andrew Hengst
Route 20
Bouckville, NY 13310, USA
Tel & Fax: (315) 893-1810
5 Rooms, Double: $120–$180
Open: mid-Mar to Dec 31
Credit cards: all major
www.karenbrown.com/oldelandmark.html

Although, Buffalo is New York State's second largest city; it is surprisingly easy to navigate, intimate in size, and boasts a wealth of handsome Second Empire residences. Delaware and Elmwood span the length of downtown; from a luxurious park ringed by gorgeous homes on one end, to the town square and waterfront on the other. Buffalo is home to four of Frank Lloyd Wright buildings, enjoys theater and opera, and deserves more attention and acclaim. Built in 1869, and abandoned for 25 years according to the owners, we were thrilled to learn the city's handsome red brick estate had been converted to a luxury hotel. A discreet brass plaque identifies the property. When you climb the stairs, planked by griffin statuary, the magnificent, massive wood doors magically open. The term "Butler" takes on new meaning as the Mansion's Butlers greet you and attend to your every need and wish; from "pampering your palate" at breakfast, to complimentary transportation to events and restaurants. With evening turndown treats, such as strawberries dipped in chocolate laced with Grand Marnier, the hotel prides itself in making a statement in service and hospitality. Architecturally the rooms are grand and spacious and the public rooms are popular for private functions. The decor is quite modern and incorporates the crafts and talents of locals. *Directions:* Located at the corner of Edward Street and Delaware Avenue.

THE MANSION ON DELAWARE AVENUE
Owners: Dennis Murphy, Geno & Diana Principe
Innkeeper: Geno Principe
414 Delaware Avenue
Buffalo, NY 14202, USA
Tel: (716) 886-3300, Fax: (716) 883-3923
28 Rooms, Double: $169–$425
Open: all year, Credit cards: all major
www.karenbrown.com/mansion.html

Innkeepers who care about their guests in a truly personal way, who come to know them, and who are devoted to fulfilling their needs must have been trained by Julie and John Sullivan. They set the standard in the hospitality industry for creating a superb guest experience, a standard exemplified by the touches in the bedrooms that include all the amenities a guest would want—extra towels, a hairdryer, plenty of places to sit and relax, a wood-burning fireplace that's set and lit by the innkeeper before you retire for the evening. In the early evening guests enjoy a selection of wonderful hors d'oeuvres on the glassed-in porch, visiting with the innkeepers while enjoying drinks such as freshly pressed apple cider. Dinners are served nightly on request for a minimum of six people. Breakfasts are fabulous and include a selection of fresh fruit presented on a silver tray—there were probably a dozen varieties of fruit on the morning we were at the inn. The hot entrée selections would make a restaurant blush in the variety of offerings, accompanied by local sausage or thick slices of bacon. There were egg dishes, pancakes, French toast, and freshly baked muffins accompanied by jams that were sensuous in their richness of flavor. As we drove away from the inn, we knew that we had been treated by our hosts in an unparalleled way. *Directions:* Leave I-90 at exit 43, turning right on Route 21. Turn left at Route 488, then first right on East Avenue to the stop sign. Continue ¾ mile.

MORGAN-SAMUELS INN
Innkeepers: John & Julie Sullivan, Brad Smith
2920 Smith Road
Canandaigua, NY 14425, USA
Tel: (585) 394-9232, Fax: (585) 394-8044
5 Rooms, Double: $119–$295
3 lake villas
Dinner by reservation only
Closed: Christmas, Credit cards: all major
Select Registry
www.karenbrown.com/nymorgansamuels.html

Welcome to Friends Lake Inn; welcome to our own style of hospitality in upper New York where late spring explodes with beauty and warm summers brim over with things to do at the lake, on the trails, or at the edge of the pool. Fall, with its vivid colors, is an artist's dream, and winter brings peace and quiet interrupted by the holidays and decorations from tip to toe. Such is the year at the Friends Lake Inn. The Adirondack Lodge rooms are the most popular of the guestrooms. The Great Room has a king bed with head and footboards made of tree limbs, while its oversized stone hearth and fireplace spread glow and warmth. Other bedrooms, most with canopy beds, have more traditional décor but, whatever the style, all rooms are comfortable and have private baths. Second-floor rooms overlooking the lake have access to a private balcony where many a good hour can be spent watching the trees grow and the lake shimmer with the changing light. Guests have the use of a common room with Craftsman and Adirondack furniture and on the first floor you find the main dining room and attractive bar. Dinner is served five nights a week off season and every night in high season. The award-winning restaurant is known for its new-American cuisine. *Directions:* Leave I-87 at exit 25 onto Route 8 west for 3½ miles. Turn left at Friends Lake Road, bear right at the fork for 1 mile then turn right for 8/10 mile to the inn.

❄ ▰ CREDIT ☎ P ¶ ≈ ✝ 🏃 👫 ⛷ 🚣

FRIENDS LAKE INN
Innkeepers: John & Trudy Phillips
963 Friends Lake Road
Chestertown, NY 12817, USA
Tel: (518) 494-4751, Fax: (518) 494-4616
17 Rooms, Double: $325–$475*
*Includes breakfast & dinner
Open: all year, Credit cards: all major
Select Registry
www.karenbrown.com/nyfriendslake.html

Clarence is a great base for visiting Niagara Falls, attending the theater, antiquing, or exploring the area, and the Asa Ransom House is the perfect place to stay in Clarence. This full-service inn serves dinner to its guests six nights a week in two dining rooms and the Snug, the inn's pub. On Friday and Saturday the inn offers a modified American plan, which includes dinner in the room rate. There is great attention to detail here in every aspect of the inn's operation and guests' needs and comfort are the owners' primary concerns. The nine bedrooms, all but one with working fireplaces, are furnished with antiques and reproductions and are exceptionally comfortable in every detail. My favorite was decorated in blue and white with a canopy bed and coordinated fabrics on the upholstered chairs where you can sit and read that good book you brought to finish before turning in for the night. Each room has a hidden TV, radio, telephone, modem, and its own controls for heat and air conditioning. Many of the bedrooms also have their own porches or balconies—great to sit on but especially wonderful for the fresh air that you'll enjoy. The inn also has a spectacular gift shop packed with lots of goodies that you can take home as a remembrance of your stay. *Directions:* Traveling east, from I-90 take exit 49 to Rte 78, go left for 1 mile then right on Rte 5 for 5-3/10 miles. Traveling west, take exit 48A, go south on Rte 77 for 1 mile and right on Rte 5 for 10 miles.

❄ ☕ 🎿 CREDIT ☎ P ⑪ 🚭 🚶 🖼 ⛷ 🧍 👫

ASA RANSOM HOUSE
Innkeepers: Abigail & Robert Lenz
10529 Main Street
Clarence, NY 14031, USA
Tel: (716) 759-2315, Fax: (716) 759-2791
Toll Free: (800) 841-2340
9 Rooms, Double: $105–$175
Serving breakfast & dinner daily Tues-Sun
Closed: Jan, Credit cards: all major
Select Registry
www.karenbrown.com/nyasaransom.html

You find the Pig Hill Inn on Main Street in one of the most scenic little villages on the Hudson River. It is a cozy and welcoming inn; its simple charm and stylishly furnished bedrooms provide the traveler with pleasant overnight accommodations and the ability to wander about the town to shop, to eat, and to enjoy a break from the everyday world. You enter the inn through a Victorian-style greenhouse conservatory where breakfast is served in the mornings; alternatively, you can eat on the terrace—unless you decide to breakfast in bed. The inn prides itself on serving breakfast in bed, accompanied by a copy of the New York Times, and this delicious experience is hard to turn down. There are nine bedrooms in the inn, some with fireplaces or wood-burning stoves, and five have private bathrooms with claw-foot or whirlpool tubs. Quilts top four-poster queen and king beds. If you'd be content with staying in Cold Spring for a few days, forget the car—take the train from New York (one hour) and just enjoy. If "doing" is your thing, close by you can visit West Point, the Boscobel, Dia, Roosevelt and Vanderbilt mansions. *Directions:* From New York, take the Taconic State Parkway north, exiting at Route 301 west to Cold Spring to Main Street. The inn is on the left at the corner of Main and Rock Streets.

PIG HILL INN
Owners: Henry & Vera Keil
Innkeeper: Emily Aunas
73 Main Street
Cold Spring, NY 10516, USA
Tel: (845) 265-9247, Fax: (845) 265-9154
9 Rooms, Double: $150–$250
Open: all year, Credit cards: all major
www.karenbrown.com/nypighillinn.html

The Inn at Cooperstown, a fine example of Second Empire architecture, makes a stately impression as you round the corner on Chestnut Street. It was originally built as a hotel in 1874 in three sections and operated as an annex to a posh resort across the street. Later in the century it was converted into a family home. The original design makes this building ideal for an inn and it now has two sections, one having been torn down to make a garage. Within these walls the best features have been preserved and you find 17 comfortable rooms for guests. Bedrooms are simply furnished and all have private baths. Curtains frame the windows and shades pull down to shut out the night and bring coziness to your late-night book reading. There are no telephones or TVs in the bedrooms but these are available in the common rooms on the first floor, all of which have been beautifully redecorated this past year. Across the hall is the dining room where the inn serves an expanded Continental breakfast. The innkeeper's dedication to extending hospitality to guests, in the same way that they have been welcomed for more than 100 years, is most admirable. *Directions:* From I-90 take exit 30 to Route 28 south to Chestnut Street to the inn. From I-87, take exit 21 to Route 23 west to Route 145, then Route 20 west to Route 80 west to Chestnut Street. From I-88 take exit 17 to Route 28 north to Chestnut Street.

INN AT COOPERSTOWN
Innkeepers: Sherrie & Marc Kingsley
16 Chestnut Street
Cooperstown, NY 13326, USA
Tel: (607) 547-5756, Fax: (607) 547-8779
17 Rooms, Double: $169–$325
Open: all year, Credit cards: all major
Select Registry
www.karenbrown.com/nyinnatcooperstown.html

Enjoying 7 acres of woodlands and gardens, Cromwell Manor Inn, an imposing structure with great columns fronting its brick façade, sits high on a hill with a spectacular view of the Hudson Highlands and offers thirteen guestrooms with private baths in two buildings. The Manor House is elegantly furnished with period antiques and fine reproductions. On the entry level you find the living room and the dining room where guests are served a full gourmet breakfast. The Chimney's Cottage, built in 1764, offers romantic bedrooms with a more rustic country decor. The mansion's original owner's ancestors can be traced back to England's Oliver Cromwell. There's much to do in this area: West Point, for example, is just 5 miles away and many other historical sites, such as the homes of the Roosevelts and the Vanderbilts, are nearby—and there's always antiquing, the wineries, and all sorts of sporting activities. *Directions:* From New York City drive north on I-87 to exit 16. At the end of the ramp, turn right onto 32N for 1-3/10 miles. Make a right at Smith Clove Road and travel for almost 9 miles (the road name changes twice). Cromwell Manor is on your left.

CROMWELL MANOR INN
Innkeepers: Jack & Cynthia Trowell
174 Angola Road
Cornwall, NY 12518, USA
Tel: (845) 534-7136, Fax: none
13 Rooms, Double: $165–$370
Open: all year
Credit cards: all major
www.karenbrown.com/nycromwellmanor.html

"Take from this inn its amity, take from this hearth its warmth, return them not—but return." This quote from the inn's simple information brochure says it all, and I promise, after being embraced by the warmth and hospitality of Old Drovers, you will do exactly that—return. Going back to when it first offered accommodation and food to drovers as they herded cattle from New England to the New York City markets, this inn has repackaged its welcome and its wonderful old Colonial charm. Crackling fires complete a perfect ambiance already staged with creaking, wide plank floors, massive, wood beams, handsome old stone walls. The inn's five bedrooms have been redecorated and are now elegant abodes for guests. Besides relaxing in the library or in the living room or breakfasting in a dining room with hand-painted scenes of nearby historical sites, there's more to do outside this inn than there are hours in the day. However, no matter what the day's activities were, you must plan to return to enjoy a candlelit dinner served in the inn's downstairs dining room. The soft light of candles and a little indirect light give charm and intimacy to a dinner with someone you love. The inn's setting beckons you outdoors—for a walk, to sit under the trees, to go antiquing, or to explore the countryside. *Directions:* On Route 22 north from Brewster through Wingdale, there is a billboard instructing you to turn right on East Duncan Hill Road.

OLD DROVERS INN
Innkeeper: David Wilson
East Duncan Hill Road
P.O. Box 100
Dover Plains, NY 12522, USA
Tel: (845) 832-9311, Fax: (845) 832-6356
5 Rooms, Double: $190–$550
Dinner on weekends
Closed: Jan, Credit cards: all major
Relais & Châteaux
www.karenbrown.com/nyolddrovers.html

North of New York City in the Catskill Mountains there is a 135-year-old country estate that is now an inn housed in three buildings: the Manor House, the Carriage House, and the Cottage. Rooms differ in décor as befits the architecture of their building. Both the Carriage House and the Cottage, built from lumber milled on the property, carry an Adirondack theme with beamed ceilings and stone fireplaces. The Eagle's Nest, the Cottage's most elegant room, has a living room with vaulted ceiling and stone fireplace, upstairs king bedroom and bath, and a full kitchen. In the Manor House, where furnishings are traditional, the Cardinal Room, used by Cardinals Spellman and Hayes, is a large corner room with a gas fireplace and whirlpool tub. The inn has two parlors, a billiard room, and a formal dining room where a full breakfast is served, either on the glassed-in porch during winter or the screened porch in summer. As you ascend the winding staircase from the entry hall, there are paintings, prints, and other memorabilia to catch your eye. A stay here is like spending the weekend at grandmother's house—but with a fireplace in your bedroom and a whirlpool tub in the bathroom. Summer and winter activities are yours to enjoy with the lake being the biggest attraction. *Directions:* From Monticello, take Route 42 south for 4½ miles then turn left at the Lake Joseph Estates sign (Lake Joseph Drive) and drive ¾ mile, following signs to the inn.

❋ 🍵 🏊 CREDIT ☎ 🏠 🍸 P ≈ 🎿 ♿ 👫 🎿 ⚓

INN AT LAKE JOSEPH
Innkeepers: Ivan & Ru Weinger
162 Lake Joseph Road
Forestburgh, NY 12777, USA
Tel: (845) 791-9506, Fax: (845) 794-1948
15 Rooms, Double: $170–$385
Open: all year
Credit cards: all major
www.karenbrown.com/nyinnatlakejoseph.html

A hundred-foot veranda is one element of the striking façade that The White Inn presents to the world in Fredonia, New York. The inn is traditional in feel and in the way that its owners have decorated it for their guests. Most of the common areas of this inn are spacious—the lobby and reception area, the dining room, and the bar/lounge are large and have high ceilings that make the rooms seem even larger. Hallways on the second and third floors are wide and have interesting furniture and art hanging on the walls. There are 23 bedrooms, each with a private bath, and 11 are larger suites. The rooms are decorated not in high style but with comfortable furnishings and décor from the 19th century or reproductions thereof. The dining room, a charter member of the Duncan Hines Family of Fine Restaurants, serves breakfast, lunch, and dinner seven days a week to guests and non-guests. All conferencing and banqueting facilities are available (there are four meeting rooms) and the inn also hosts weddings on site. The inn is well located for attending performances at the Chautauqua Institution or at the Fredonia Opera House. *Directions:* Leave I-90 at exit 59 and at the light turn left onto Route 60 south. At the second light turn right onto Route 20 west for 1¼ miles to the inn on the right.

❄ ☕ 🎿 🏧 ☎ ♿ P ⑀ 🖼 🔔 ☂ ⚲ 🚶 🥾 ⚘

THE WHITE INN
Innkeepers: Robert Contiguglia & Kathleen Dennison
52 East Main Street
Fredonia, NY 14063, USA
Tel: (716) 672- 2103, Fax: (716) 672-2107
Toll Free: (888) 373-3664
23 Rooms, Double: $79–$179
Open: all year, Credit cards: all major
www.karenbrown.com/nywhiteinn.html

Although relatively new, this 26-room lodge is already developing a comfortable and familiar charm. Its Arts and Crafts decor is complemented by mission-style furniture—simple, yet warm and inviting. The great room looks out through the trees of the forest to the dramatic rock cliffs of the Shawangunk Mountains: it's a breathtaking view and if you're a rock climber, you'll know of the famous challenges of scaling this mountain wall. For non-climbers, walking trails in the forest beckon and there's a wide deck along the back of the lodge where you can sit and absorb it all—vicariously. The cleanly decorated guestrooms have king- and full-size beds, and bathrooms with every amenity, and most rooms have the bonus of decks. The photographs of local artist Steve Jordan decorate each room—great photographs and reason alone to come stay at Minnewaska. Guests enjoy an expanded Continental breakfast in front of the wood stove in the great room and homemade cookies and beverages in the afternoon. There's a fitness center in the building, which is wonderful for that daily workout. Under the guidance of its owners and staff, Minnewaska Lodge is acquiring the patina and comfort of a favorite leather chair. *Directions:* Leave the New York State Thruway (I-87) at exit 18, turn left on Route 299 and drive 6 miles to the end. Go left on Route 44/55 to the inn immediately on the right.

MINNEWASKA LODGE
Owner: Paul Schwartzberg
Manager: Rebecca Frost
3116 Route 44/55
Gardiner, NY 12525, USA
Tel: (845) 255-1110, Fax: (845) 255-5069
26 Rooms, Double: $135–$319
Open: all year, Credit cards: all major
www.karenbrown.com/nyminnewaska.html

Carrie Harron Collins began work on her dream home in 1885 and several years later the 48 men she hired finished her castle. This castle, like most, is one of which dreams are made and the interiors are handsomely crafted of cherry, chestnut, and mahogany. The richness of these woods and the intricate carving of staircases, railings, and other architectural details add to the fantasy-like feel of the interiors. With the inn's setting on Seneca Lake and its serene grounds, this is a lovely place for those who have always fantasized about staying in a castle. Recently constructed, a building that neighbors the castle, called the Vinifera, offers guests twenty additional lakefront rooms and suites. Find historical charm in the chambers of the original Castle or romantic luxury in the Vinifera. The property now also boasts two dining options. Edgar's in the castle enjoys the awe-inspiring interior of the stone castle with excellent cuisine and a memorable setting overlooking the lake. Stonecutters is more informal offering eclectic tavern fare, a sunken bar and an outdoor patio with fire pit and more. *Directions:* Take I-90 to exit 42, then Route 14 south to Geneva to the inn.

BELHURST
Innkeeper: The Reeder Family
P.O. Box 609
Geneva, NY 14456, USA
Tel & Fax: (315) 781-0201
47 Rooms, Double: $70–$365
2 cottages
Open: all year, Credit cards: MC, VS
www.karenbrown.com/nybelhurstcastle.html

Built as a private home in 1914, subsequently becoming a monastery and now an upscale inn, Geneva on the Lake is a property with a unique style and personality. Its various lives have left their mark on the building as rooms date back to different periods of the inn's history. Owned by Alfred and Aminy Audi, the inn is furnished throughout with the furniture and decorative accessories made by the Stickley furniture company, which results in a very coordinated look, as opposed to the more eclectic mix usually found in inns. Seating both looks and is comfortable, whether it be sofas, side chairs, rockers, or chairs for the dining-room table. There is a large variety of accommodations at the inn, ranging from single rooms to two-bedroom suites. My favorite, The Loft, with its lovely cherry mission furniture, is at the top end. It has a cathedral ceiling, a loft furnished with chairs, rockers, and big floor cushions, all positioned to look out at the lake, and a sitting room with views of the lake, the formal gardens, and the pool. The Library Suite makes use of the home's original library and is handsome with its floor-to-ceiling black-walnut paneling, bookshelves, and wood-burning fireplace. The inn serves dinner seven nights a week, accompanied by live music, in a room that overlooks the lake. Numerous packages for staying at the inn are available, as are wedding and conference facilities. *Directions:* Take I-90 to exit 42 to Route 14 south for about 7 miles—the inn is on the left.

GENEVA ON THE LAKE
Innkeeper: William J. Schickel
1001 Lochland Road, Route 14
Geneva, NY 14456, USA
Tel: (315) 789-7190, Fax: (315) 789-0322
Toll Free: (800) 343-6382
29 Rooms, Double: $212–$1,214
Open: all year, Credit cards: all major
Select Registry
www.karenbrown.com/nygenevaonlake.html

What's special about this inn, and makes it stand tall among other inns, is its innkeepers; there are few who match the easy charm of Kim and Mark—and this would be reason enough for staying at the Greenville Arms. What's unusual and fun about this inn is that it runs a series of workshops for artists and quilt artists, from novice to expert, with a different instructor each week. Travelers in the area are welcome to stay at the inn even if not participating in one of the classes. The guestrooms are located in three buildings: the main inn offers several rooms with both a queen and a single bed, while in the carriage house just across the babbling stream and in the new building some rooms have two-person spa tubs. On Sunday through Friday the Greenville Arms serves a set dinner and on Saturday guests are provided with menus from local restaurants. Special features of the property include a swimming pool, croquet court, and flowering gardens. Guests can enjoy the activities of the Hudson River Valley and of the northern Catskill Mountains, which range from antiquing to water sports on the Hudson and skiing in the mountains. The Greenville Arms is the former home of William Vanderbilt who in 1889 left New York City for a more tranquil existence. *Directions:* From New York, drive north on I-87 to exit 21B onto Route 9W, heading south. After 2 miles get onto I-81, driving west for 13 miles to Greenville where you turn left at the traffic light to the inn on the right.

❄ 🛷 🛋 CREDIT ❣ P 🍴 🏊 🚶 🏃 👫 🐎 🎿 🛶

GREENVILLE ARMS 1889 INN
Innkeepers: Kim & Mark LaPolla
P.O. Box 659
Greenville, NY 12083, USA
Tel: (518) 966-5219, Fax: (518) 966-8754
Toll Free: (888) 665-0044
13 Rooms, Double: $115–$235
2 cottages
Meals Sun through Fri for inn guests only by reservation
Open: all year, Credit cards: MC, VS
www.karenbrown.com/nygreenvillearms.html

This 1841 home on 6 acres, built on classic Georgian Colonial lines and listed in the National Register of Historic Places, is now a bed and breakfast inn with five guestrooms. The house has seven working fireplaces, double living rooms with large crystal chandeliers, and elegant wallpapers throughout—the antique paper on the dining-room walls is especially lovely. The formal dining room continues the theme of Federal-period elegance found in the other rooms of the house. Of the three bedrooms on the second floor, each is lovely and enjoys its own private bathroom. Canopy beds are in style here, with four-poster beds of substance and great style. On the third floor are two additional bedrooms, each with bath and double Jacuzzi. Interestingly shaped windows provide views into the lovely yard with its swimming pool, gardens, and plantings of shrubs and trees. The inn serves a full gourmet breakfast with recipes garnered by the innkeeper who attended the Culinary Institute of America. An attractive ballroom wing with parquet flooring has been added to the house and is used for weddings and other functions. The country inn is in a quiet setting where a walk down the road will refresh your senses. The Roosevelt homes, West Point, and the Vanderbilt estates overlooking the Hudson River are close by. *Directions:* From New York, take the Taconic State Parkway and turn right at Carpenter Road then first left at Bykenhulle Road.

BYKENHULLE HOUSE
Innkeepers: Bill & Florence Beausoleil
21 Bykenhulle Road
Hopewell Junction, NY 12533, USA
Tel: (845) 221-4182, Fax: none
5 Rooms, Double: $145–$165
Open: all year, Credit cards: MC, VS
www.karenbrown.com/nybykenhulle.html

In honor of the genius responsible for this beautiful inn, Lynnette christened her new venture in innkeeping as the William Henry Miller Inn. Ironically, Cornell's first student of architecture never graduated because of his immediate success. Built in 1880 and stunning in its architectural detail with stained glass, chestnut woodwork, numerous fireplaces, and brilliant use of space; fortunate is the traveler to snare one of the inn's nine rooms. Seven guestrooms are located up the grand stairway of the main house. For more privacy, two guestrooms are offered in the garden carriage house. All the rooms are individual in their decor and appeal. In the main house, the second floor rooms are spacious with high ceilings. Rooms on the third floor are converted from what were once where the grandchildren received music lessons, cozy under angled ceilings. My favorite, The Library, incorporates a sitting area in the circular alcove of the turret. Its pretty decor of soft greens goes well with the shuttered windows. My favorite feature of this inn is the innkeeper herself, Lynnette. Sincere in her wish to make her guests feel relaxed and welcome, she considers the greatest compliment "guests who feel comfortable enough to put their feet up!" While a continental breakfast in your room will be honored, enjoy an elegant feast by candlelight in the regal dining room. *Directions:* Exit Route 96B on Aurora Street. The inn is on the corner of Buffalo and Aurora, just past Ithaca Commons.

WILLIAM HENRY MILLER INN
Innkeepers: Lynnette Scofield & David Dier
303 North Aurora Street
Ithaca, NY 14850, USA
Tel: (607) 256-4553, Fax: (607) 256-0092
Toll Free: (877) 256-4553
9 Rooms, Double: $130–$210
Closed: Dec 24 to Jan 12, Credit cards: all major
Select Registry
www.karenbrown.com/miller.html

The Lamplight Inn is a romantic 1890 Victorian inn located halfway between Saratoga Springs and Lake George. Here, in the countryside, you can begin to feel the magnificence of the Adirondacks. The roads are lined with trees and there are views of meadows around every bend in the road. The inn sits on top of a hill, as if it commands all that it overlooks. It is pure Victorian, and the common rooms and bedrooms reflect this style. There are patterns on bedspreads, curtains, carpets, and pillows reminiscent of the bygone era. There is a large dining room, a comfortable living room, and a wrap-around porch—which was part of the architecture of this period—all designed with great entertaining in mind. The house was built for a wealthy lumberman (an eligible bachelor) in the Gothic style and was used as his summer home. There's a magnificent chestnut keyhole staircase, crafted in England, which leads up to the bedrooms. Linda and Gene purchased the home in 1984 and, together, created the bed-and-breakfast inn that exists today. Breakfast in the morning includes fruit, freshly baked bread or muffins, homemade granola—followed by a non-egg special and egg menu, breakfast meat, and famous home-fried potatoes. A great variety of events and seasonal activities are available the year-round. *Directions:* From the south, take the Northway I-87 to exit 21, then take Lake Luzerne/Lake George exit on Rte 9N south for 11 miles to the inn.

LAMPLIGHT INN BED & BREAKFAST
Innkeepers: Gene & Linda Merlino
231 Lake Avenue
P.O. Box 130
Lake Luzerne, NY 12846, USA
Tel: (518) 696-5294, Fax: (518) 696-4914
Toll Free: (800) 262-4668
13 Rooms, Double: $99–$239
Closed: Christmas, Credit cards: all major
Select Registry
www.karenbrown.com/lamplight.html

As morning comes silently across the lake, with rays of sunshine and the promise of a new day, breakfast in front of the cabin fire or in the lodge's dining room tempts you with blueberry pancakes with coconut custard, or cheddar scrambled eggs with a caramelized onion and potato rosti with mushrooms. Read the newspapers in front of the fire, take a walk along the lakefront, then it's time for lunch and a nap. Enjoy some exercise in the afternoon, soothe your muscles in the soaking tub, put another log on the fire, and watch the changing shadows of the day's end. Sip a glass of wine in the den before a dinner made special by the final light on the lake, good conversation, and great wine—a dinner that might include caramelized parsnip soup with chestnuts, roasted garlic, and a wild mushroom timbale, duck, beef, or fish magically prepared and artistically presented, and a bittersweet chocolate and peppermint confection for dessert. Walk back to the cabin, listening to the still of the night, pile another log on the fire, relax to the sound of soft music, climb onto the featherbed, pulling up sheets of softest cotton, then float off into your dreams. These are the moments of a day at the Lake Placid Lodge and they make the memories of a lifetime. *Directions:* Take I-87 to exit 30 to Lake Placid. Drive for 30 miles on Route 73 to Route 86 west then drive through the village for 1½ miles to the sign for the Lodge—turn right and drive ½ mile to the inn.

LAKE PLACID LODGE
Innkeeper: David Garrett
Whiteface Inn Road
P.O. Box 550
Lake Placid, NY 12946, USA
Tel: (518) 523-2700, Fax: (518) 523-1124
34 Rooms, Double: $350–$950
Open: all year, Credit cards: all major
Relais & Châteaux
www.karenbrown.com/nylakeplacidlodge.html

The Genesee Country Inn sits right on Spring Creek, a trout stream with waterfalls where you can fish and relax in the morning, walk to the Genesee Country Museum (a fabulous experience with craftsmen demonstrating the trades of a former day) in the afternoon, take day trips into Rochester, follow the path of the Erie Canal, bike, golf, and hunt for antiques. There's a lot more to keep you busy a little farther a field, including visiting Niagara Falls (an hour and a half away), driving into Ontario, or continuing on to Toronto. The inn has ten comfortably furnished bedrooms with sitting areas. All of the rooms have private bathrooms, individual heat and air-conditioning controls, direct-dial telephones, and TV/VCRs, and some have fireplaces and a view to the water. During the 1800s the inn was a plaster mill and then a sawmill. Around 1917 this lovely old mill with 2½-foot-thick stone walls was converted into a duplex for employees and then in 1982 the private residence became the Genesee Country Inn. While it fronts onto a street with a church across the way, at the back there is a lovely sun room overlooking a serene setting of pond and stream where guests can relax in a hot tub. *Directions:* From I-90 take exit 47 to Rte 490E. Take first exit to LeRoy, Rte 19S. Follow inn signs to North Rd. Take a left onto North Rd and follow it for 3 miles. At the stop sign, turn right onto Rte 36S to Mumford. At the flashing light in Mumford take a right and travel two blocks to the inn.

GENESEE COUNTRY INN
Owner: Fran Pullano
Innkeeper: Kim Rasmussen
948 George Street, P.O. Box 340
Mumford, NY 14511-0340, USA
Tel: (585) 538-2500, Fax: (585) 248-2488
Toll Free: (800) 697-8297
10 Rooms, Double: $109–$185
Closed: Christmas week, Credit cards: MC, VS
Select Registry
www.karenbrown.com/nygenesee.html

Good things always come in threes and the Casablanca Hotel is the first of three boutique hotels crafted by Henry Kallan in New York (although he is part owner of yet another). This one, just east of Broadway on 43rd Street, round the corner from Times Square and the theater district, has a Moroccan flavor, which makes it fun and different. Rooms are not large, but everything that the traveler needs is right there at the ready. Throughout the day guests may have international coffees and teas, fresh fruit, cookies, and cappuccino or espresso are always there for the asking. Each weekday evening Rick's Café, where breakfast is served, hosts a wine and cheese reception every night except Sundays, and, as in the other Kallan properties, there's a piano where on Friday evenings a selection of popular songs transports you to another world. There's a great little outdoor patio where you can look up and see sky and drink in the air of New York. All the hotel services you could imagine are available here including secretarial service and a concierge. *Directions:* Located centrally in New York City in the heart of Times Square, the theater district, entertainment, business, and shopping. You can be in the downtown financial district of Wall Street in fifteen minutes by subway.

❄ ☕ ✄ 💳 ☎ 🛗 ⛾ P ⛴ ♿

CASABLANCA HOTEL
Owner: Henry Kallan
Manager: Peter Jurecka
147 West 43rd Street
New York, NY 10036, USA
Tel: (212) 869-1212, Fax: (212) 391-7585
Toll Free: (888) 922-7225
43 Rooms, Double: $275–$405
Open: all year, Credit cards: all major
www.karenbrown.com/nycasablanca.html

Home away from home—at a hotel like the Elysée . . . and at a great price—this is truly possible. When the doorman greets you, it's obvious service will be high on the list of memories. It's quiet, it's friendly, and above all, it's refined and yet alive. Rooms range from smaller, standard-size rooms to suites with separate beds and sitting rooms. The décor is traditional with warm, wood furniture and armoires that provide ample space for your clothes and the TV. French scenic and floral prints convey a classy message of comfort. Wallpaper in soft neutrals adds to the distinguished atmosphere. My favorite room (I could have been at home in any) had a king bed and opened onto a small solarium with curved frosted-glass delivering natural light into the space. Furnished with cane and bamboo furniture, one would almost welcome a lovely, soft rain to stay inside. Bathrooms, tiled in marble, contain every imaginable amenity. On the second floor, above the lobby, is a sitting room where breakfast is served: fresh juices, fruit, yogurt, hard-boiled eggs, cereals, and an array of pastries. In the evening, a selection of wines and cheese and crackers is offered. *Directions:* Located about a block off Fifth Avenue between Madison and Park Avenues, this hotel is close to all the shopping, museums, and restaurants one could wish to visit—and within reasonable walking distance of the theater district. Good bus and subway transportation to all of Manhattan.

HOTEL ELYSÉE
Owner: Henry Kallan
Manager: John Avina
60 East 54th Street
New York, NY 10022, USA
Tel: (212) 753-1066, Fax: (212) 980-9278
Toll Free: (800) 535-9733
101 Rooms, Double: $295–$625
Open: all year, Credit cards: all major
www.karenbrown.com/hotelelysee.html

There's a new destination in New York, one that travelers who crave the new and exciting will want to experience. The Hotel Gansevoort, overlooking the Hudson River, is located in an area many have never visited. It's time to come to this part of lower Manhattan with its galleries, design boutiques, restaurants, and accompanying nightlife. As you walk through the tall glass doors into the lobby, it's the very high ceilings, the softly muted and rich earth colors, the background music, and the warm welcome that instantly communicate this will be a special experience. Standard room, suite, penthouse—makes no difference as long as you can get into this very popular property. Leather headboards framed in rich woods, richly textured fabrics, plushy seating, feather beds and hypo-allergenic down duvets, flat-screen TVs, direct DID, fax, cordless telephones, and in-room safe are now the mark of hotels who understand today's sophisticated traveler. Add a rooftop heated, outdoor pool with underwater music and colored lighting, a restaurant and bar, 360-degree views, and who would want to venture out from the hotel at all? *Directions:* In lower Manhattan, take a taxi or the E subway to 14th Street, which is 8th Avenue. Walk one block west to 9th Avenue, then one block south to the Hotel.

❄ ⛷ 💳 ☎ 🏠 🛗 🏋 P 🍴 🚭 ≈ 🖼 🔔 ♿

HOTEL GANSEVOORT
Owner: Henry Kallan
Manager: Elon Kenchington
18 Ninth Avenue at 13th Street
New York, NY 10014, USA
Tel: (212) 206-6700, Fax: (212) 255-5858
Toll Free: (877) 426-7586
187 Rooms, Double: $345–$5,000*
*Breakfast not included: $19-$21
Open: all year, Credit cards: all major
www.karenbrown.com/hotelgansevoort.html

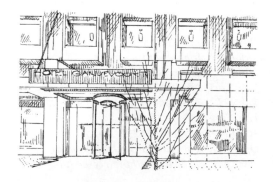

The Hotel Giraffe is one of those boutique hotels that looks smart, feels smart, and is smart. This one is located on Park Avenue South at 26th Street, and for those who either have business in this part of Manhattan or just want the luxury of a uniquely designed hotel, the Giraffe is hard to beat. Decor is European Art Modern from the 1920s and 1930s—warm wood and lush textures of velvets and leather were fashionable then and are reproduced here with sophisticated colors in upholstered chairs, headboards, and wall coverings. Twelve-foot-high ceilings and floor-to-ceiling windows draped with sheer silver curtains, groupings of chairs and sofas, and a grand piano softly playing the songs of this period all add to the atmosphere. In the bedrooms subtle colors, ivory diamond-quilted satin bedcovers, chocolate-leather headboards, and pearlized platinum wallcoverings are glamorous and feel good. More than half the rooms have French doors opening to a tiny balcony. The suites have pullout sofa beds and there's a penthouse that's nothing short of glamorous. *Directions:* Located on Park Avenue South, below Mid-Town in a fashionable residential and business community with good restaurants, the Giraffe provides easy access via public transportation to lower Manhattan, Mid-Town, and the Upper East Side.

HOTEL GIRAFFE
Owner: Henry Kallan
Manager: Nalini Sirjoo
365 Park Avenue South at 26th Street
New York, NY 10016, USA
Tel: (212) 685-7700, Fax: (212) 685-7771
Toll Free: (877) 296-0009
52 Rooms, Double: $325–$950
Open: all year, Credit cards: all major
www.karenbrown.com/nygiraffe.html

Staying at the wonderful Inn at Irving Place is to experience living in a brownstone in a New York neighborhood, feeling like you are at home. The credit is due to the friendly home-like style of the inn and the reality of being part of Manhattan; where neighborhood restaurants with street-side dining, small markets, and boutiques are enjoyed by the families who live here. Irving Place is famous for its afternoon tea parties held in Lady Mendl's Tea Salon & Dessert Parlor. The inn's twelve rooms are individually decorated with lots of old-fashioned comfort in a style reminiscent of the brownstone era of New York. The Madame Olenska room, where I stayed, had a king bed piled with welcoming pillows and a comforter that was just waiting to be pulled up for an afternoon nap, if you could avoid the temptation of curling up in the window seat overlooking the comings-and-goings on Gramercy Square. This is a hotel, however, that has digital electronics: TV, radio, two-line telephone, dataport, VHS. In the evening, the Cibar Lounge has designer martinis, Belgian beer, and appetizers. Next door, the Pure Food and Wine restaurant has a raw bar and a good selection of wines. Breakfast can be served in bed or downstairs where the morning newspaper is available. *Directions:* Located in lower Manhattan with easy access to downtown and the financial district, and within walking distance of the subway to Mid-Town and the Upper East Side.

❄ ☕ 💳 ☎ 🏠 ⛾ P 🍴 🖼 🚶 🚶‍♂️

INN AT IRVING PLACE
Owner: Naomi Blumenthal
Innkeeper: Shawn Rettstatt
56 Irving Place
New York, NY 10003, USA
Tel: (212) 533-4600, Fax: (212) 533-4611
Toll Free: (800) 685-1447
12 Rooms, Double: $325–$495
Open: all year, Credit cards: all major
www.karenbrown.com/nyirvingplace.html

The Library Hotel is one of several new boutique hotels in New York. With its library theme, this hotel is fun and different, using the Dewey decimal system to number its bedrooms. Each floor is designated for one of the system's ten classifications and books in the bedrooms reflect the appropriate classification. Guestrooms are classified either petite or deluxe, and there are eight junior suites, one with its own terrace. Rooms come with all the amenities including access to a video library of the American Film Institute's top 100 films. The hotel's facilities include a reading room, a poetry garden with an absolutely delightful terrace on top of the building, and a business center with free access to high-speed internet service, a computer, and a printer. The ground-floor lobby and reception area is spacious and high-ceilinged, and graced with a grand piano. Wine and hors d'oeuvres are offered to guests on weekdays. Passes are available to a nearby fitness center. Cappuccino, coffee, tea, fruit, and cookies are available throughout the day. The Library takes staying at a hotel to a new level—as do its sister properties, Casablanca, Hotel Giraffe, Hotel Elysée, and the new Gansevoort. These properties are warm and personable, and in a world that only goes faster, they are great places to stop and enjoy. *Directions:* Located centrally in New York with easy access to the theater districts, fashionable Mid-Town stores, the Rockefeller Center, and major transportation centers.

❄ ☕ 🛴 💳 ☎ 🛗 Ⴒ P ᵗᵗ ♿

LIBRARY HOTEL
Owner: Henry Kallan
299 Madison Avenue at 41st Street
New York, NY 10017, USA
Tel: (212) 983-4500, Fax: (212) 499-9099
Toll Free: (877) 793-7323
60 Rooms, Double: $325–$435
Open: all year, Credit cards: all major
www.karenbrown.com/nylibrary.html

On a quiet, tree-lined street, a block from New York's Central Park, is a little bit of Europe set in the refined Upper East Side of Manhattan yet still accessible to Midtown, just five blocks away. For many, this is the real New York—away from the frenetic hustle and bustle of people and traffic. The Plaza Athénée greets you as if you are coming home: whether it's the European style or the very attentive service or the exquisite attention to detail matters not, for the comfort one feels is instant and enveloping. The guestrooms and suites are reminiscent of fine homes—thoughtfully furnished, gracious, and comfortable. You can't go wrong, for the luxurious fabrics and the comfort of chairs, sofas, and, of course, the beds seem tuned to the music of your soul. Bathrooms are lavishly appointed with all the amenities you'd expect and more. The highly rated restaurant, Arabelle, features a stylish decor in a stunning gold-domed room. Bar Seine is not only a refuge for guests of the hotel, but is a favorite lounge for the discerning Manhattanite. The Plaza Athénée offers elegant, comfortable surroundings and outstanding service, enabling guests to enjoy a truly indulgent stay. *Directions:* Located in the fashionable Upper East Side, close to major museums, Central Park, and the boutiques and galleries of Madison Avenue.

PLAZA ATHÉNÉE
Manager: Bernard Lackner
37 East 64th Street at Madison Avenue
New York, NY 10021, USA
Tel: (212) 734-9100, Fax: (212) 772-0958
Toll Free: (800) 447-8800
150 Rooms, Double: $555–$3,600*
*Breakfast not included: $35
Open: all year, Credit cards: all major
www.karenbrown.com/nyathenee.html

Exciting! is the word that best describes this 164-room, 29-suite hotel. Just about perfectly located in Times Square and the theater district, their brochure says that The Time is all about redefining hospitality, defining style, a multi-sensory hotel experience, and it truly is a different place to stay. The senses are tantalized when you leave an elevator and find yourself watching a small monitor with an abstract or defined graphic, image, or message. When you sit in the lounge, a series of these captivating screens marches down the wall—a sort of multimedia projection system. In each bedroom the headboard and bedspread are in one of the primary colors (red, yellow, or blue) with a small container of jellybeans and a flagon of fresh scent in the same hue. Rooms are sleek and contemporary, yet have all the amenities that travelers might expect, including Bose wave radios, dual-line telephones with data ports and voice mail, and fax/printer/copier. VCRs, DVDs, and cell phones are available upon request. On top of it all is a triplex penthouse with terraces. With private function space, on this penthouse level you can have a meeting, stay the night, or just relish the luxury that surrounds you. Right off the lobby there's a restaurant serving delicious Tuscan cuisine. *Directions:* Located centrally in New York City in the heart of Times Square, the theater district, entertainment, business, and shopping.

❋ ⚡ ▭ ☎ ♨ ⛹ ⅄ P ¶ ♿

THE TIME
Owner: Vikram Chatwal
224 West 49th Street
New York, NY 10019, USA
Tel: (212) 246-5252, Fax: (212) 245-2305
Toll Free: (877) 846-3692
164 Rooms, Double: $255–$505*
*Breakfast not included
Open: all year, Credit cards: all major
www.karenbrown.com/nythetime.html

The Beekman Arms is truly a village inn and one from which you can walk to Rhinebeck's many antique stores, shops, and restaurants. Its 67 rooms are located in the original, pre-Revolutionary building and in seven guesthouses designed in the American Carpenter Gothic style of architecture at the Delamater Inn. The Beekman Arms is old and with its beams, low ceilings, great paneling, and wide floorboards is reminiscent of an old tavern, which it has and which contains, in addition to a dining room, a great bar area with a long polished counter and many stools where you can eat or have a drink. Bedrooms in the Arms are traditionally furnished and you cannot escape the feeling that you are in an ancient building. Delamater House, originally designed by one of America's first architects, functions as a conference center as well as a bed and breakfast facility. Its guestrooms are appointed with reproduction furniture, gas fireplaces, desk areas, and data ports. Bathrooms have showers and tubs, and though not large, provide the traveler with all that's needed. A Continental breakfast is served in the garden room. Rhinebeck is at the heart of many attractions in the Hudson River Valley, appealing to those interested in history, antiques, and galleries. *Directions:* Take the I-87 New York State Thruway to exit 19 to Rhinecliff Bridge to Route 9G south. Get onto Route 9 south and drive 2 miles to Rhinebeck village—the inn is on the right.

❄ ☕ 🎿 🔲 ☎ P 🍴 🚭 ♿ 🛷 🎋 👫 🐎 🎿

BEEKMAN ARMS–DELAMATER INN
Innkeeper: George Banta
6387 Mill Street, Route 9
Rhinebeck, NY 12572, USA
Tel: (845) 876-7077, Fax: (845) 876-2530
Toll Free: (800) 361-6517
73 Rooms, Double: $110–$300
Open: all year, Credit cards: all major
www.karenbrown.com/nybeekman.html

The University Club of Rochester was built in 1929 and was the center of social activities for its members for over 70 years but now it has a new life as a warm and inviting inn with high standards of service. Each of the bedrooms is individually decorated and great attention to detail has been given to ensure that the guest has everything needed or even contemplated. Silky Egyptian-cotton sheets dress feather beds and top-of-the-line towels hang in the bathrooms—all touches that tell guests that they are special. Many of the rooms have fireplaces, several have Jacuzzi tubs, some have multi-head showers and convenient kitchenettes. Tavern 26, where complimentary breakfast is served to the inn's guests, is located on the first floor and has a wonderfully convivial and welcoming atmosphere, like an old English pub. The inn offers excellent facilities for meetings or private functions, including the cherry-paneled library, the parlor, and the grand ballroom. The Inn on Broadway is in the heart of Rochester within a short walk of museums, theaters, shops, and other restaurants. *Directions:* From Buffalo take I-90 to Route 490 east to exit 13 (Inner Loop) to East Avenue. Turn right onto East Avenue, then at the next light, turn right on Broadway. The inn is on the left.

❄ 🍽 CREDIT ☎ 🏨 P ♉ ⚘ ♿ 🏌

INN ON BROADWAY
Innkeeper: Brendon McElduff
26 Broadway
Rochester, NY 14607, USA
Tel: (585) 232-3595, Fax: (585) 546-2164
Toll Free: (877) 612-3595
25 Rooms, Double: $175–$275
Serving lunch Tues-Friday
Open: all year, Credit cards: all major
www.karenbrown.com/nyinnonbroadway.html

The Point is an Adirondack great camp secluded on the shores of Saranac Lake where the resident genies make absolutely every wish come true. This is an inn where, from the moment you arrive at the gate or are met at the plane, the innkeepers attend to your every desire: a Scotch, a glass of Sonoma chardonnay, a favorite food, a chocolate treat, or a brandy on the porch overlooking the lake. The Point's staff knows which water sport you most love and at what time of day you'll want to do it; which trail you're likely to walk and whether you'll want a picnic at the far cove. Guests at The Point are treated like family. They gather for an evening aperitif, perhaps on the boat for a sunset cocktail cruise in black ties and long gowns, and then sit down to dinner at one of two large round tables in the living room where they enjoy good conversation, great food, and superb wine. Guests at this very special camp—no more than 22 at any one time—are housed in cottages in rooms that are not high-style but are extraordinarily comfortable, cozy, and geared to provide the utmost of privacy and relaxation. There are beamed ceilings, stone fireplaces, and comfortable chairs in which to relax with a good book and a glass of wine. Come to The Point—you'll not be disappointed: in fact, you'll be rewarded many times over. *Directions:* Located not far from Lake Placid. Directions available with confirmation of reservation.

THE POINT
Innkeepers: David & Christie Garrett
P.O. Box 1327
Saranac Lake, NY 12983, USA
Tel: (518) 891-5674, Fax: (518) 891-1152
Toll Free: (800) 255-3530
11 Rooms, Double: $1,250–$2,600*
*Includes all meals
Open: all year, Credit cards: all major
Relais & Châteaux
www.karenbrown.com/nythepoint.html

Arriving at the Batcheller Mansion Inn is a little like arriving at a fantasy park as it greets you with its High Victorian Gothic architecture with influences from the French Renaissance, Italy, and Egypt. All of which is to say that this is an exceptional piece of architecture! When you add the red-and-gray slate mansard roof, the ivory stucco façade, the painted clamshell arches, dormers, bays, balconies, and a conical tower resembling a minaret from the Arabian Nights, you know that this will be a fun experience. Interestingly enough, when you're standing in the great front hall, life settles down a bit and the decor is more restrained Victorian. A formal drawing room and a large library have several sitting areas, a grand piano, and a card table for games, and in the formal dining room you find a large table and several smaller tables set for two. A full breakfast is served on weekends and a Continental during the week. There are nine bedrooms, six of which are suites, tucked into the corners of the upper two floors, some with bathrooms that twist and turn under the eaves. Saratoga Springs is a great center of activity with the arts, the college, the lakes, and museums—and, of course, for horse-racing aficionados, it's been the place to be during the racing season for over a century. *Directions:* From Albany, take I-87 north to exit 13 then drive north for 3 miles to the traffic light at the Holiday Inn. Turn right and the inn is the third building on the right.

❄ ☕ 💳 ☎ ⍟ P ❀ ✝ 🚶 👭 🐎 ⛷ ⚓

BATCHELLER MANSION INN
Innkeeper: Sue McCabe
20 Circular Street
Saratoga Springs, NY 12866, USA
Tel: (518) 584-7012, Fax: (518) 581-7746
Toll Free: (800) 616-7012
3 Rooms, Double: $120–$400
Open: all year, Credit cards: all major
www.karenbrown.com/nybatcheller.html

An 1885 Queen Anne Victorian within an easy walk of the center of Saratoga Springs is now a seven-room bed and breakfast inn. Its decor is Victorian in every sense of the word, with flowered wallpaper, flowered prints on bed coverings, canopies with lace, and beds whose headboards and footboards echo the elaborate style of the period. Common areas include an inviting living room on the first floor for relaxing and chatting with the innkeepers or fellow guests, a formal dining room where breakfast is served, and a porch from which you can watch the world go by. The inn is surrounded by old fashioned gardens that create a peaceful, in-town ambiance. There are telephones with data ports and voice mail in each bedroom, a fax machine and copier on the premises, and early breakfast if you need it—all geared for the corporate traveler whose life while staying at this inn would certainly be made easier. For the leisure traveler Saratoga Springs is the center of much activity. Besides celebrating the horse-racing season, a tradition for over a century, this town focuses on the arts with dance, theater, museums, and in June and July performances of the New York City Ballet and the Lake George Opera. Westchester House is located in a residential neighborhood, just a quick walk from the main street of town with all its shops, antiques, and restaurants. *Directions:* From Albany, take I-87 to exit 13, driving north for 4 miles to the sixth traffic light. Turn right onto Lincoln to the inn.

❄ ☕ ✂ 💳 ☎ P 🚭 🖼 ✝ 🏃 🚶 🐎 ⛷ 🚣

WESTCHESTER HOUSE BED AND BREAKFAST
Innkeepers: Bob & Stephanie Melvin
102 Lincoln Avenue
Saratoga Springs, NY 12866, USA
Tel: (518) 587-7613, Fax: (518) 583-9562
Toll Free: (800) 579-8368
7 Rooms, Double: $145–$475
Closed: Dec & Jan, Credit cards: all major
Select Registry
www.karenbrown.com/nywestchester.html

Life a hundred years ago probably had its share of challenges, but even then one of life's pleasures would have been a stay at Hobbit Hollow Farm. This five-room bed and breakfast inn is set on the hill overlooking Skaneateles Lake, with wide porches on which rocking chairs await your arrival. The side entrance to the inn brings you into a large entryway with a full-length mural of life in the country. Hobbit Hollow's double living rooms on the ground floor are furnished with large, comfortable chairs and sofas facing the fireplace—no place better to relax with an early-morning cup of coffee or after returning from dinner. The bright-yellow-painted dining room with its formal mahogany table is a cheery place to begin the day with a great farm breakfast. Four bedrooms are large and beautifully furnished with antiques, some having queen mahogany four-poster beds so grand that you need a step stool to climb into them. The windows in these elegant rooms with their fireplaces and comfortable side chairs are framed in lovely floral fabrics, full and rich, pleated and puffed, which flow to the floor where they puddle in repose. The fifth room is also attractively furnished but slightly smaller. Venture into town to shop or sample the restaurants, one of which, the Sherwood Inn, is under the same management as the inn. *Directions:* Leave I-90 at exit 40 onto Rte 34, drive south to Rte 20. Take Rte 20 to Rte 41A, go south for just over 1½ miles to the inn.

HOBBIT HOLLOW FARM
Owner: Noreen Falcone
Innkeepers: Celeste Holden & Betsy Barrett
3061 West Lake Road
Skaneateles, NY 13156, USA
Tel: (315) 685-2791, Fax: (315) 685-3426
5 Rooms, Double: $120–$270
Open: all year, Credit cards: all major
Select Registry
www.karenbrown.com/nyhobbithollow.html

"New" and "marvelous" would be words to describe this inn, spa, and restaurant. From the moment you walk through the front door to be greeted with genuine warmth, you feel a sense of luxury and a desire to stay for a long while. The spa is definitely at the center of activities but you could stay in a guestroom in one of the four châteaux-style buildings overlooking the pond and the waterfall and forget the world outside your room. Rooms, decorated with a French-country theme, are spacious and comfortable, with gas fireplaces, sitting areas, and color schemes of either blue and gold or red and gold. Beds are covered with down comforters in French-country fabric and bathrooms have French soaking tubs and European tiled walk-in showers. Colored ceilings with hand-hewn beams bring a warmth and glow to rooms and corridors. Windows look out to the pond and the Monet-style gardens, and when the windows are open, it's restful to listen to the water splashing into the stream below. Mirbeau's 10,000-square-foot spa includes a classically designed resting area where you await your treatment, a heated foot massage pool, a studio for mind and body classes, a cardio/strength room, herbal steam baths, and dry saunas. There's a restaurant within the walls where imaginative cooking is reason enough to visit Mirbeau—but it's only one of the several treats beyond the entrance gate. *Directions:* Leave I-90 at exit 40, taking Route 34 south to Route 20 to the inn and spa.

❄ ✍ 💳 ☎ 🚻 🏋 🍸 P 🍴 🌺 ♿ 🎿 🚶 🐎 ⛷

MIRBEAU
Manager: Joachim Ohlin
851 West Genesse Street
Skaneateles, NY 13152, USA
Tel: (315) 685-5006, Fax: (315) 685-5150
Toll Free: (877) 647-2328
34 Rooms, Double: $165–$395*
*Breakfast not included: $12
Open: all year, Credit cards: all major
www.karenbrown.com/nymirbeau.html

Way back in 1807 The Sherwood Inn was a stagecoach stop and travelers would emerge from their carriages to have a meal or to spend the night. Today's travelers stop for the same reasons but there is a lot more to the town of Skaneateles than there was then—now there are antique shops, boutiques, and restaurants for travelers to enjoy, not to mention the lake and all the boating activities. The inn sits at the heart of all this, a wonderful place to base yourself while you enjoy all the area has to offer. There are 24 antique-appointed guestrooms offering king, queen, and twin beds, some with canopies, and there's a wide choice for your consideration—some have fireplaces, some are larger, some smaller, some face the lake, and some look to the rear. They are simply but comfortably furnished and each room enjoys its own private bath. The Sherwood Inn has a large dining room and banquet rooms which were renovated last year and feature two fireplaces and a lovely wine bar and two dining porches from which you can enjoy unbeatable views of the lake. The inn also has a full-service tavern with lots of atmosphere—a great place to meet your friends. *Directions:* Take I-90 to exit 40 and Route 34 south to Auburn. Drive east on Route 20 to Skaneateles to the inn on the left.

THE SHERWOOD INN
Owner: William B. Eberhardt
Innkeepers: Julia Bergan & Linda B. Hartnett
26 W. Genesee
Skaneateles, NY 13152, USA
Tel: (315) 685-3405, Fax: (315) 685-8983
Toll Free: (800) 374-3796
24 Rooms, Double: $105–$225
Open: all year, Credit cards: all major
Select Registry
www.karenbrown.com/nythesherwood.html

Inns that sit high on hills overlooking lakes benefit from their very special locations, and the Taughannock Farms Inn is no exception. As you drive down the western shore of Cayuga Lake you pass mile upon mile of beautiful shoreline and few homes. This indeed appears to be an area of serene beauty, and yet not far to the south is the city of Ithaca with its colleges, businesses, and potential guests of this inn, which was built in 1873 by a wealthy Philadelphian as his summer estate and known as the Jewel of the Finger Lakes. The furnishings were brought from Philadelphia and augmented by imports from England and Italy, and some of these original furnishings are found in the inn today. The 150-seat dining room has a tiered porch so that guests can have unobstructed views of the lake. Bedrooms are housed in various locations—the original building, where you also find the restaurant; a guesthouse with three bedrooms; a second guesthouse with two bedrooms; and two bedrooms that are part of the owner's home. A new 10-room guesthouse has opened and all rooms face the lake. This is a seasonal inn, open from April through December. Taughannock Farms is located in the center of the Finger Lakes wine district, a favorite destination for inn guests. *Directions:* Take I-90 to exit 41 to Route 318 east for 4 miles. Drive south on Route 89 for approximately 34 miles to the inn on the right.

❄ ☕ ⚕ 🅲🆁🅴🅳🅸🆃 🖨 P ⫲ ⊘ ✝ 🕴 👫 🍷

TAUGHANNOCK FARMS INN
Innkeepers: Tom & Susan Sheridan
2030 Gorge Road
Trumansburg, NY 14886, USA
Tel: (607) 387-7711, Fax: (607) 387-7721
Toll Free: (888) 387-7711
18 Rooms, Double: $95–$400
2 guesthouses
Open: Apr to Jan, Credit cards: all major
Select Registry
www.karenbrown.com/nytaughannock.html

Inns that not only pamper you with great accommodations but also conveniently have a restaurant with an extensive menu are a real reward for travelers at the end of a day's journey. At The William Seward Inn the gracious team of Jim and Debbie Dahlberg see that their guests' every need is attended to, with the attention to detail that makes you want to stay on longer. The main building's style of architecture is 19th-century Greek Revival and the more recently added carriage house blends well with the grace of the earlier structure. In the big house there are living and dining rooms and 12 bedrooms for guests. The living room provides that level of comfort you feel at home and it's a great place to greet fellow guests or to chat with the owners about the many activities awaiting you in the area. The inn's bedrooms are all wonderfully decorated and thought has been given to ensure that if you want to read in bed, there are good reading lamps, and that if you want to sit and talk with your traveling companion, there are comfortable chairs for doing so. In the carriage house the rooms are larger than the ones in the original building—and those are already very spacious—and the owners have been able to add spa tubs to the long list of amenities available to guests. *Directions:* Leave I-90 at exit 60 onto Route 394, driving south for 4 miles to the inn on the left.

❄ ☕ ☕ 💳 ☎ 🏠 P ⑪ ♿ 🚶 🐎 ⛷

THE WILLIAM SEWARD INN
Innkeepers: Jim & Debbie Dahlberg
6645 Portage Road
Westfield, NY 14878, USA
Tel: (716) 326-4151, Fax: (716) 326-4163
Toll Free: (800) 338-4151
12 Rooms, Double: $70–$185
Dinner by reservation, Wed-Sun
Closed: Christmas, Credit cards: all major
Select Registry
www.karenbrown.com/nywilliamseward.html

In the northern Catskills west of the Hudson River there's the lovely little town of Windham and the place to stay in town is the Albergo Allegria. It has fourteen bedrooms and seven suites, each with private bathroom, and some of the king beds can be converted into twins. Cozy down comforters are the way of life here and they are guaranteed to provide you with a heavenly night's sleep. Rooms are decorated in Victorian style, but not with that fancy fussiness so often seen. The five carriage-house suites enjoy the added luxury of two-person spa tubs. Within the inn you find a guest living room with fireplace and a lovely, bright room where a full breakfast is served, with delicious entrées like gourmet omelets, stuffed French toast, Belgian waffles, and herb frittatas. Twenty-one rooms might seem a lot to manage but the innkeeper and her extended family have it all under control. In the evenings after dinner at one of the nearby restaurants, you may borrow one of the inn's 400 videos. An added bonus here is a conference room for the use of corporate guests. The inn's landscaped grounds contain perennial flowerbeds that provide great color in the summer and enjoyment to guests. Albergo Allegria, Italian for inn of happiness, seems just that! *Directions:* Take I-87 to exit 21 onto Route 23 west for 24 miles. Turn left onto Route 296 to the inn on the left.

ALBERGO ALLEGRIA
Innkeeper: Lenore Radelich
43 Route 296
P.O. Box 267
Windham, NY 12496, USA
Tel: (518) 734-5560, Fax: (518) 734-5570
21 Rooms, Double: $99–$299
Closed: 2 weeks in Apr & Nov, Credit cards: MC, VS
Select Registry
www.karenbrown.com/nyalbergoallegria.html

Places to Stay
Pennsylvania

Places we recommend tend to project the personality of the people behind the business, and, here, because of Oralee, the Golden eagle is exceptional. We met her meticulously tending her side garden, a task she enjoys, taking advantage of a warm afternoon and a few quiet hours between lunch service and afternoon check-in. Oralee is impressive, and her love of this inn, that extends to embrace the town, is infectious. When asked how she came to own the inn, she admitted it was all by chance. She and her husband discovered Bedford when traveling the turnpike and stranded by a snow storm. They subsequently returned to relax in the village that had captured their hearts. Oralee's husband is no longer involved, but she is ever present and her example sets the standard for her team. Bedford is best known for its neighboring Old Bedford Village—a recreated pioneer-type village with working crafts persons. Just down from the intersection of main street, the dark, green-painted, brick façade of the inn is easy to spot. Climb the steps to the entry and discover the attractive dining room. Guestrooms are located atop the main stairs, as well as off from the screened porches at the rear of the inn. I especially loved the three rooms (1, 2 and 3), furnished in lovely antiques, found in the main house on the first level. *Directions:* Located on Rte 30, 2 miles south of Exit 146 off the Pennsylvania Turnpike.

ORALEE'S GOLDEN EAGLE INN
Innkeeper: Oralee Kieffer
131 East Pitt Street
Bedford, PA 15522, USA
Tel: (814) 624-0800
Fax: (814) 623-9020
Double: $99–$149
Open: all year
Credit cards: MC, VS
www.karenbrown.com/bedfordgoldeneagle.html

Built in 1885 in a blend of Gothic, Italianate, and Queen Anne architectural styles, this building seemed destined to one day become an inn—and so it has at the hands of its present owners. The architectural details of Reynolds Mansion are well worth noting—the marble vestibule, the mirrors, the stained-glass windows, the Eastlake woodwork, and the inlaid parquet floors. There are six suites for guests, each of them spacious, each with a fireplace, and each with a spa tub or steam shower in the bath. The fireplace mantles throughout Reynolds Mansion (which, interestingly enough, was built by a bachelor for his own use) are varied in style but all especially interesting in their carving and in the tile that was used to trim them. On the first floor there are three common rooms, one of which the owners have made into a games room with a billiard table, a card table, and plenty of games to be enjoyed. The main parlor is at the front and is flooded with light from large windows. A full breakfast is served in the dining room each morning and there are restaurants for fine dining just a few blocks away from the inn. *Directions:* Leave the I-80 at exit 161, taking Route 26 south to the Bellefonte exit, then Route 550 into town. At the third light turn right onto Allegheny Street, then at the second light turn left on Linn—the inn is on the right.

REYNOLDS MANSION
Innkeepers: Charlotte, Joseph Jr. & Joseph Heidt III
101 West Linn Street
Bellefonte, PA 16823, USA
Tel: (814) 353-8407, Fax: (814) 353-1530
Toll Free: (800) 899-3929
Double: $125–$325
Closed: Dec 24 & 25, Credit cards: all major
Select Registry
www.karenbrown.com/pareynoldsmansion.html

In 1858 Robert Heysham Sayre moved his family into this large Gothic Revival mansion in what has become the Fountain Hill National Historic District. His grand house is now a handsome inn where you can happily stay while enjoying the many activities: music educational institutions—for which Bethlehem is noted. Sweeping lawns and landscaped grounds surround this inn, giving it its own parklike setting. The Sayre Mansion reflects the architecture of this period with high ceilings, large rooms, and lots of space. Guestrooms, all with private bath, have been updated to include wireless access, flat screen TV, and voice mail. The grandest of the bedrooms are those of the Sayres, furnished with pieces appropriate for the time and the lifestyle that the family must have had when they lived there. Room 30, on top of it all in the conservatory, is a spacious, grand, and very unique experience. Third-floor bedrooms are under the eaves, which create some very special spaces for you to enjoy. A particular treat at this inn is to be had in the Wine Cellar where you can choose a wine from those on display and then taste it with a selection of artisan cheeses. The Sayre Mansion is an especially fine inn in which to have a wedding, family reunion, conference, or some function where the luxury of space is important. *Directions:* Take I-78 to the Bethlehem exit. Follow Route 412 into Bethlehem to the corner of Third and Wyandotte Street—the inn is on the right.

THE SAYRE MANSION
Owners: Grant & Jeanne Genzlinger
Innkeeper: Carrie Ohlandt
250 Wyandotte Street
Bethlehem, PA 18015, USA
Tel: (610) 882-2100, Fax: (610) 882-1223
Toll Free: (877) 345-9019
21 Rooms, Double: $145–$275
Open: all year, Credit cards: all major
Select Registry
www.karenbrown.com/sayremansion.html

Seemingly part of the Amish Country Homestead complex that provides a rewarding overview into Amish culture, the independently owned and newly built AmishView Inn affords travelers wonderful accommodation. Neither country inn nor bed & breakfast, it is a small hotel of fifty rooms and suites that is well located and managed by a team who believes that "Great Service always makes the difference." Appropriate to its name, the hotel is set against the acreage of an Amish farm. The hotel's entry and reception open to a vast living room set with numerous tables and chairs and comfortable seating that, mornings, also serves as the breakfast room. Guestrooms are found off the wide corridors and most overlook the back farmland. Spacious and comfortable the rooms are furnished with handsome, reproduction mahogany furniture including bed, armoire and writing desk. In addition to the common amenities, rooms are also equipped with microwaves, refrigerators, coffee makers, luxurious soaps and even make-up mirrors-all at a very reasonable price. A chef is present every morning to prepare omelets, waffles, eggs to order, sausage, bacon and more. Facilities include an indoor pool, spa and fitness center. This is a great place to stay if traveling as a family with a wonderful location and excellent value. *Directions:* Located on Old Philadelphia Pike (Route 30) to the east of Lancaster between Bird-in-Hand and Intercourse.

AMISHVIEW INN & SUITES   *New*
Manager: Jennifer Binkle
3125 Old Philadelphia Pike
Bird-in-Hand, PA 17505, USA
Tel: (717) 768-1162, Fax: (717) 768-3006
Toll Free: (866) 735-1600
50 Rooms, Double: $109–$329
Open: all year, Credit cards: all major
www.karenbrown.com/paamishview.html

On the outskirts of Bloomsburg, the Inn at Turkey Hill is convenient to the interstate and yet miles away in terms of setting, mood, and ambiance. Once a working farm, the property's 1839 white, two-story, brick farmhouse serves as the heart of the inn. Here you will find the reception and be introduced to the intimacy and feeling of tradition and family that dominates the ambiance of this lovely country inn. Off the reception are a cozy tavern and three dining rooms: the Stencil Room, the Mural Room, and the Greenhouse. The Greenhouse, a favorite with guests, is a glassed-in side porch overlooking the lush greenery of the garden, central pond, and gazebo. In the main farmhouse there are just two charming guestrooms, located at the top of a side stair above the reception. A newer wing of rooms stretches and steps down the length of the property and houses both standard rooms and suites. Appropriately adjacent to the farm's dramatic red barn is the newest addition, The Stables, whose deluxe rooms are large, luxurious, and comfortably appointed. All guestrooms are very attractively furnished with reproduction pieces and are equipped with TVs, direct-dial phones, and high speed internet. One of my favorites is number 6 which enjoys both a wood burning fireplace and an in-room jacuzzi! *Directions:* Traveling the I-80, exit at 236 driving south toward the traffic light, turn left at the light and the next available left is into their driveway.

INN AT TURKEY HILL
Innkeeper: Andrew B. Pruden
991 Central Road
Bloomsburg, PA 17815, USA
Tel: (570) 387-1500, Fax: (570) 784-3718
23 Rooms, Double: $109–$225
Open: all year, Credit cards: all major
Select Registry
www.karenbrown.com/paturkeyhill.html

Glendorn is a very private family camp, which after many generations of exclusive use by the Dorn family is now open to the public. The compound has a gated entrance and a long, winding drive to the lodge where you are met and escorted to your accommodations. It's a privilege to become a part, however briefly, of a retreat where you feel as if you are a guest of the family for the weekend and it's fascinating to look through the photo albums showing generations of Dorns. There's a cozy, pine-paneled library with chairs and a sofa in front of the fireplace, with a table and chairs to the side. The living room has a massively large stone fireplace and a vaulted ceiling, and it is in this room that guests gather for cocktails before dinner. Tables are set for two so that your time at dinner can be private and the discreet, unhurried service means that you can enjoy your meal at your leisure. Accommodations at Glendorn are either in the main lodge, in the guest house, or in one of the cabins on the property (some with multiple bedrooms) where the only sounds you're likely to hear are of the brook flowing and rippling as it winds through the grounds. Glendorn also hosts executive retreats, but it is really about another kind of retreat—one where you and someone special can escape to relax and to rejuvenate. *Directions:* Take I-86 to Route 219 south through Bradford to Glendorn.

GLENDORN
Manager: Daniel J. Abrashoff
1000 Glendorn Drive
Bradford, PA 16701, USA
Tel: (814) 362-6511, Fax: (814) 368-9923
Toll Free: (800) 843-8568
9 Rooms, Double: $495–$795*
7 cabins, *Includes all meals
Restaurant open to non-residents if space available
Open: all year, Credit cards: all major, Relais & Châteaux
www.karenbrown.com/paglendorn.html

Noel and Jane McStay are the owners of a country inn that's very special—an inn where you will feel like and be treated as a member of the family. The greeting here is genuine and when you step into one of the guestrooms, you'll feel perfectly at home. There are five bedrooms in the main house, four rooms and two suites in the Carriage House, and four rooms in the Springhouse. The Carriage House deluxe rooms have soaring ceilings, ancient, hand-carved beams reflecting their barn origins, and doors which open to decks and views of quiet rolling countryside including a distant pond glimpsed through trees. Wing chairs by the fireplace beckon you to sit and read and the king canopy bed assures you of a good night's sleep. The Fairville Inn is the embodiment of elegant comfort. The innkeepers serve a full breakfast with a hot entrée each morning. The Fairville Inn is a great stopping point for an extended stay in the Brandywine Valley, being centrally located for a lot of sightseeing. There's great natural beauty in the surrounding towns and driving with no particular destination is very fulfilling. Close by are the Winterthur Museum, the Brandywine River Museum, Longwood Gardens, and the Hagley Museum. *Directions:* Located on Route 52, 8 miles north of I-95, exit 7, Wilmington, or 2 miles south of Route 1.

FAIRVILLE INN
Innkeepers: Jane & Noel McStay
506 Kennett Pike, Route 52
Chadds Ford, PA 19317, USA
Tel: (610) 388-5900, Fax: (610) 388-5902
Toll Free: (877) 285-7772
13 Rooms, Double: $150–$250
Open: all year, Credit cards: all major
Select Registry
www.karenbrown.com/pafairville.html

A country estate dating back to the 1850s, Lancaster County with its rolling hills and large farms, and the presence of the Amish community evidenced in many ways but most obviously by the horse-drawn buggies rolling along the county's byways—all these are reasons for visiting this part of Pennsylvania. The Inn at Twin Linden, a manor house surrounded by flower-filled gardens, offers a warmth that's easy to feel but not easy to duplicate. Innkeepers Norm and Sue Kuestner offer a very comfortable inn with a variety of accommodations to suit any traveler. The Garden Gate and the Palladian Suites are deluxe retreats with their own private entrances. The Garden Gate provides ultimate seclusion in a separate building over the carriage house with a balcony porch overlooking a peaceful garden setting and farm fields as far as the eye can see. The Palladian enjoys a sitting room with a view that will turn minutes into hours as you gaze across the distant fields and farms. A multi-course breakfast with a hot entrée is served in one of the dining rooms where on Saturdays dinner is available. Tea is provided in the afternoon—a great refresher of energy that will see you through to dinner, after which you're assured of a great night's sleep. *Directions:* Take Route 76 to exit 326 (Pennsylvania Turnpike). Drive west on the Turnpike for two exits to exit 298 at Morgantown, taking Route 10 south to Route 23 west for approximately 5 miles to the inn.

❄ ☕ ✄ 💳 P ⵊ 🏌 🚶

INN AT TWIN LINDEN
Innkeepers: Norm and Sue Kuestner
2092 Main Street
Churchtown, PA 17555, USA
Tel: (717) 445-7619, Fax: (717) 445-4656
Cellphone: (866) 445-7614
8 Rooms, Double: $125–$265
Open for Sat dinner by reservation
Open: all year, Credit cards: all major
www.karenbrown.com/painnattwinlinden.html

Set off from a busy interchange, all that is visible on first sight is a side profile of a modern, ivy-covered, two-story building, one of two side additions that extended the original home. Step into the expanse of the back garden with brick paths that descend down to the lake's edge to view the front entrance with its dramatic columns. Inside, every nook and cranny becomes a display of collectibles; hallways are a bustle of costumed waitresses traveling between the bakery (on view behind a glass partition), the kitchen, and the three restaurants. Ashley's is for the true gourmet, while the Old South Restaurant offers bountiful family-style meals. My favorite, Stonewall's Tavern is cozy and intimate with tables set within adjoining small rooms under low-beamed ceilings. There are set tours, but guests are welcome to explore on their own. Playing on the theme of the movie, Gone with Wind, the rooms of Tara are lavishly decorated with floral wallpapers, decorative carpets, reproduction antiques, and new brass beds. Doors of unoccupied rooms are left open and cordoned off, making it easy to peak in and get a feel for the home. Though not inexpensive, I recommend Tara for comfortable accommodation, a good meal, and a convenient stopover. *Directions:* From I-80, take exit 4B to Route 18N, travel north 7 miles, the hotel is located on the east side at the intersection of PA 258.

TARA–A COUNTRY INN
Owners: Jim & Donna Winner
Innkeeper: Deborah DeCopua
2844 Lake Road
Clark, PA 16113, USA
Tel: (724) 962-3535, Fax: (724) 962-3250
Toll Free: (800) 782-2803
27 Rooms, Double: $225–$425
Open: all year, Credit cards: all major
Select Registry
www.karenbrown.com/tara.html

As my husband pointed out I must have uttered "beautiful" more than a thousand times when we visited the various rooms of Lesley's Mountain View Country Inn. I was enchanted by this elegant inn housed in a complex of weathered barn and a two-story, stone 1850s country house. Lesley, herself, greeted us under the awning at the handsome wine-colored door of the barn and proudly showed us the attractive bar and intimate dining rooms. Not inexpensive, the menu offers fine dining at tables that are embraced by walls that incredibly once were stables. In terms of accommodations, there are four guestrooms with their own outside entrance below the barn restaurant. There are an additional four guestrooms in the nearby stone Georgian Farmhouse. Accessed from the front porch, guests in the farmhouse enjoy shared use of the charming public rooms. Period furnishings and antiques are common throughout. On a hillside, beautifully landscaped with fruit trees and lawn, the inn enjoys a pastoral setting and sweeping views of the surrounding Laurel Mountains. *Directions:* From the I-76 (PA Turnpike) take exit 91, travel 1 mile east on Rte 31 and then turn south (right) onto Mountain View Road and travel 0.5 miles to the inn.

LESLEY'S MOUNTAIN VIEW COUNTRY INN
Innkeepers: Gerard & Lesley O'Leary
327 Mountain View Road
Donegal, PA 15628, USA
Tel: (724) 593-6349, Fax: (724) 593-6345
Toll Free: (800) 392-7773
8 Rooms, Double: $150–$210
Open: all year, Credit cards: all major
www.karenbrown.com/lesleys.html

The town of Eagles Mere, with its mountain and lake setting, moderate climate, and natural beauty, sprang up because wealthy Philadelphians were attracted to the cool, clean mountain air, the pristine lake, and the surrounding forests. Here you find the comfortable Eagles Mere Inn, where the Glaubitzes offer a wonderfully warm welcome and go out of their way to make their guests' visit memorable. A stay at Eagles Mere includes a delicious gourmet five-course dinner and a full country breakfast. The individually decorated guestrooms are simple, but all have private bathrooms and are decorated with antiques and reproduction pieces. In the main house I particularly liked the luxury of space afforded by the end Innkeeper's Suite and Tilly's Room, a pretty room named for the innkeepers' daughter. In the Garden House, rooms 11 and 12 enjoy their own ground-floor entrance, while 13, 14, and 15 share a side of the building and would be perfect for a family traveling together. Room 17 looks out through French sliding doors to a deck and garden. As you settle on the front porch in one of the Shaker rockers, don't forget that you must take the Laurel Path, a 2-mile walk around the perimeter of the lake, especially pretty in late spring when the massive rhododendrons and mountain laurel are in bloom. *Directions:* From the south, enter town on Route 42, pass the old town clock, and turn right on Mary Avenue to the inn.

EAGLES MERE INN
Innkeepers: Matthew & Barbie Gale
1 Mary Avenue
Eagles Mere, PA 17731, USA
Tel: (570) 525-3273, Fax: (570) 525-3904
Toll Free: (800) 426-3273
19 Rooms, Double: $169–$269*
*Includes breakfast & 5-course dinner
Closed: 2 weeks at Christmas, Credit cards: MC, VS
Select Registry
www.karenbrown.com/paeaglesmere.html

College towns invariably have an inn, and the Lafayette Inn, sitting high on a hill up by the college, is one of the nicest in Easton. Its owners, Paul & Laura, provide extraordinary hospitality to those who stay there. Part of their secret is that they are open and friendly and ready to provide assistance to their guests—whether they want to go to the Crayola factory and store, to the Martin Guitar Company, or to attend the weeklong music festival in neighboring Bethlehem. Guests will feel well cared for with special touches, such as the freshly made cookies and fresh fruit in the living room, and the nearby refrigerator stocked with soft drinks. Breakfast begins at 7 am for corporate travelers who must get on their way, but it's a great breakfast to linger over if your schedule is more relaxed. Outside the dining room with its many windows is a lovely patio where flowers and a fountain tempt you to settle. The inn's eighteen bedrooms on four floors are comfortably furnished, each with a private bath. Two have a separate sitting area with a day bed in case there's a third person in your group. Close by you will find some really fine dining and when you return to the inn, you can enjoy that cookie jar and a few minutes with the innkeepers. *Directions:* Leave I-78 at exit 22, driving north through Easton and north on Third Street toward Lafayette College. Go up the hill to the corner of Cattell and Monroe Streets. The inn is on the left.

LAFAYETTE INN
Innkeepers: Paul & Laura Di Liello
525 West Monroe Street
Easton, PA 18042, USA
Tel: (610) 253-4500, Fax: (610) 253-4635
Toll Free: (800) 509-6990
18 Rooms, Double: $125–$225
Closed: all year, Credit cards: all major
Select Registry
www.karenbrown.com/palafayette.html

The rustic restoration of a long-neglected family farm has created a place where elegance and the simplicity of country living converge. Glasbern is a paradise for those who love country barns, with buildings framed and adorned in the original post-and-beam architecture that has always graced the property. The barn's soaring spaces, walls of stone, and a fireplace provide a grand dining environment any season of the year. This struck me as especially true after having stayed in several Victorian inns where rooms tend to be cozy and small. Other barns have been brought to the property where they have been converted into wonderful accommodations for travelers—both those who are away on business and those who are exploring the neighboring countryside. There's no denying that this style of architecture is a favorite of mine—it's different, it's inviting, and it welcomes you in. The restaurant serves dinner to both guests and the public, and the food is imaginatively prepared and beautifully presented. Many of the dishes feature pasture raised meat from the farm. Located only a few miles from urban areas with major business, Glasbern enables you to stay in the countryside with only a short commute to the business community and makes a great base for exploring the beauty of Pennsylvania. *Directions:* Take I-78 to exit 49B for Fogelsville (Rte 100). Turn left at the first light then go for 3/10 mile and turn right at Church Street. After 6/10 mile, turn right at Pack House Road.

GLASBERN
Innkeeper: Al Granger
2141 Pack House Road
Fogelsville, PA 18051, USA
Tel: (610) 285-4723, Fax: (610) 285-2862
36 Rooms, Double: $175–$450
Open: all year, Credit cards: all major
Select Registry
www.karenbrown.com/paglasbern.html

The Baladerry Inn is ideally situated for travelers who are interested in the history of the Civil War. The perfect way to see the battlegrounds and understand the battles would be to bike across the neighboring fields where more than a century ago the conflict that tore apart our nation took place. (A local shop will deliver bikes to the inn.) The inn has ten bedrooms, five in the main house and five (including the Carriage House Suite) in a separate building. The rooms are comfortably decorated with antique and reproduction furnishings, with basic bathrooms. My favorite room was at the top of the creaking, weathered stairs in the part of the house that dates to 1830: named for the charming wallpaper in delicate primrose, the room offers either a king or twin beds, overlooks the garden, and has a private bathroom located across the hall. In the common room in the original building there is a dining area near the wood fireplace. Located in a country setting, Baladerry sits up on a hill and lawns slope down to the street below. Its gardens add color in season to the rolling hills steeped in military history, and terraces and a tennis court invite the guest to enjoy the spacious grounds. *Directions:* From Route 15 exit on the south side of Gettysburg at Baltimore Street. Travel north 1 mile, take a left at McAllister Mill Road, a left onto Blacksmith Shop Road, and a left onto Hospital Road.

BALADERRY INN AT GETTYSBURG
Innkeeper: Suzanne Lonky
40 Hospital Road
Gettysburg, PA 17325, USA
Tel: (717) 337-1342, Fax: none
Toll Free: (800) 220-0025
10 Rooms, Double: $135–$235
Open: all year, Credit cards: all major
Select Registry
www.karenbrown.com/pabaladerry.html

The Brafferton Inn, an historic home built in 1786, has only recently become the Hodge Family business. Joan, her son Brian, his wife Amy Beth, are a wonderful team who extend guests a warm welcome to Gettysburg and their new home. This attractive fieldstone house of red brick with shuttered windows and flowering window boxes and a handsome blue door is well located just a block off Lincoln Square. Inside the public salons introduce an inviting country ambiance with antiques and provincial fabrics. Five guestrooms are found up the stair, and seven are located in the converted Carriage House. A central courtyard creates a seamless transition from one building to the other and also provides passage to a lovely back garden and deck. From the Old Master Bedroom with its four poster bed and fireplace to The Battle Room whose mantel still proudly bears a bullet from the Civil War, the rooms are comfortable and unique which is in keeping with the history of the buildings. A few doors down, above the Hodge's Artworks Store (once the butcher shop) and in a building referred to as Lane Studios, are at total of six more guestrooms, a bit more modern and spacious. Breakfast is served in a cozy room just off the parlor whose walls are painted with a beautiful mural by the renowned Virginia Jacobs McLaughlin. *Directions:* Take the York Street Exit (Rte 30) off Hwy 15 and travel in the direction of downtown.

THE BRAFFERTON INN **New**
Innkeepers: Joan, Brian & Amy Hodges
44 York Street
Gettysburg, PA 17325, USA
Tel: (717) 337-3423
18 Rooms, Double: $80–$195
Open: all year, Credit cards: all major
www.karenbrown.com/pabrafferton.html

This lovely hotel, located just a block from the Lincoln Square and the Wills House where Abraham Lincoln composed his Gettysburg Address, has its own impressive ties to history. It occupies the first plot of land that James Getty sold in 1787 to a Mr. Troxell, who then in 1804, opened a roadhouse for travelers attracted to Pennsylvania's western frontiers. In the two hundred years of its existence the building has served as a hotel, a hospital for the wounded of Gettysburg's battles, an apartment complex and a youth hostel. In 1995 it reverted back to its original purpose, a resting spot for travelers. However, the remarkable difference is the luxury of appointments of today's James Gettys Hotel. Accommodations are appropriately termed suites as they each enjoy a sitting room, separate bedroom, private bath and kitchenette. Since the only public area is the intimate entry and reception, breakfast goodies are stocked each evening in the guest room refrigerators when staff provides turn down service. Stephanie McSherry oversees the direction of the hotel and sets a wonderful example of welcome and hospitality for her staff. Artwork is conveniently provided by her father's neighboring gallery. *Directions:* Take the York Street Exit (Rte 30) off Hwy 15 and travel in the direction of downtown to Lincoln Square. Chambersburg is one of the roads that spokes off the square.

JAMES GETTYS HOTEL   New
Innkeeper: Stephanie McSherry
27 Chambersburg Street
Gettysburg, PA 17325, USA
Tel: (717) 337-1334, Fax: (717) 334-2103
Toll Free: (888) 900-5275
12 Rooms, Double: $145–$250
Open: all year, Credit cards: all major
www.karenbrown.com/pajamesgettys.html

Fourteen miles east of Gettysburg in the town of Hanover sits the Beechmont Inn whose seven bedrooms provide comfort to the traveler visiting the area and whose genial hosts make sure that the visit is a pleasant one. Tom and Kathryn, originally from the gracious Midwest, St. Louis, Missouri, moved here to take over the Beechmont Inn. Kathryn is redecorating each room, one by one, and with each completion the inn reflects more and more her elegance and refined taste. I loved the Garden Gate Suite, warmed in colors of soft green and salmon, whose entrance is either off the inn entry or by a private door off the back porch shaded by a gorgeous and mature magnolia tree. Many of the rooms boast fireplaces. Six of the inn's bedrooms have adjoining private baths, while one has its private bath down the hall. The hosts provide a full breakfast and there is a guest refrigerator with bottled water and soft drinks. The library has many interesting books for browsing, a selection of games to play, and a help-yourself cookie jar. Tom and Kathryn have taken up residence in the back Carriage House. They are nearby, attentive hosts, and sincere in their wish that your stay will be a memory that lingers joyously. *Directions:* Take I-195 to I-695 north, I-795 west to Maryland, and then Route 30/Pennsylvania Route 94 north to Hanover.

BEECHMONT INN
Innkeepers: Tom & Kathryn White
315 Broadway
Hanover, PA 17331, USA
Tel: (717) 632-3013, Fax: (717) 632-2769
Toll Free: (800) 553-7009
7 Rooms, Double: $99–$169
Open: all year, Credit cards: all major
Select Registry
www.karenbrown.com/pabeechmont.html

The Sheppard Mansion, a grand, three-story edifice built in 1913 as a private residence, regally dominates almost an entire block in the town of Hanover. Architecturally grand, both inside and out, it has a red-brick exterior trimmed in white marble, entries fronted by grand columns, and tall chimneys and dormer windows piercing the roofline. Once inside, you will be overwhelmed by the elegance and grandeur of the home. Oriental carpets enhance beautiful hardwood floors, gorgeous polished-wood trims and yards of fabric adorn doorways, and high ceilings are paired with dramatic moldings. Public rooms are lavish and you find exquisite antiques and incredible art everywhere. The formal dining room is lovely with its gorgeous paned windows and hand-painted frieze and the dinner menu is superb under the creative talents of Matthew. The guest den is a cozy place to enjoy the large-screen TV, play a game or the piano, or enjoy a glass of sherry. The breakfast room, open to the garden porch, is light and airy with green-and-white lattice wallpaper, bamboo window shades, a black-and-white-tiled floor, and a beautiful plaster-cast ceiling with hand-painted relief. Your innkeeper, Tim, is devoted to his guests and you will be charmed by his devoted shadow, Punch (French Bull Terrier). There is a total of nine guestrooms but only five bathrooms, so on any given night only five bedrooms are rented. *Directions:* Located at the intersection of Routes 116 and 194.

❄ ■☕ CREDIT ☎ P 🚭 ❀ 🖼 🔔

SHEPPARD MANSION B&B
Innkeepers: Kathy Sheppard Hoar & Timothy Bobb
117 Frederick Street
Hanover, PA 17331, USA
Tel: (717) 633-8075, Fax: (717) 633-8074
Toll Free: (877) 762-6746
9 Rooms, Double: $140–$220
Open: all year, Credit cards: all major
Select Registry
www.karenbrown.com/pasheppard.html

A hotel built in 1927 in the English Arts and Crafts style of architecture, The Settlers Inn has been under the loving care of the Genzlingers for more than 25 years. They strive to preserve the heritage of their property and the tradition of hospitality. The large entry hall/living room features a fireplace where 4-foot-long logs burn almost all day and night. Bedrooms are handsomely furnished, many with queen iron or brass beds, and offer amenities such as air conditioning and wireless internet. The decor respects the character of the home and as they are all individual, from 101 with its leather seating, warm rusts and creams selected for its color scheme and a wonderful side deck to the smallest room in the house, 215, pretty and charming with a white iron bed set against a delicate yellow and blue patterned wallpaper—it is truly hard to select a favorite. The bathrooms deserve mention as almost all of them have been beautifully remodeled and many include Jacuzzi tubs. In addition to the dining room with its award winning wine list, you'll find, just off the living room, a charming bar with a small-tavern-like ambiance, with several small tables, bar stools cozying up to the bar, and an outdoor terrace for dining in good weather. Fishing on the property is a great attraction. *Directions:* Leave I-84 west at exit 7 onto Route 390 north then take Route 507 north to Route 6 west for 2½ miles to the inn.

THE SETTLERS INN
Innkeepers: Jeanne & Grant Genzlinger
4 Main Street
Hawley, PA 18428, USA
Tel: (570) 226-2993, Fax: (570) 226-1874
Toll Free: (800) 833-8527
21 Rooms, Double: $150–$250
Open: all year, Credit cards: all major
Select Registry
www.karenbrown.com/pasettlers.html

This exclusive destination estate spa and boutique bed and breakfast in Bucks County, once the home of Pulitzer-prize winning playwright George S. Kaufman, is surrounded by 100-acres of pasture and woodland views. Sixteen luxurious suites in the 1740 manor house, guest cottage and barn feature whirlpool tubs by the fireplace, full body steam showers, sunrooms, private balconies and terraces. The décor ranges from European and American antiques, Arts and Crafts to East Asian themes. The spa offers exceptional all-natural products and services in private in-suite treatment rooms. A gourmet brunch is presented in the conservatory overlooking the trellis gardens, swimming pool and pond. Wine and cheese is served in your suite upon arrival and comes with a fully stocked courtesy wet bar, flat-screen TV, Bose CD. Close to New Hope and Peddler's Village shops, antiquing, museums, wineries, fine restaurants and the Delaware River. *Directions:* On Route 202 between New Hope and Doylestown, ½ mile west of Lahaska. From New Jersey take Route 202 south; from the south take I-95 north to Route 276 to Route 611 north. In Doylestown take Route 202 north.

❄ ▭ 🏊 ⊟ ☎ ▽ P ≈ ♿ 🎿 🚶

BARLEY SHEAF FARM
5281 York Road
Holicong, PA 18928, USA
Tel: (215) 794-5104, Fax: (215) 794-5332
16 Rooms, Double: $250–$750
Open: all year, Credit cards: all major
Select Registry
www.karenbrown.com/pabarleysheaf.html

I must admit it was not only the AAA four-diamond award but also the name of the village in the midst of Amish country in Lancaster County that caught my attention and drew me to this wonderful property, whose level of service and quality of accommodation are actually more in keeping with an elegant country inn than a B&B. This attractive, white-shuttered, two-story building dates back to 1909 and in the main house the decor is very Victorian, respecting the period of the home. On the entry level are two guest salons, the formal dining room where a five-course, gourmet, candlelit breakfast is served each morning, and a kitchen with a refrigerator stocked with beverages for guests. Spanning the length of the home on the third floor under the angled rooflines is the dramatic Grand Suite. Behind the main house, stretching along the garden path to the back lawn and gazebo, are a number of cottages housing some gorgeous, beautifully designed accommodations—the Grand Suites and the Country Homestead Suites. I loved these rooms with their small, welcoming candlelights in the windows, country reproduction furnishings, attractive stenciling, Berber carpets, and fireplaces. We peeked into the Beiler Suite, which was lovely with a theme of horses and a sitting area apart from the bedroom. *Directions:* Located on Main Street (Rte 340).

※ ▬ ☕ 📇 ☎ Ⴁ P ❀ 🖼 ⚓ 🏌

THE INN & SPA AT INTERCOURSE VILLAGE
Owners: Elmer & Ruth Ann Thomas
Innkeeper: Ruth Ann Thomas
Route 340, Main Street, P.O. Box 598
Intercourse, PA 17534, USA
Tel: (717) 768-2626, Fax: (717) 768-7622
Toll Free: (800) 664-0949
9 Rooms, Double: $169–$369
Open: all year, Credit cards: all major
Select Registry
www.karenbrown.com/paintercourse.html

The Inn at Whitewing Farm, spread over 43 pastoral acres in southern Chester County, is a delight in any season. It is close to many of the area's attractions including the adjacent Longwood Gardens, the Winterthur Museum, and the Brandywine River Museum with its exhibits of the paintings of the Wyeth family. Whitewing, whose core is an 18th-century farmhouse, is actually a cluster of buildings in which there are seven bedrooms and three suites, all meticulously decorated rooms that provide a feeling of being an overnight guest at a friend's horse farm in the picturesque countryside. The suites enjoy fireplaces and comfortable sitting areas. A new barn houses a common room on the second floor, a marvelously warm room with burgundy-painted walls, and a dining room on the first floor with individual tables set in front of a fireplace and windows looking out onto the landscape. The stables have been converted into bedrooms, which are smaller than some of the newer suites. One building has three bedrooms so that family or friends can be together. The inn serves a full breakfast—you'll need it for all there is to do in the area and on the property where guests have the use of tennis courts, and a swimming pool. *Directions:* Leave I-95 at exit 7 (Wilmington, DE), go north at Rte 52; turn left onto Rte 1. Drive about ¾ mile to the traffic light. Turn right on Rte 52 for 1-1/10 miles to Valley Rd. Turn left and drive 7/10 mile to the inn on the right.

❄ 🍴 🏊 P 🌷 🏊 🏃 🐕 ♿ ⛳

INN AT WHITEWING FARM
Innkeepers: Ed & Wanda DeSeta
Manager: Cathleen Ryan
P. O. Box 98, 370 Valley Road
Kennett Square, PA 19348, USA
Tel: (610) 388-2664, Fax: (610) 388-3650
7 Rooms, Double: $155–$269
3 suites
Closed: Dec 23 to 26, Credit cards: none
Select Registry
www.karenbrown.com/pawhitewing.html

Spanish-style mansions in the Amish world of Lancaster County are definitely not the norm, which makes The King's Cottage a nice change—particularly from the Victorian style of so many inns in this area. With a stucco exterior and tile roof, this structure distinguishes itself nicely. This inn was built as a private home in the early 1900s. It is now listed in the National Register of Historic Places and has won an award for preserving its historical heritage. The living room is large and especially comfortable, offering many places to relax and enjoy good conversations. The inn's bedrooms, each with private bath, are decorated traditionally and have queen or king beds. The largest, the Majestic Chamber, features an ornately carved king bed, crystal chandelier, marble-faced fireplace and a two-person whirlpool tub. The Carriage House, behind the inn, features a king canopy bed, a fireplace, and a two-person Jacuzzi spa tub. A full breakfast is served in the formal dining room each morning. There's a lot to do in this area, with live entertainment and antiquing high on the list, though driving through the quiet countryside a few minutes from this inn would also be a favorite. *Directions:* Take Rte 30 to the Walnut St exit, turn right at the end of the ramp then left at the second light at Ranck Ave. Turn left at the second stop sign onto East Orange St and go one block. Turn right onto Cottage Ave. The inn is the last building on the right.

❄ ☕ 🛷 CREDIT ☎ P ♿ 🚶 👫

THE KING'S COTTAGE
Innkeepers: Janis Kutterer & Ann Willets
1049 East King Street
Lancaster, PA 17602, USA
Tel: (717) 397-1017, Fax: (717) 397-3447
Toll Free: (800) 747-8717
7 Rooms, Double: $145–$270
1 cottage
Open: all year, Credit cards: MC, VS
Select Registry
www.karenbrown.com/pakingscottage.html

Throughout Lancaster County there are winding roads connecting sprawling farmlands and towns of great age and charm. Here and there in this landscape there are bed and breakfast inns, most of them out in the country where the rural setting guarantees that the loudest noise the traveler hears is of singing birds, the ripple of a stream, and wind in the trees. Swiss Woods is one such inn and it has the additional bonus of being right near a lake over which it looks, at least in the wintertime when leaves are off the trees. The owners have decorated their inn with warm and comfortable country touches. Casual upholstered pine furniture in the living room sits in front of a wood-burning, stone fireplace. Bedrooms have four-poster pine beds and flowered linens, which are but an extension of the flowering gardens outside. The oval breakfast table at which the owners serve a full breakfast with a hot entree each morning is set in front of French doors looking out to the countryside. This is an inn where afternoon tea is served, and it's easy to imagine that a long walk in the surrounding countryside before tea in front of the fire would be just the perfect way to end the day. *Directions:* From Lancaster go north on Route 501 for 11 miles and after passing the 501 Motel, turn left at the next crossroads. Go 1 mile on Brubaker Valley Road to the lake and turn right onto Blantz Road. Do not cross the bridge at the lake. Swiss Woods is the first property on your left.

❄ ☕ 🛷 💳 P 🏌 🥾

SWISS WOODS
Innkeepers: Werner & Debrah Mosimann
500 Blantz Road
Lititz, PA 17543, USA
Tel: (717) 627-3358, Fax: (717) 627-3483
Toll Free: (800) 594-8018
6 Rooms, Double: $110–$180
1 suite
Closed: Christmas, Credit cards: all major
Select Registry
www.karenbrown.com/paswisswoods.html

With a charming cream stucco and green shuttered home that dates from 1740 as its heart, a series of newer buildings designed to resemble homes of the same period transition to either side of the country home and dot the edge of the Delaware River. Achieving the appearance of a quaint colonial village, this, in fact, is the 1740 House Country Inn. Find the outdoor stand that reads, "Your window on the River. Your door to Bucks County." and you will find the reception located in the original home. The old creaking floors, open fireplace and wood paneling create a cozy ambiance for the sitting room and intimate bar. Spanning the length of the home at back, with an expanse of window that frames the river and woods is the breakfast room where tables are set on the old brick floor. Offered from 8:30 to 10am a continental breakfast buffet is the morning fare. All the guestrooms are thoughtfully decorated with country furnishings and fabrics; all have river views and private terraces or decks; however, my favorite room is located at the top of the steep stair in the original home. In red checks and provincial prints, the "bedroom" of room six can be partitioned off by sliding shuttered doors from its sitting room which runs the length of the upstairs. A full wall of window opens to a deck and unobstructed river views! *Directions:* Located on Hwy 32 to the north of New Hope.

1740 HOUSE COUNTRY INN   **New**
Innkeeper: Joyce Cooke
3690 River Road
Lumberville, PA 18933, USA
Tel: (215) 297-5661, Fax: (215) 297-5243
23 Rooms, Double: $170–$325
Closed: Christmas & January
Credit cards: all major
www.karenbrown.com/pa1740house.html

The Mercersburg Inn is one of the few 20,000-square-foot Georgian mansions that have become inns and the owners have used the space beautifully. Rooms are larger than large (rare these days), ceilings are high, and large-scale furniture fits the proportions of the windows and the many fireplaces. The inn's staircase is a memorable one, with a double set of stairs sweeping upwards toward the second floor. There are 15 bedrooms and bathrooms tucked here and there on the second and third floors of the mansion, with a choice of queen and king beds. Some of the bathrooms are of the size of bedrooms in today's homes and represent an era when claw-foot tubs and large porcelain sinks were popular. My favorite room, up on the third floor, was decorated in colors of blue and yellow and had a king bed with many pillows just inviting an afternoon read or perhaps even a nap. The gas fireplace had been installed so that it could be seen from both the bedroom and the bathroom. Other bedrooms were much larger—I suppose the term would be grand—but they are all of another era when gracious living without the pace of today's world was the norm. The inn serves a full breakfast in the dining room and on a glassed-in side porch, and a candlelight dinner is available on Thursdays, Fridays, Saturdays, and Sundays. *Directions:* Take I-81 to exit 3, driving west on Route 16 for 10 miles to Mercersburg. The inn is on the left at the junction of Routes 16 and 75.

MERCERSBURG INN **New**
Innkeepers: Lisa & Jim McCoy
405 South Main Street
Mercersburg, PA 17236, USA
Tel: (717) 328-5231, Fax: (717) 328-3403
15 Rooms, Double: $135–$275
Dinner Thur through Sun
Closed: Dec 24 & 25, Credit cards: MC, VS
Select Registry
www.karenbrown.com/pamercersburg.html

This is a handsome two-storey stone and shuttered home that graces Main Street of Mercersburg. Dating back to 1786 the home was built by the widow of William Smith Jr., founder of Mercersburg, the birthplace of President James Buchanan. It was her grandson, a doctor, that added on to the original core to incorporate a medical office. In 1890 it was purchased by Mrs. Fenderick who added the Greek Revival architectural elements. Take note of the stained glass arched over the entry door as well as the Bezel lampposts on the banisters that are original works of Comfort Tiffany & Company who befriended the Fendericks while they were working at the academy. Lucky for the traveler, it is the present owners, Melanie and Ross Bates, who converted the residence to an inn. Launching what they termed "their third attempt at retirement" they have committed their heart to the business. They offer three lovely rooms found at the top of the main stairway. A fourth room without a private bath can connect to form a two room suite. A handsome dining room, rich in dark wood paneling and warmed by an open fireplace is where a bountiful breakfast is served mornings at 8:30. Tea and sweets tempt you to return in the afternoon, which is also a lovely time to enjoy the expanse of back and side garden. *Directions:* Take I-81 to exit 3. Drive west on Route 16 for 10 miles to Mercersburg. Turn right on Main Street to the inn on the right.

SQUIRE SMITH INN   New
Innkeepers: Melanie & Ross Bates
47 N. Main Street
Mercersburg, PA 17236, USA
Tel: (717) 328-9040
Toll Free: (877) 445-5218
3 Rooms, Double: $120–$280
Open: all year, Credit cards: all major
www.karenbrown.com/pasquiresmith.html

This striking Grande Dame was slated for demolition until the architectural team of Strubb and Schneider stepped in to restore it and give it back to Milford. Constructed as a home in 1868 it later served as a hotel welcoming such dignitaries as John F. Kennedy. The three story white building with black shuttered windows and a large wrap-around porch was being readied for its grand opening at the time of our visit. Still a construction zone, we donned our "hard hats" and felt privileged to tour what will become one of the region's trendiest hotels. Many architectural details such as the original Swiss marble tiles and handsome hardwood floors and ceilings have been preserved. The reception is off one side of the wide central hallway and a lovely dining room off the other. The combined 45 years of European hotel experience of Jennifer and Michael guarantee a high standard of service. Rich beiges and creams set the color scheme and comfortable beds are topped with European duvets. Standard, deluxe and superior identify room categories based on size (Although all are small, they couldn't be enlarged because of the restrictions imposed on historic buildings.) and whether they are corner rooms or corner rooms with terraces. Public areas include the dining room, back garden and the very chic basement, Bar Louis. *Directions:* From Scranton travel east to exit 46 and then take Rte 6, 3 miles south to Milford.

FAUCHÈRES   New
Innkeepers: Jennifer Hazen & Michael DiLonardo
401 Broad Street
Milford, PA 18337, USA
Tel: (570) 409-1212, Fax: (570) 409-1251
16 Rooms, Double: $250–$325*
*Minimum stay: 3 nights on weekends in high season
Open: all year, Credit cards: all major
www.karenbrown.com/pafaucheres.html

Owned by the National Park Service, this lovely inn is located just outside the town of Milford, nestled in 70,000 acres of park and overlooking the greens of the nine-hole golf course. It has operated as an inn since the 1850's but until it came under the direction of Jamie and Yvonne Klausmann just three years ago, with just one bathroom for all twelve guestrooms, it could only be described as rustic. Now, after extensive renovations the inn advertises twelve wonderful rooms, all with private bath. The reception area is just off the wrap-around porch. Once inside you will be embraced by a cozy mountain retreat. Chairs and sofas set on old plank floors and clustered round the open fireplaces tempt one to linger. The original main dining room is very inviting with its tables elegantly set with white linens on pine floors before an expanse of windows that frame the surrounding greenery. Downstairs both golfers and guests congregate in the popular pub. The guestrooms are all located in the main house and vary in size and attractive décor. Three rooms enjoy their own porch. With the Delaware Water Gap National Recreation Area at its doorstep, guests can spend the day exploring parkland, waterfalls, hiking trails and return at day's end to be embraced by the comfort and ambiance of this grand country estate. *Directions:* From Scranton travel east to exit 46 and take Rte 6, 3 miles south to Milford.

※ ■☕ 💳 ☎ P ‖ 🚭 ♿ 🎿 🚶 🚶‍♂️ 🏇 🎣

CLIFF PARK INN   *New*
Innkeepers: Jamie & Yvonne Klausmann
155 Cliff Park Road
Milford, PA 18337, USA
Tel: (570) 296-6491
Toll Free: (800) 225-6535
12 Rooms, Double: $149–$249
Open: all year, Credit cards: all major
www.karenbrown.com/pacliffparkinn.html

Stroll down the wide main street in New Berlin and feel the charm of a small, country town where everyone knows everyone else. The Inn at New Berlin has Victorian appeal, candles in the windows to beckon you inside, fine dining to please your palate, rooms designed with your comfort in mind, and innkeepers whose personal touch spreads glitter on every imaginable moment of your stay. Nancy and John run their inn with the highest standards of hospitality and service. The inn has a wide variety of guestrooms with offerings of fireplaces, spa tubs, and canopy beds. At the top of the stairs in the main house, rooms are beautifully decorated in a Victorian style to complement the history of the home. In a building, the Aurand, that once housed the family country store, are very handsome, luxurious bedchambers, two enjoying their own intimate living rooms. This is also where you will find Grandma Molly's Kitchen, John's mother's kitchen now abundantly stocked with cookies, snacks, and beverages. Enjoy the peace and beauty of the rolling farmlands, watch the Amish horse and buggy travel down the road at a pace of a bygone era, and, more than anything, sit on the porch of the Inn at New Berlin and enjoy life as it is meant to be. *Directions:* Leave Route 80 at the Lewisburg exit, taking Route 15 south to Route 45 west for 4 miles. Turn left onto Dreisbach Mountain Road, continue 5 miles, turn right onto Market Street.

INN AT NEW BERLIN
Innkeepers: John & Nancy Showers
321 Market Street
New Berlin, PA 17855, USA
Tel: (570) 966-0321, Fax: (570) 966-9557
Toll Free: (800) 797-2350
11 Rooms, Double: $139–$209
Dinner Wed through Sun, Brunch Sat & Sun
Closed: first 3 weeks of Jan, Credit cards: all major
Select Registry
www.karenbrown.com/painnatnewberlin.html

Another innkeeper cautioned me that this Inn would, "knock my socks off!" Indeed, this is a beautiful property set behind private gates, on a 5 acre estate close to the village of New Hope. A cluster of brick, stone and wood buildings huddle below the circular drive. The main house, the owner's home, contains the reception, breakfast room and garden conservatory as well as the Manor Suite. Steps terrace down to the pool that overlooks the woodland, stream and stone bridge. The Tower Suite with its own living room, bedroom and bathroom is located in an adjoining building. Climb a stair from the living room of the Tower Suite to access the Tower Suite Loft a cozy room rented only in conjunction with the Suite. Four additional rooms are tucked away across the courtyard in the Carriage House. One enjoys its own entrance and three are off an interior stair and share a common sitting area. My favorite two rooms mirror each other: Pond Vista and Orchard Retreat—both corner rooms that enjoy serene views and open on to decks. As we toured the inn I recalled the fellow innkeeper's comment and agreed that, yes, this is a superlative hotel, but I decided it is owners, rather than the inn's physical attributes that make this property exceptional. In fact, Lynne was just voted innkeeper of the year! *Directions:* From Philadelphia take 1-95 North to New Hope exit 51. Turn north onto Taylorsville Rd. Turn left onto Lurgan Rd.

THE INN AT BOWMAN'S HILL   *New*
Innkeepers: Mike & Lynne Amery
518 Lurgan Road
New Hope, PA 18938, USA
Tel: (215) 862-8090, Fax: (215) 862-9362
6 Rooms, Double: $325–$525
Closed: Christmas, Credit cards: all major
Select Registry
www.karenbrown.com/pabowmanshill.html

The Latham Hotel is a small, European-style hotel with that personal ambiance and service that is often hard to find—very appealing to sophisticated travelers. Its location is just about perfect: just off Rittenhouse Square on Walnut Street at the intersection of 17th Street. Within blocks of the hotel are all of Philadelphia's best shops and specialty boutiques, the center of Philadelphia's performing arts—most especially the home of the Philadelphia Orchestra—and the best restaurants in the city. The hotel's guestrooms vary in size, but even the smallest of the three styles is more than comfortable, with every amenity, from toiletries in the bathroom to robes, turndown service, complimentary newspaper, and free use of the fitness center. The rooms are decorated more or less in standard hotel furniture, draperies, bedding, and carpeting, but everything is clean and fresh looking. An especially handy service is the use of a small business center where you may access your email, use the printer, or make a photocopy at no charge. Jolly's Grillroom and Bar, featuring a classic American grilled menu, is available for breakfast, lunch, and dinner. Close by you find Independence Hall, the Liberty Bell, and all of Philadelphia's historic section. *Directions:* From I-95 take I-676 west to the first exit, Broad Street. Follow the exit ramp to the traffic light, turn right onto Vine Street, and at the second light turn left to 17th Street. The Latham is eight blocks down on the left.

❋ ⚓ ▭ ☎ ♁ ☗ P ¶ ♿ ⚐

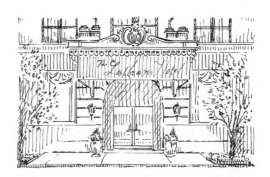

LATHAM HOTEL
Manager: Alex Cohen
17th at Walnut Street
Philadelphia, PA 19103, USA
Tel: (215) 563-7474, Fax: (215) 563-4034
Toll Free: (877) 528-4261
139 Rooms, Double: $119–$149*
*Breakfast not included
Open: all year, Credit cards: all major
www.karenbrown.com/palatham.html

The Penn's View Hotel is a nice, affordable alternative to the hustle and bustle of a midtown hotel and is conveniently located just three blocks from Independence National Park. Remembering my own visit to the Liberty Bell and Independence Hall decades ago, I would say that a visit to these historic structures is a must for young children, who will find the park rangers' stories fascinating and instructive. The hotel's bedrooms all have private baths and a nice Continental breakfast is available from early in the morning in the dining room. My room at the hotel was extra large, with a king bed, desk, small conference table, and gas fireplace. I missed having a comfortable chair and a good reading light as an alternative to sitting in bed. The marble bathroom was huge and had the longest spa tub with shower that I'd ever seen. Next to the inn in the same building is the Panorama restaurant with the "largest wine bar in the world"—a unique experience.
Directions: From I-95 south: take the Central Philadelphia Historic District exit, staying left at the bottom of the ramp to Second Street. Go to Market Street, drive left for one block to Front Street, then left to the hotel. From I-95 north: travel around the airport to exit 20 (Historic District). At the end of the ramp turn left onto Columbus Boulevard and get in the left lane to Dock Street. Turn left on Dock to Front Street, go to Market Street, turn left—the hotel is on the left.

PENN'S VIEW HOTEL
Manager: Carlo Sena
Front & Market Streets
Philadelphia, PA 19106, USA
Tel: (215) 922-7600, Fax: (215) 922-7642
Toll Free: (800) 331-7634
50 Rooms, Double: $159–$255
Restaurant serving lunch weekdays, dinner nightly
Open: all year, Credit cards: all major
www.karenbrown.com/papennsview.html

A bed and breakfast inn in the middle of any city is rare and this one is a gem, both in terms of its central location and the quality and service it offers its guests. The Rittenhouse Square Bed & Breakfast was created in a 1900s carriage house in the prime residential section of Philadelphia. The staff is exceptionally friendly and helpful in guiding you to the historic sites and informing you about nearby restaurants. Philadelphia is wonderful to visit in that you can walk to almost anything you might want to do, which is particularly desirable in a city that has tiny narrow streets making driving somewhat difficult. Guestrooms are well equipped and have nightly turndown service. My room on the third floor had a king bed, comfortable seating, good lighting, cable TV, and especially nice fabrics in the bed coverings and drapes. The marble-tiled bathroom was complete with all the amenities you'd expect to find in an inn of this caliber. In the mornings, coffee (or tea) is available early and then there is a nice Continental breakfast with fresh fruit, juice, cereals, and pastries served in a bright and cheery breakfast room. *Directions:* From the Philadelphia airport take I-76 west to the South Street exit. At the light turn right on South Street, left on 16th Street, and left on Walnut Street. Drive one block and turn left on 17th Street then right at Rittenhouse Square Street (the inn is on the right).

RITTENHOUSE SQUARE BED & BREAKFAST
Manager: Harriet Seltzer
1715 Rittenhouse Square Street
Philadelphia, PA 19103, USA
Tel: (215) 546-6500, Fax: (215) 546-8787
Toll Free: (877) 791-6500
16 Rooms, Double: $259–$599
Closed: Dec 24 & 25, Credit cards: all major
Select Registry
www.karenbrown.com/rittenhousesquarebb.html

I would bring my kids to Philadelphia to hear national park rangers telling the stories of the founding of the United States of America, and I would stay in the wonderfully convenient Thomas Bond House, built in 1769, just steps away from the park. The Thomas Bond has ten bedrooms and two suites, each with private bath, and several rooms have more than one bed or have a sofa bed or a connecting room. The amenities of a bed and breakfast inn are all yours to enjoy—a Continental breakfast during the week and a full breakfast on the weekends; wine and cheese in the evening; freshly baked cookies and games for the kids. The Thomas Bond Room, with its lovely Chippendale furniture, has a magnificent rice-canopy four-poster bed, a fireplace, whirlpool tub with shower, and a double-size sofa bed. There's a similar room one floor up, and then there are smaller rooms with pencil beds, wrought-iron beds, a cannonball pine bed, etc. The area around the inn consists of buildings from the same era so you really feel part of the town and the society of that earlier life. *Directions:* From I-95 south: take exit 22, stay in the right lane downhill to Callowhill Street. Get in the left lane and go through the light onto Second Street to the inn. From I-95 north: take exit 20 and at the end of the ramp turn left onto Columbus Boulevard. At the fifth light turn left onto Dock Street, go to Front Street, and turn right.

THOMAS BOND HOUSE
Innkeeper: Rita McGuire
129 South Second Street
Philadelphia, PA 19106, USA
Tel: (215) 923-8523, Fax: (215) 923-8504
Toll Free: (800) 845-2663
10 Rooms, Double: $105–$190
2 suites
Open: all year, Credit cards: all major
www.karenbrown.com/pathomasbond.html

Located in Pittsburg's "Shadyside" district, The Inns on Negley enjoy a wonderful proximity to the University, Carnegie Museum, and one of the city's most beautiful residential districts. Accommodations are housed in two separate buildings on opposite sides of Negley Street. Each address enjoys a front porch, but the building facades are architecturally quite different. One is gray and white stone, the other is made of brick. At 703 Negley, The Appletree, guestrooms are named for different species of apples. One of the more popular rooms, the Cortland, is a suite with a handsome four-poster bed. My favorite is a cozy Granny Smith in a décor of creams and reds with shuttered windows in the bedroom and side sitting room. You will be pleased with any room. Across the street at 714 Negley, the décor is described by the manager as a little more French and elegant. This location hosts many private weddings, conferences and parties. In both buildings there are lovely salons and dining areas. Two chefs oversee the breakfast offering and, in the welcome note, guests are given a choice of entrees. On the day of our visit the offering was either cornmeal pancakes with blueberry syrup or an open-face sandwich of asparagus and smoked salmon on a poached egg. *Directions:* From the airport, follow signs for Pittsburgh, then take 279 N to 376 E. Exit 376 at Forbes Ave/Oakland. Take Forbes Ave, turn left on Moorwood Ave, Right on Fifth Ave, and left on Negley.

THE INNS ON NEGLEY
Owner: Liz Sullivan
Manager: Jackie Karkowski
703 and 714 South Negley
Pittsburgh, PA 15232, USA
Tel: (412) 661-0631, Fax: (412) 661-7525
Double: $150–$220
16 Rooms & 8 suites at each address
Open: all year, Credit cards: all major
Select Registry
www.karenbrown.com/negley.html

Fortunate for the traveler, a highway that would have required demolition of the brick Priory and its adjacent church, was relocated and the buildings spared. The complex attracted the interest and commitment of Ed and Mary Graf, who converted it in 1986 to an upscale hotel. Located in the Pittsburgh's Deutschtown District, within walking distance of the Warhol Museum and near the sport stadiums, The Priory has established a wonderful reputation and many loyal, returning guests. Under the example set by their son, John, the staff exudes graciousness, warmth of welcome and professional attentiveness. John's wife, Suzanne, busy raising their family, is, however, responsible for many details and decisions that go on behind the scenes to ensure guest comfort. The Priory has just 24 rooms, three of which are two-room suites. All are handsome and uncluttered in their décor. There is no elevator; so those who might find negotiating the old stairways difficult might want to request the ground floor suite. In the public areas, flowers abound and there is a lovely salon warmed by a fireplace where wine is offered evenings. Just beyond is the Library, which also serves as the honor bar. A hearty buffet breakfast is set in a beautiful paneled pantry. Guests can choose to dine in the elegant dining room or in the lovely garden courtyard. *Directions:* Exit the I 279 north at 7c, travel 3 blocks west on E. Ohio, turn left on Cedar for 3 blocks, then left on Pressley.

THE PRIORY HOTEL
Innkeepers: John & Suzanne Graf
614 Pressley Street
Pittsburgh, PA 15212, USA
Tel: (412) 231-3338, Fax: (412) 231-4838
Toll Free: (866) 377-4679
24 Rooms, Double: $149–$215
Open: all year, Credit cards: all major
www.karenbrown.com/thepriory.html

Buhl Mansion is a grand tribute to a couple, the Buhls, who made a fortune in steel, and then generously shared their wealth by giving so much back to the town and region. They ensured that a park, golf course and the library would be maintained forever on the funds left. Quite tragically, as they were childless, their home eventually left the family. Over the next several decades the home endured a revolving door of owners and overtime it was gutted and reduced to shambles as chandeliers, furnishings, fireplaces, and the grand stairway were dismantled and sold to cover debts. Vagrants even burned moldings to heat their camping spots. Modern day philanthropists, Mr. and Mrs. Winner, sight unseen, purchased the home to save it from demolition, and invested a fortune to restore the home. With the exception of the woodwork and fireplaces of the rooms found at the top of the stairs, which could not be reached and vandalized because of the missing stairs, everything is new. Opulent and grand, the décor is lavish with every luxurious detail included. Neighbored by retail establishments, the heavy stone-turreted mansion is set back off the road, nestled in its own gardens. Breakfast is offered at the mansion, but for lunch or dinner guests travel the six miles to its sister property, Tara–A Country Inn in Clark. *Directions:* From I-80 take exit 4B to Rte 18N, then travel north to East State Street and turn left. Continue for 2.8 miles to Buhl Mansion on the left.

BUHL MANSION
Owners: Jim & Donna Winner
Innkeeper: Laura Ackley
422 East State Street
Sharon, PA 16146, USA
Tel: (724) 346-3046, Fax: (724) 346-1702
Toll Free: (866) 345-2845
10 Rooms, Double: $325–$475
Open: all year, Credit cards: all major
Select Registry
www.karenbrown.com/buhl.html

I had heard Carnegie House was inspired by Edward Lutyen's Greywalls, but it wasn't until I stepped into its lobby that I appreciated the similarity. Newly constructed, it is an attractive gray building with white trim nestled in tall, wispy trees and stretches at back along the expanse of lush green lawn of the Tofttrees' Golf Course. Inside, one is immediately captivated by the understated and refined elegance and sense of being transported to Scotland. Rooms are paneled in rich woods or traditional papers; decorated with the beautiful fabrics used in the furnishings and window coverings; and include oriental carpets, paintings, and bookcases filled with old books—creating an ambiance of olde world. In the living room with its adjoining club-bar, I almost felt I was in Gullane. To dine here is a memorable experience, in either the handsome dining room or under the shaded trellis of the back veranda. The menu features local and Scottish specialties. The guestrooms are a lovely haven in their own right, spacious with comfortable seating and modern bathrooms. But more than the elegant accommodations, it is the dedication of Peter and Helga that makes Carnegie House exceptional. They are proud to adhere to the saying, Ceud Mille Failte—A Thousand Welcomes and a very professional, European, standard of service. *Directions:* Traveling 322 west from State College, take the Toftree's exit north one block to Cricklewood Dr east.

CARNEGIE HOUSE
Innkeepers: Peter & Helga Schmid
100 Cricklewood Drive
State College, PA 16803, USA
Tel: (814) 234-2424, Fax: (814) 231-1299
Toll Free: (800) 229-5033
22 Rooms, Double: $150–$275
Open: all year, Credit cards: all major
www.karenbrown.com/carnegie.html

Located on the road that parallels the river, across from the entrance to Merle Phillips Park, the River View Inn enjoys a wonderful location and is proud of its status as Sunbury's first inn. Purchased initially as a real estate investment, Mathew and David saw its potential for hosting overnight travelers. Although this is an attractive two-story clapboard-sided building, from the façade one would never anticipate the elegance of its interior. Cross the threshold and the richness of its décor will amaze you. Lovely paintings, gorgeous fabrics, warm colors, handsome furnishings and personal treasures (Mathew's Grandmother's button collections among others) together affect an ambiance of an intimate, beautiful residence. Off the entry one can settle in the living room which then opens to the adjoining, dining room or climb the stairs to the inn's six guestrooms which all enjoy an element of river view. Burgundy and Regal share a hall bath. On the corner of the third floor, the bedroom area of Lake Augusta has corner windows, and the bathroom with its clawfoot tub sits positioned in front of the dormer window commanding the best view. My favorite is on the second floor, the Overlook Room, with a full wall of bay windows and unobstructed river views. *Directions:* Easily accessible from routes 11 and 15, the inn is located on route 61 (Front Street) at the corner of Chestnut Street along the river frontage.

RIVER VIEW INN   **New**
Innkeepers: Matthew Strauser & David Hollabaugh
103 Chestnut Street
Sunbury, PA 17801, USA
Tel: (570) 286-4800, Toll Free: (866) 592-4800
6 Rooms, Double: $98–$129
Open: all year, Credit cards: all major
www.karenbrown.com/pariverview.html

Places to Stay—Pennsylvania

What's magical about Bridgeton House is that it sits above the Delaware and if you reserve one of the rooms overlooking the river—several have French doors leading to private screened porches off the bedrooms—you can laze the day away as you watch the river, the boats, and the people drift by. The most special of all the rooms is the luxurious penthouse suite—it's superlative, with 900 square feet of space divided into a sitting area with panoramic views of the river and countryside, a bedroom area, a bathroom, and a dressing room. Second most special is the Boat House, which is in a separate cottage with a sitting room, bedroom, 2-person whirlpool, outdoor sitting area, and garden. The inn has been imaginatively decorated by the owners whose artistic talents have found an outlet: color and design flow with great imagination throughout the house. Some of the guestrooms have canopy beds and fireplaces. The Delaware Canal State Park is a block away and provides miles upon miles of hiking, biking, jogging, and bird watching. You can while away the day swimming, canoeing, fishing, and floating on an inner tube or there are the more serious antiquing, shopping, art galleries, and museums to divert your attention from just plain doing nothing at the inn. *Directions:* From Lambertville drive north on Rte 29 to Frenchtown where it ends. Turn left onto Bridge St, cross the river, turn right on Rte 32 north. The inn is 3½ miles north.

BRIDGETON HOUSE ON THE DELAWARE
Innkeepers: Bea & Charles Briggs
1525 River Road
Upper Black Eddy, PA 18972, USA
Tel & Fax: (610) 982-5856
Toll Free: (888) 982-2007
8 Rooms, Double: $139–$379
1 cottage
Open: all year, Credit cards: all major
www.karenbrown.com/pabridgeton.html

Places to Stay
Virginia & West Virginia

The Capitol Building, Colonial Williamsburg

The Morrison House is so wonderful that it's hard to think of how it could be improved. Replicate an 18th-century Federal manor in the heart of old-town Alexandria, surrounded with boutiques and interesting things to do; have a staff that provides a level of service that's so personal that you feel completely at home; tuck in a bar and grille and there you have the ideal place to stay in the Washington, D.C. area. The hotel is only 10 minutes from downtown Washington and 3 miles from National Airport, and the Metro is a 10-minute walk away. My room had a carved four-poster king bed, a love seat next to a great reading light, an armoire that doubled to hold my clothes and hide the TV, a marbled bathroom with two vanities, oversized towels, and all the amenities you could possibly want. The hotel's location is such that I was able to open a window for fresh air without being bothered by noise. There are three suites, but I can't imagine who would need one, considering the comfort of the bedrooms. The dinner in the grille was nothing short of sublime. The Morrison House's gourmet restaurant with its extensive wine list adds the final touch of perfection. *Directions:* From the Washington Beltway take Route 1 north to King Street, go right on King for one block, then turn right on S. Alfred to the inn on the left.

MORRISON HOUSE
Owner: Peter Greenberg
General Manager: Bert le Roux
116 South Alfred Street, Alexandria, VA 22314, USA
Tel: (703) 838-8000, Fax: (703) 684-6283
Toll Free: (800) 367-0800
42 Rooms, Double: $199–$399*
*Breakfast not included: $10 to $35
Open: all year, Credit cards: all major
Relais & Châteaux
www.karenbrown.com/vamorrison.html

An escape to Hillbrook is like a trip to the heart of the English countryside. This charming old timbered home, a jumble of angled roofline, chimney stacks, small-paned glass, and dormer windows, steps down the hillside surrounded by lush lawn shaded by trees. Families of ducks and geese grace the ponds, walking bridges span the gurgling stream, a swing hangs in the breeze, and human-size chessmen are set on a chess board sculpted in the lawn. In addition to accommodation, Hillbrook is popular for its delicious meals, which include a three-course lunch and a gourmet seven-course dinner, and its cozy tavern. Inside the long, narrow inn, rooms take advantage of every nook and cranny. The ambiance is intimate and cozy with the patina of old woods, creaking floors, soft lighting, paintings, Oriental carpets, shelves of books, crackling fires, and small tables set with candles. In the main house five guestrooms range from the enchanting Lookout, tucked under the eaves, to the most dramatic and spacious, The Bamford Suite, which enjoys a sitting area and bedchamber in front of an open fire and a private porch. The four suites in the garden cottage have luxurious bathrooms and handsome furnishings set on gorgeous terracotta tile floors. *Directions:* From Rte 7 east or west, take Rte 340 north. Travel ¾ mile and then take Rte 611 west. Travel 5½ miles to the stop sign, go right, and the entry is 1 mile down on the right.

HILLBROOK
Innkeepers: Carissa & Christopher Zanella
4490 Summit Point Road
Charles Town, West Virginia 25414, USA
Tel: (304) 725-4223, Fax: (304) 725-4455
Toll Free: (800) 304-4223
9 Rooms, Double: $200–$325
Restaurant: Meals & afternoon teas, open Thur-Sun
Open: all year, Credit cards: all major
www.karenbrown.com/wvhillbrook.html

The Boar's Head Inn is a very attractive full-service hotel with one of the region's finest restaurants, an intimate lounge bar, lovely accommodation, and a sport and fitness center (complimentary to hotel guests), all set on 573 acres and conveniently located near the university. I almost didn't consider the Boar's Head as, with 171 guestrooms, it is a larger property than we usually include, but from the moment I entered the reception area I was charmed. The lobby is reminiscent of Olde England, with dark woods, low, wide beams, and handsome antiques and paintings. The restaurant is housed in an old mill that was actually relocated here. Guestrooms are all well appointed, traditional in decor, and enjoy wonderful modern appointments and luxurious amenities. The standard rooms are a great value. Be sure to ask for rooms in the Hunt Club or in the 600 and 700 series overlooking the lake. We saw a lovely standard room, 622, which had a king bed and its own deck. Room 724, one of the inn's seven suites, has a living room equipped with sofa bed and also enjoys its own deck and lake view. Loving the ambiance of old, my favorite rooms are the cozy Jefferson Alcove rooms (311, 312, and 313), which are tucked under the old exposed eaves and decorated with antiques. *Directions:* From the east or west, travel the I-64 to exit 118-B in Charlottesville. Continue 1½ miles and exit at Route 250 west. Turn left onto Route 250 and drive 1 mile—the inn's entrance is on the left.

BOAR'S HEAD INN
Manager: Jorg Lippuner
200 Ednam Drive
P.O. Box 5307
Charlottesville, VA 22903, USA
Tel: (434) 296-2181, Fax: (434) 972-6019
Toll Free: (800) 476-1988
171 Rooms, Double: $188–$675*
*Breakfast not included: $14.95
Open: all year, Credit cards: all major
www.karenbrown.com/vaboar.html

Incorporated within the Silver Thatch Inn is a two-story log cabin built on the site of an old Indian settlement. The cabin was constructed in the late 18th century by Hessian troops who, captured by the colonists, were marched south to Charlottesville. Subsequently, the property became a boy's private school in the first half of the 19th century, then a melon farm and a tobacco plantation, and in 1937 the home of the dean of the University of Virginia. All these lives and the transformations they brought with them have given character to this wonderfully harmonious structure that now has seven bedrooms, each named after a Virginia-born president, and a Wine Spectator Award-winning restaurant, where contemporary cuisine is just part of an intimate, romantic evening. There's also an English pub in which to begin or end an evening at the inn. The bedrooms, while cozy in size, are very comfortably furnished and each has its own private bath. There's much to do in Charlottesville including visits to Thomas Jefferson's Monticello, Ash Lawn-Highland, the University of Virginia, the Blue Ridge Mountains, and neighboring wineries. *Directions:* From the south: 6 miles north of the intersection of Route 29 and the 250 bypass, turn right on Hollymead Dr. From the north: 1 mile south of Airport Road, turn left on Hollymead Dr.

❄ ☕ CREDIT P ⅋ ≈ 🛶 🚶‍♂️ 🚶‍♀️

SILVER THATCH INN
Innkeepers: Jim & Terri Petrovits
3001 Hollymead Drive
Charlottesville, VA 22911, USA
Tel: (434) 978-4686, Fax: (434) 973-6156
Toll Free: (800) 261-0720
7 Rooms, Double: $150–$185
Dinner Tues through Sat, Sun brunch
Open: all year, Credit cards: all major
Select Registry
www.karenbrown.com/vasilverthatch.html

This inn is a real charmer: it's an old plantation at the end of a long drive set in the Virginia countryside close to many historical sites and wineries. You walk to the front door among fragrant old boxwood, enjoying the flowering gardens, and feel the warmth of hospitality as soon as you enter the main part of the house, built in 1732. The inn is known for its food—the owners are chefs themselves—and there are several small, intimate dining rooms. In the evenings before dinner there is a reception at which complimentary wine is served and you have the opportunity to meet the family that has owned this inn since 1977. In addition to the main building, added on to in later years, there are eight guest cottages, once all part of this working plantation. The carriage house, the summer kitchen, the slave quarters, and the smokehouse, dating from 1699 to 1880, have all been made into very special accommodations with uniquely different decor. The inn invites you to laze by the pool, stare into space, eat the best of the local foods, and enjoy what's become known as "southern hospitality." (Note that the rates includes staff gratuities.) *Directions:* From Charlottesville: take I-64 east to exit #136. From Washington, D.C.: take I-66 west to Route 29 south then Route 15 south to Zion Crossroads. Turn left on Route 250 east for 1 mile to Poindexter Road and go left. The inn is 3 miles along on the left.

PROSPECT HILL PLANTATION INN
Innkeeper: The Sheehan Family
P.O. Box 6909, 2887 Poindexter Road
Charlottesville (Trevilians), VA 22906, USA
Tel: (540) 967-0844, Fax: (540) 967-0102
Toll Free: (800) 277-0844
13 Rooms, Double: $295–$575*
*Includes all meals
Closed: Christmas, Credit cards: all major
Select Registry
www.karenbrown.com/vaprospecthill.html

The Cedar Gables Seaside Inn is a converted private home where your focus is the view out back of the water front and the intervening saltwater marshes—beautiful in summer when they're green and lush and wave in the breeze, and equally interesting in winter with their brown stalks rising and falling with the incoming and outgoing tides. There are four bedrooms in this inn, all very different and all having a slightly different orientation to the water. On the third floor there's the Captain's Quarters with a king brass bed, fireplace, and its own private and spectacular copula staged with tall chairs, binoculars and a telescope where you can take in the sea views. The elegant Oriental Suite, also with a balcony overlooking the water, is beautifully decorated with pieces collected in the Orient. Lori's Room, which shares a waterview deck with Little Oyster Bay, has a Persian rug on yellow pine flooring, a fireplace, writing desks, and a love seat, which can be made into a twin bed. In Little Oyster Bay there's a queen iron bed, a fireplace, and a view to the bay from the window. Add a year-round porch where breakfast is served and an outdoor pool and hot tub and this is indeed a place to linger, away from it all. *Directions:* Take Rte 13 down the Delmarva Peninsula to 175 east to Chincoteague, cross the bridge onto the island and turn left on Main St. Go right on Taylor St to its end, then left on Deep Hole Rd. Proceed through the "S" turn then take a right on Hopkins Lane.

CEDAR GABLES SEASIDE INN
Innkeeper: Claudia Kesseler
6095 Hopkins Lane
P.O. Box 1006
Chincoteague, VA 23336, USA
Tel: (757) 336-6860, Fax: (757) 336-1291
Toll Free: (888) 491-2944
4 Rooms, Double: $165–$190
Open: all year, Credit cards: all major
www.karenbrown.com/vacedargables.html

The Oaks Victorian Inn in Christiansburg is a charming inn on the National Register of Historic Places with wonderful innkeepers whose every moment is directed toward making your stay not just a good one, but a memorable one. With great imagination and lovely decor, they offer every comfort to today's traveler. My bedroom on the first floor was a delight to stay in, with a comfortable bed, good reading lights, a TV/DVD tucked out of sight in an armoire, a refrigerator stocked with soft drinks, and wireless internet access for that necessary work on the computer. Breakfast the morning I was there was Belgian waffles served with a small scoop of pecan ice cream, slivered almonds, and fresh berries, then a slice of cantaloupe melon served with blueberries and blackberries. There is a Victorian library with a great selection of current magazines, movies, and books and a living room for guests, both with gas fireplaces. There is a lovely garden out back (with a Victorian cottage also providing accommodations) and an appealing terrace on which to relax or eat one of those fabulous breakfasts. *Directions:* Take I-81 south to exit 114 (Main St) and drive for 2 miles. From Blue Ridge Pkwy take Rte 8 (MP165) west for 28 miles.

THE OAKS VICTORIAN INN
Innkeepers: Lois & John Ioviero
311 East Main Street
Christiansburg, VA 24073, USA
Tel: (540) 381-1500, Fax: (540) 381-3036
Toll Free: (800) 336-6257
7 Rooms, Double: $150–$185
Open: all year, Credit cards: all major
Select Registry
www.karenbrown.com/vaoaksvictorian.html

This distinguished, three story brick residence sits opposite the legal courts in the historic old town of Fairfax. Originally built as a private home it was later converted to law offices and in the 1980s it opened its rooms to accommodate paying guests. Fairfax is home to George Mason University, and the Bailiwick Inn and Restaurant caters to its students, their families, tourists and members of the court. Although not responsible for converting the residence to an elegant town hotel, Bonnie W. Mc Daniel, took over the business three years ago and it has flourished under her direction. Just off the entry are two regal salons, partitioned by sliding doors and individually warmed by fireplaces. Each of the twelve guestrooms upstairs are all elegant in their appointments and vary in their individual décor from the creams and whites of the bridal suite to the handsome Robert E. Lee. Christina's, named for Bonnie's daughter, is the inn's restaurant and offers cozy corners at the back of the inn and overflows to tables set in the walled garden. Sweet Christina's, a block away is Bonnie's newest venture and will offer light luncheons, coffee, tea and feature some of her grandmother's cherished recipes: red velvet cake, sweet potato pie and lemon coconut cake. *Directions:* Take I 66 to exit 60and follow route 123 S. Chain Bridge Road toward Fairfax. Pass Main Street and the inn is located on the corner of Sager.

THE BAILIWICK INN   New
Innkeeper: Bonnie W. McDaniel
4023 Chain Bridge Road
Fairfax, VA 22030, USA
Tel: (703) 691-2266, Fax: (703) 934-2112
Toll Free: (800) 447-8679
12 Rooms, Double: $170–$355*
*Breakfast not included
Closed: Christmas, Credit cards: all major
Select Registry
www.karenbrown.com/vabailiwick.html

The romance of plantation life in the 17th century comes to us today through inns whose owners have fallen in love with the architecture and society of that period. Warner Hall dates back to 1642 and the Stavenses have taken this plantation house with its 17th- and 18th-century bones and re-created a home and a style that will delight the traveler. Every detail of the inn is one to relish for this restoration is so well done and so much has been preserved that one can only marvel at the end result. Rooms are large and gracious, beginning with the wide front hall from which you look down over the lawns to a distant view. The furnishings are beautifully chosen and look as if they may have been there for a hundred years—except that they now display lovely fabrics and trims. On the far side of the inn is a glassed-in porch with white wicker furniture where breakfast is served. Dinner in the dining room with its mahogany tables set with silver and crystal is a most romantic experience. The eleven bedrooms continue the gracious style of the home with magnificent beds, comfortable seating, large windows with expansive views of the surrounding countryside, and bathrooms that contain steam showers, spa tubs, and every amenity you could ever want. *Directions:* From Washington, D.C. take I-95 south to Route 17 south to Gloucester. Stay on Route 17 south to White Marsh and turn left on Route 614. Go 2-3/10 miles then turn right onto Route 629 for 1 mile to Warner Hall Rd.

INN AT WARNER HALL
Innkeepers: Troy & Theresa Stavens
4750 Warner Hall Road
Gloucester, VA 23061, USA
Tel: (804) 695-9565, Fax: (804) 695-9566
Toll Free: (800) 331-2720
11 Rooms, Double: $155–$245
Open: all year, Credit cards: all major
Select Registry
www.karenbrown.com/vawarnerhall.html

The General Lewis Inn is one of more than 60 buildings that make up Lewisburg's National Historic District with nearby Civil War sites. Patrick Henry and Thomas Jefferson stood at the inn's front desk when they registered and visited one of the many local mineral springs resorts, popular with the antebellum aristocrats so many years ago. The living room, a 1929 addition to a home built in 1834, is filled to brimming with antiques and collectibles gathered over the years by the inn's founder. Bedrooms are simply furnished, mostly with double beds, but with some queen bed options. Some have canopy beds, which add to the nostalgic and historic feeling of this property. Rooms are equipped with bureaus, desks, TVs, and air conditioning, and all have private, but, small, basic bathrooms. The master bedroom has two double beds and a love seat where you can sit and read. The two-bedroom suite is perfect for those traveling with family or friends. The inn has a dining room serving old-fashioned meals including fried chicken, country ham, and mountain trout. This is a good location from which to explore this era of our nation's history. *Directions:* Take I-64 to Lewisburg exit 169, then Route 219 south for 1½ miles to Route 60 east where you turn left. The inn is three blocks up on the right.

THE GENERAL LEWIS INN
Innkeeper: The Morgan Family
301 East Washington Street
Lewisburg, West Virginia 24901, USA
Tel: (304) 645-2600, Fax: (304) 645-2601
Toll Free: (800) 628-4454
23 Rooms, Double: $99–$168*
*Breakfast not included: $8
Open: all year, Credit cards: all major
Select Registry
www.karenbrown.com/wvgenerallewis.html

The Joshua Wilton House, once the home of one of Harrisonburg's prominent citizens, is an inn and restaurant located within a walk of downtown and James Madison University. It has been restored in the Victorian tradition of its earlier life and is a comfortable place to stay while touring the Shenandoah Valley. The inn's five bedrooms, which are all located on the second floor, are unusually large, which makes them feel very gracious. Room 4, especially attractive with its turret sitting area, has rose-garden wallpaper, a large canopy bed covered with lace that matches the window fabrics, a Victorian armoire, and a Queen Anne desk. Room 1 overlooks the patio and the terraced gardens. In the best Victorian tradition, it has a large walnut bed and armoire and an elegant walnut vanity with marble top. While my visit did not take place on a night that the restaurant was open, I saw that the dinner menu offered half a dozen appetizers including salmon, mussels, mushrooms, sea scallops, and a tempting tomato-orange-basil soup. There were three salad options before a choice of entrées including honey macadamia-crusted Mahi Mahi and a pan-seared duck breast, and an ever-tempting array of desserts. *Directions:* Take I-81 south to exit 245, going west on Port Republic Road to Main Street and turn right. Drive north approximately 1 mile to the inn on the right.

JOSHUA WILTON HOUSE INN & RESTAURANT
Innkeepers: Ann Marie Coe, Mark Newsome & Sean Pugh
412 South Main Street
Harrisonburg, VA 22801, USA
Tel: (540) 434-4464, Fax: (540) 432-9525
Toll Free: (888) 294-5866
5 Rooms, Double: $100–$150
Dinner Tue through Sat
Open: all year, Credit cards: all major
Select Registry
www.karenbrown.com/vajoshuawilton.html

Another of the historic inns in Virginia is Maple Hall, a plantation established in 1850 on 56 acres located just off Route 11 north of the town of Lexington. The inn may be viewed from Route 64 as you travel north. This is an imposing structure with massive columns supporting its three floors and a grand staircase which leads to a hallway running from front to back. Lined up on both sides of this hallway, the bedrooms are modestly furnished but have everything that you would want including air conditioning and a complete bath. There are fireplaces in several of the bedrooms. Apart from the sixteen rooms and five suites, Maple Hall offers guests a swimming pool, fishing pond, and tennis courts. Breakfast is served in a downstairs room—you can bring it up to the porch or enjoy the luxury of breakfast in your own room. The town of Lexington and the historic sites of Generals Stonewall Jackson and Robert E. Lee are part of our nation's history and are well worth visiting. There is also the George C. Marshall Museum, commemorating another general from another war and another man who served his country well. *Directions:* From I-81 take exit 195 to Route 11 north where you will find a large sign to the inn.

MAPLE HALL
Owner: The Peter Meredith Family
Innkeepers: Roxanne & Don Fredenburg
3111 North Lee Hwy
Lexington, VA 24450, USA
Tel: (540) 463-6693, Fax: (540) 463-2114
Toll Free: (877) 283-9680
16 Rooms, Double: $90–$170
Open: all year, Credit cards: all major
www.karenbrown.com/vamaplehall.html

The Goodstone Estate is nestled on 265 acres in the rich farmland and horse country of Virginia. It seemed fortunate and serendipitous that we happened on this peaceful and tranquil property. The reception, breakfast room, and four guestrooms are found in The Carriage House where guests settle in front of the large stone fireplace to sip a complimentary beverage or enjoy a traditional afternoon tea. The restaurant, where guests can enjoy either breakfast or an evening meal, enjoys a peaceful setting overlooking the creek. Climb a steep flight of stairs to what was one of my favorite rooms, the cozy and romantic Hayloft, decorated in the soft blue-cream reminiscent of the French countryside and set under angled eaves. The former stables house some of the most popular accommodation: the Mare's and the Stallion Suites, both large corner rooms with cozy interiors. The other guestrooms are found in separate buildings on the property and each building has a lovely common area. Behind the ivy-covered ruins of the original house a pool is set in an expanse of lawn, looking out to rolling hills. A round of golf, use of canoes and bikes are included in the tariff. *Directions:* From Rte 50 West in Middleburg, turn right at the light onto N. Madison St. Go one block to the fork, bear right, and continue on Foxcroft Rd for 2½ miles. Turn Left on Snake Hill Rd and immediately left.

GOODSTONE INN & ESTATE
Manager: Brian Cook
36205 Snake Hill Road
Middleburg, VA 20117, USA
Tel: (540) 687-4645, Fax: (540) 687-6115
Toll Free: (877) 219-4663
17 Rooms, Double: $470–$600*
*Includes breakfast, golf & afternoon tea
Open: all year, Credit cards: all major
www.karenbrown.com/vagoodstone.html

Hunt country in Virginia is a delightful area of gently sloping hills, winding roads, whitewashed fences, and gracious homes peeking out behind trees, a world away from Washington, the bustling suburbs, the shopping centers, and busy highways with heavy traffic. It takes a while to realize that there are no fast-food joints, that the highways wind a bit, that speed limits are 50, and that at night there are no streetlights along its byways. Middleburg, the area's most delightful village, is the home of the Red Fox Inn. Originally built in 1728 as a tavern, the Red Fox is now a complex of several buildings, some of which are down the street in between private homes. Some guest quarters have living rooms with fireplaces and one or more bedrooms with queen and king beds—all have private baths. The decor is comfortable but not grand. Most of the accommodations are in old buildings and the lower ceilings add to, rather than detract from, the experience of a stay at the inn. The restaurant serves dinners and hearty luncheons in a charming mélange of dining rooms that date back to the 18th century. The front door of the inn opens onto Middleburg's attractive main street where you can enjoy the array of shops that beckon not only you but also the residents of this lovely part of horse country. *Directions:* From Washington, D.C. take I-66 west to Route 50 west to Middleburg.

RED FOX INN
Innkeeper: Turner Reuter
2 East Washington Street
P.O. Box 385
Middleburg, VA 20118, USA
Tel: (540) 687-6301, Fax: (540) 687-6053
Toll Free: (800) 223-1728
10 Rooms, Double: $150–$325
1 cottage
Open: all year, Credit cards: all major
www.karenbrown.com/varedfox.html

In 1750, to protect settlers from Indian raids, Colonel Charles Lewis built a stockade on 3,200 acres of fertile land in western Virginia's Allegheny Mountains. Today, Fort Lewis is still a safe haven, with all the modern comforts for a romantic getaway. Guestrooms are available in the Main Lodge, in separate log cabins with rockers on covered porches and stone fireplaces, or at Riverside House. The timbered-and-stucco structures have been hand-hewn and lovingly assembled like a puzzle. These warmly decorated cabins have front porches, large rooms, fireplaces, ceiling fans, and handmade quilts on the beds. Rooms in the Riverside House, sequestered a few miles away on the upper tract, are always the angler's first choice. In the main lodge the silo has been renovated to provide three very individual bedrooms. There's a hot tub for guests to enjoy after a day's activities or just before turning in after counting the stars. Evenings are highlighted by a drink in the Tobacco Bar followed by delicious American-style cuisine served in the historic Lewis Gristmill. It takes a bit to reach the Lodge, so plan to stay a while and unwind—enjoy the mountains and the beauty of the surrounding countryside, hike, walk, swim, and take it all in. *Directions:* From Staunton take Rte 254 west to Buffalo Gap, then Rte 42 to Millboro Springs. Take Rte 39 west for 7/10 mile then turn right on Rte 678. Drive almost 11 miles to Rte 625 and go left to the inn.

FORT LEWIS LODGE
Innkeepers: John & Caryl Cowden
603 Old Plantation Way
Millboro, VA 24460, USA
Tel: (540) 925-2314, Fax: (540) 925-2352
16 Rooms, Double: $175–$275*
3 cabins
*Includes breakfast & dinner
Open: Apr to Nov, Credit cards: MC, VS
Select Registry
www.karenbrown.com/vafortlewislodge.html

If you plan to visit Chincoteague and the wildlife refuge of Assateague but would prefer to stay away from the tourist hustle and bustle, I would recommend the Garden and the Sea, a few minutes north in the quiet village of New Church. As you turn from the highway you can see ahead the magnificent structure of this inn, which encompasses three buildings, one Victorian, one 1850s, and one new. Here you find all the comforts of home—and more—in eight appealing guestrooms. Those in the original and 1850s buildings have tall ceilings and lend themselves to that Victorian decor of patterned fabrics and floral carpets. All offer sitting areas and private bathrooms with whirlpool tubs except one, which has an old cast-iron claw-foot bathtub. In the new house the decor of the very private suite is more contemporary and the bathroom features a two-person spa tub. One building has three rooms, which are very spacious, bright, and cheery, and would make a great place for families or friends to come together to linger over coffee or to stroll in the early-morning or the late-afternoon light. The innkeepers here take their guests on river cruises when time permits. This is one of the few inns where you may bring your pet—or enjoy those of the owners. You can also now enjoy a new swimming pool. *Directions:* Take Route 13 south on the Delmarva Peninsula to New Church to Nelson Road on the right (also marked 710)—the inn is just ahead on the right.

❄ ☕ 🎿 💳 🐾 🏋 P ‖ 🏊 ♿ ✝ 🏃 👫 ⛷

GARDEN AND THE SEA INN
Innkeepers: Tom & Sara Baker
4188 Nelson Road
P.O. Box 275
New Church (Chincoteague), VA 23415, USA
Tel: (757) 824-0672, Fax: none
Toll Free: (800) 824-0672
7 Rooms, Double: $85–$225
Dinner Fri & Sat in season
Open: all year, Credit cards: all major
www.karenbrown.com/vagardenandsea.html

Pause and reflect back to the winter of 1863-64 when several thousand troops pitched their tents protectively outside the mansion, which served as the headquarters of the army of Northern Virginia III Corps. Generals Hill, Jackson, and Lee were guests. This inn, listed in the National Registry of Historic Places, was once a working plantation of 2,800 acres—a self-sufficient community of its own. As you wander about its rooms, it's easy to imagine those earlier times. The rooms of the inn have tall ceilings and large windows and invite you to bring the outside in. A four-floor staircase spirals through the Italianate Victorian's large central hall, which runs from front to back of this property. Bedrooms are large and have their own private baths. Canopies hang from the ceilings, fabrics are lovely, and fireplaces abound. Three-course breakfasts are served in the lower-floor dining room or on the brick terrace. There is much to do besides enjoying the porches and relaxing in this picturesque setting. Wineries are nearby, towns are fun to explore, Monticello and Montpelier await your visit, and the history of two wars that created and tore apart our country is everywhere around you. *Directions:* From Washington, D.C.: take I-95 south to Fredericksburg, then Route 3 west to Route 20 to Orange. From Richmond or Charlottesville: take Route 64 to Route 15 north to Orange. The inn is on the left on the approach to town from the south.

MAYHURST INN
Innkeepers: Pat & Jack North
12460 Mayhurst Lane
Orange, VA 22960, USA
Tel: (540) 672-5597, Fax: (540) 672-7447
Toll Free: (888) 672-5597
8 Rooms, Double: $150–$225
Open: all year, Credit cards: all major
www.karenbrown.com/vamayhurst.html

Great food and charming innkeepers are the winning combination you'll find at the Ashby Inn. The inn was converted from an 1829 residence set in a tiny Virginia hamlet of just a few historic homes on a quiet bypass from the major highway. The dining rooms are intimate and small, with low beams, lovely paneling, and wide floorboards and there is also a side terrace where most of the year you can enjoy food prepared expertly in the adjoining kitchen. There are ten bedrooms to choose from, six in the main building and four in an old schoolhouse that has been magically transformed into accommodations you'll find hard leave, with high ceilings, fireplaces, and comfortable love seats and chairs. Porches for evening air and morning musings are all part of the schoolhouse experience. The bathrooms are designed totally with your comfort in mind and include all the amenities that you could possibly expect, including bottled water. My first stay was in the New England Room with its country-painted furniture, pencil-post bed, and Oriental rugs. My second was in the schoolhouse in the Settle Room with its king wrought-iron bed, wood-burning fireplace, and wonderful old Oriental rugs. *Directions:* From Washington, D.C. take I-66 west to exit 23 then Route 17 north for 7½ miles. Turn left onto Route 701. The inn is at the intersection of Route 701 and Route 759.

❄ 🍺 💳 ☎ P 🍴 🚶 👫 🐎

ASHBY INN & RESTAURANT
Owners: Jackie & Charles Leopold
Innkeeper: Deborah Cox
692 Federal Street
Paris, VA 20130, USA
Tel: (540) 592-3900, Fax: (540) 592-3781
Toll Free: (866) 336-0099
10 Rooms, Double: $145–$250
Closed: Jan 1, Jul 4, Christmas, Credit cards: MC, VS
Select Registry
www.karenbrown.com/vaashbyinn.html

Everything about this inn is setting and view. Perched on a hillside this inn was constructed with the architectural intent to maximize and frame the sweep of the river as it dramatically cuts a path through the valley below. Wooden buildings washed in a warm earth tone, trimmed in white crest the hillside and are banded at every opportunity by an expanse of deck—places to perch and enjoy the tranquility and beauty of the setting. Upon arrival when you enter off the front porch the views exposed through the expanse of window that bands the back will draw you immediately across the great room to the views. Guestrooms stagger along the length of the building, each cornered and angled to enjoy privacy but whose windows, once again, frame the spectacular vistas. Named for their grandchildren, they are tasteful and luxuriously appointed and their décor is subtle and understated so as once again to enhance, rather than compete with the magnificence of the setting. A full breakfast is offered daily and dinner is offered Friday, Sunday and Monday. Alternate dining is available at the restaurant, Bank, Food & Drink. *Directions:* Traveling south on I-81 take exit 118B/Hwy 460 west to Blacksburg. Continue on 460 and take the Pearisburg-Ripplemead business exit turning left towards Pearisburg. Turn left at the first light (Wal-Mart) and then an immediate left onto Virginia Heights Dr. Follow it for 1.3 mi as it becomes Riverbend Dr. Turn left at River Ridge Dr. to the inn on the right.

INN AT RIVERBEND   *New*
Innkeepers: Linda & Lynn Hayes
125 River Ridge Drive
Pearisburg, VA 24134, USA
Tel: (540) 921-5211, Fax: (540) 921-2720
7 Rooms, Double: $130–$240
Open: all year, Credit cards: all major
Select Registry
www.karenbrown.com/variverbend.html

Historic properties are occasionally so wonderful that they wait for the right persons to come along at the right time to restore them to their original glory. Granted that a building with original Tiffany windows and a 35-foot stained-glass ceiling in a lobby that must without doubt be one of the most beautiful in the world (faux marble pillars and a 70-foot ceiling are really impressive) is a good start, but this hotel goes on to give the visitor all the service and amenities one would want. The southern style of service is a special one indeed and in this hotel, originally opened in 1895, it begins with the gentleman who opens your car door. There are 57 different styles of bedrooms, giving the hotel some interesting options for unique decorating. The rooms are comfortably furnished with reproduction antiques and each has a good sitting area with a desk and data port. There is a formal restaurant, Lemaire, which is unusual in that there are many smaller dining rooms instead of just one large one, giving the guest a feeling of privacy as in his own home. In addition, there is a less formal restaurant, TJ's, where I had a delicious dinner. This hotel is proud of its health club, exercise rooms, and swimming pool, and the YMCA is just across the street. *Directions:* From I-95 south take exit 76B to the Belvedere St exit. At the first light turn left onto Leigh St, at the next light turn right onto Belvedere St, then at the fifth light turn left onto Franklin St.

❄ ✗ ▭ ☎ 🏠 ♨ 🏋 ☗ Ⅰ P ¶ ≈ ♿ 🚶 🚶‍♀️

THE JEFFERSON
Manager: Joseph Longo
101 West Franklin Street
Richmond, VA 23220, USA
Tel: (804) 788-8000, Fax: (804) 225-0334
Toll Free: (800) 424-8014
264 Rooms, Double: $185–$1,800*
*Breakfast not included: $16.95
Open: all year, Credit cards: all major
www.karenbrown.com/vajefferson.html

Picture a wisteria-covered porch with rocking chairs from which you can watch the horses down in the meadow below or climbing the far hill and you'll have one of the best features of the Jordan Hollow Farm inn, a 200-year-old restored horse farm. The bedrooms at the inn have queen beds, fireplaces, and bathrooms (most with massage tubs). There are boarding stables on the property, cross-country skiing is available, and you could bike forever on the back-country roads. Within a short drive are swimming and fishing at Lake Arrowhead, plenty of antique and crafts shops, and, of course, the caverns for which this area is famous. The outdoors sportsman can also enjoy hiking, horseback riding, and canoeing. There is much history in the battlefields and Civil War Museums nearby. A popular attraction of the Shenandoah Valley is visiting its wineries, with their picturesque vineyards set among the rolling hills. The inn has its own restaurant where American regional cuisine featuring produce from nearby farms is served in the dining rooms of a two-story building with wide porches—an inviting setting at the end of the day. *Directions:* From Washington, D.C. take I-66 west to Exit 13. Continue on Hwy 55 into Front Royal and on to intersection of Hwy 340. Turn left on Hwy 340 south. After approximately 6 miles, turn left on Rte 624, proceed 1 mile to the stop sign, turn left on Rte 689 for approximately .5 mile. Turn right on Rte 626, Hawksbill Park Rd.

JORDAN HOLLOW FARM
Innkeeper: Gail Kyle
326 Hawksbill Park Road
Stanley, VA 22875, USA
Tel: (540) 778-2285, Fax: (540) 778-1759
Toll Free: (888) 418-7000
14 Rooms, Double: $190–$250
Closed: Jan, Credit cards: all major
Select Registry
www.karenbrown.com/vajordonhollow.html

High on a hill in the historic part of Staunton sits the Belle Grae Inn, a full-service establishment with rooms in a clustering of several buildings. In the old inn are the dining rooms, parlor, and six guestrooms decorated comfortably with some things old, some things reproduced, and some things that fit in between. The Belle Grae has a Victorian look and its furnishings are in keeping with that theme. The Belle Grae's owners have worked hard to create within the original structure a variety of accommodations — they are all very different from one another in size and feel. Talk with the innkeeper or visit their website to consider the appeal of the individual rooms to match your taste. Dinner at the Belle Grae is nice, not fancy gourmet, with ample portions served pleasantly in any of several small dining rooms rather than one large one. The inn is sentimentally named for the mountain peaks that one can view from the inn's front porch: the Betsy Belle and the Mary Gray, named for the two Scottish lasses that came to the valley and settled here as it reminded them of their homeland. Robert Burn's "Ode to Betsy Belle" is a poetic tribute to hospitality and so it seems a perfect compliment for this inn, where welcome is the priority. *Directions:* Take I-81 south to exit 222 or 225 and follow signs to Woodrow Wilson's birthplace. Turn on Frederick Street and proceed six blocks to the inn. Circle the block for convenient parking.

BELLE GRAE INN & RESTAURANT
Innkeeper: Michael Organ
515 West Frederick Street
Staunton, VA 24401, USA
Tel: (540) 886-5151, Fax: (540) 886-6641
Toll Free: (888) 541-5151
7 Rooms, Double: $99–$209
Restaurant serving dinner Wed through Sun
Open: all year, Credit cards: all major
Select Registry
www.karenbrown.com/vabellegrae.html

There's something special about inns tucked away in national forests at the end of long, climbing roads. There's also something special about buildings constructed years ago of hand-hewn logs and beams—they exude a warmth and charm that somehow speak of the effort and love that went into their being. Such is the Sugar Tree Inn, sitting at 2,800 feet in the Blue Ridge Mountains in 28 acres of forest. This is a place where dogwood, mountain laurel, rhododendron, and trillium blossom in spring with wild abandon. In summer the days are warm and the nights are cool, while in the fall an artist's palette of red and gold and every shade between clothes the sugar maples as the leaves drop into pools of swirling color. Relax on one of the many porches, enjoying the antics of chipmunks, squirrels, and hummingbirds. The inn has a number of accommodation choices—the Main Lodge, the Log House and Grey House, each with four rooms, and the Creek House with its two bedrooms. Most rooms have queen beds, but there are four with a king. All rooms have fireplaces with cozy chairs nearby, and there are quilts and comforters; some rooms have whirlpool tubs. Dinner is available Thursday through Saturday by reservation. *Directions:* From I-81 take exit 205 to Steeles Tavern, then Route 56 east for approximately 5 miles to the inn. From Blue Ridge Parkway, take Route 56 west for almost a mile to the inn.

SUGAR TREE INN
Innkeepers: Becky & Jeff Chanter
Hwy 56, Steeles Tavern, VA 24476, USA
Tel: (800) 377-2197, Fax: (540) 377-5277
12 Rooms, Double: $150–$245
1 cottage
Dinner by reservation Thurs-Sat
Open: mid-Feb to mid-Dec, Credit cards: MC, VS
Select Registry
www.karenbrown.com/vasugartree.html

The various buildings of the Inn at Vaucluse Spring nestle and perch in spots to take advantage of their unique personality and setting. Four circa-1850 buildings, the newly constructed Cottage on the Hill, and a wonderful log cabin constructed from the timbers and beams of a tobacco barn share some 100 acres of rolling land. The Mill, of course, sits on a pond and its two-story building looks out to ever-changing, lovely water views. The Gallery, which used to be just that, has a grand living space with its own fireplace overlooking surrounding gardens. Upstairs, a king-bedded room with fireplace overlooks the large guest pool. The log cabin is cozy and rustic in its decor and a large picture window frames views of the mill and pond. To sit on the porch of the elegant Federal-style Manor House, watch the sun rise or set and see the deer in the distance, take a stroll with Bisquit (she is available by appointment!), and then to go inside to a lovely dinner (Friday or Saturday only) would be hard to improve upon. Once the home of John Chumley, an artist of the Shenandoah Valley, this little bit of paradise has been well preserved by the present owners. *Directions:* From I-66 west, take exit 1B to I-81 north. Go 1 mile to exit 302. Turn left on Rte 627. Travel half a mile, then turn right on Rte 11. Drive 2 miles then turn left on Rte 638. Drive half a mile to the inn.

❄ ☕ 💳 P 🍴 🚭 ≈ 🛬 🕴 👫 🐎 🍷

INN AT VAUCLUSE SPRING
Innkeepers: Barry & Neil Myers
231 Vaucluse Spring Lane
Stephens City, VA 22655, USA
Tel: (540) 869-0200, Fax: (540) 869-9546
Toll Free: (800) 869-0525
12 Rooms, Double: $150–$295, 3 cottages
Dinner on Fri & Sat by reservation
Closed: Thanksgiving & Christmas
Credit cards: MC, VS, Select Registry
www.karenbrown.com/vauclusespring.html

What is it about mills with large water wheels and streams rushing by that draws the traveler in? They seem to be the center of a town's life and the place where the locals all drop by. The Inn at Gristmill Square has its origin in the mill built in 1771 and today there are five 19th-century buildings making up this interesting complex. The blacksmith's shop now houses a country store, the inn's office, and two guestrooms. The hardware store has seven bedrooms and the Steel House, formerly a private home, has four. The miller's former home provides four more bedrooms. Rooms are comfortably furnished and have a variety of twin, queen, and king beds. Each has bathrobes, cable TV, phone, hairdryer, refrigerator, and private bath. There are three tennis courts and an outdoor pool. The inn's restaurant is in the old mill and it's been so well preserved that many of the mill's working parts are still in place. Wood beams and individual small rooms create an inviting atmosphere for a meal. Ask for a tour of the wine cellar downstairs where it is naturally cooled by water. There's also a tiny pub with just the right number of well-worn bar stools and two tables. Warm Springs' pools are as popular today as they were years ago when guests traveled from afar to benefit from their healing powers. In winter you can enjoy skiing and skating. *Directions:* From Route 220 turn west to Route 619 (Court House Hill) to the inn.

❄ ☕ ⛷ CREDIT ☎ 🏋 🍸 P 🍴 🌿 🏊 🎣 🖼 🚶 🎿

INN AT GRISTMILL SQUARE
Innkeeper: The McWilliams Family
P.O. Box 359
Warm Springs, VA 24484, USA
Tel: (540) 839-2231, Fax: (540) 839-5770
17 Rooms, Double: $95–$160
Open: all year, Credit cards: MC, VS
www.karenbrown.com/vagristmill.html

The Corbetts moved from "big" Washington to "little" Washington (surveyed by George Washington when he was only 17 years old), having fallen in love with both the inn and the country life. While they are not the first innkeepers of the Foster-Harris House, they are quickly making improvements and decorating so that it is now a reflection of their refined taste. Enter off the front porch and to the right is an attractive guest salon, which then opens into a lovely dining room where a memorable five-course gourmet breakfast is served on the family's fine china and crystal. There are five guestrooms. The Garden Room, just off the entry, has a lovely decor of light colors and pines, and a wonderful bathroom that looks out through a wall of windows up to the surrounding mountains. At the top of the stairs is the largest room, The Mount View Suite, decorated in rich red and with an alcove sitting area from which you can watch the sun set over the mountains. My favorite was the Meadowview Room, a back bedroom, dramatic with its deep-blue walls and four-poster bed. From the bathroom you enjoy unobstructed views of the mountains and garden. In addition to breakfast, included in the room rate is afternoon tea, a silver-platter service featuring delicious baked goods prepared by the Corbetts' pastry-chef daughter. *Directions:* From Washington, D.C. take Route I-66 west to Route 29 south, then Route 211 west to Washington, VA.

FOSTER HARRIS HOUSE
Innkeepers: Diane & John Macpherson
189 Main Street
P.O. Box 333
Washington, VA 22747-0333, USA
Tel: (540) 675-3757, Fax: (540) 675-3868
Toll Free: (800) 666-0153
5 Rooms, Double: $225–$335
Open: all year, Credit cards: all major
www.karenbrown.com/vafoster.html

A legend in its own right with more awards than there is wall upon which to hang them. The Inn at Little Washington is special indeed for those who can find availability in its nine bedrooms, seven suites, and off-site private home in the countryside. If decor were the measure of comfort and pleasure, the rooms of this inn would be over the top. If food were the most important thing in the world, you would be hard pressed to find better food more beautifully presented. As if this were not enough, this is an inn that understands what service is and how it should be given—gracious and unassuming but ever present. The bedrooms are sumptuously decorated with fabulous fabrics used lavishly to create moods and comfort. Every possible amenity has been thought of, and if there were something lacking, it would be brought to you before the thought could be completed. Tea was served while I was there, and in addition to the choice of teas, there was a selection of cookies, berry tarts, and dried or candied fruit that would have made either the earlier lunch or the forthcoming dinner unnecessary—a thought not to be considered! The dining room is so spectacular that dinner already tastes good before you are even seated. The Inn at Little Washington, while expensive, is one of a kind and should not be missed. *Directions:* From Washington, D.C. take I-66 west to Route 29 south, then Route 211 west to Washington, VA.

INN AT LITTLE WASHINGTON
Innkeepers: Patrick O'Connell & Reinhardt Lynch
P.O. Box 300
Washington, VA 22747, USA
Tel: (540) 675-3800, Fax: (540) 675-3100
9 Rooms, Double: $395–$1,235
7 suites, 1 cottage
Closed: most Tuesdays, Credit cards: all major
Relais & Châteaux
www.karenbrown.com/valittlewashington.html

A warm welcome, a cozy bedroom with a four-poster French country bed and a wood-burning fireplace, a superbly prepared meal in the best French style, and a glass of sauvignon blanc made this country inn overlooking fields and ponds—a haven of pleasure. The rooms have comfortable reading chairs, good lighting to read by, fluffy terry robes, and bathrooms with all the amenities a traveler could possibly want. The restaurant is decorated with antique French copper cooking ware, which sets off and complements the warm-salmon faux-painted walls. Dinner began with a special appetizer of fresh crab croquette with citrus salad, vanilla and chili oils with cilantro; followed by wild mushroom stuffed kurobuta pork with caramelized onion and smoke bacon tart; and dessert was impossible to resist: a fudge brownie and banana split with a trio of ice creams. There is an extensive French and American wine list worthy not only of study but selective tasting. Within the inn there is also an attractive library. Alain and Celeste also have their new Villa La Campaignette with three suites and a swimming pool set in a lovely area of this Virginia hunting country, just 3 miles from L'Auberge Provencale. Breakfast is served in a charming dining room. *Directions:* From Washington, D.C. take I-66 west to exit 23. Follow 17 north to Route 50 west to Route 340 south. The inn is 1 mile along on the right.

L'AUBERGE PROVENCALE
Innkeepers: Alain & Celeste Borel
Route 340, P.O. Box 190
White Post, VA 22663, USA
Tel: (540) 837-1375, Fax: (540) 837-2004
Toll Free: (800) 638-1702
11 Rooms, Double: $155–$395
Restaurant serving dinner Wed through Sun
Closed: Jan 1 to 22, Credit cards: all major
Select Registry
www.karenbrown.com/vaauberge.html

The checklist of life must include a visit to Williamsburg, Virginia's capital from 1699 to 1780, and its marvelously restored village. This is living history and touring the buildings and talking with the merchants and tradesmen as they ply their trades make for an unforgettable experience. What's especially nice about Williamsburg is that even after the sun goes down and the buildings close you can still stroll around the village and feel as if you are part of that earlier era. You may have the opportunity to hear an evening concert or attend a special music program in the Bruton Parish Church. There are many options for overnighting in Williamsburg, but this five star Inn is elegant with the service and comfort to compliment its superb rating. Guestrooms are beautifully appointed and the public areas are lovely and enjoy tranquil garden views. The Historic Lodging defines the many Colonial homes that have been restored and are located in the village, just a few steps from the village green. My house had a living room with a desk, sofa and other seating, good lighting, and an area where you could make coffee or tea in the early morning. My large bedroom had a four-poster canopy bed and more than enough space for luggage and clothes. Breakfast was available in the neighboring inn just a short walk from any of the homes. The Inn reception services both the Inn and Historic Lodging. *Directions:* Take Route 64 east from Richmond, leaving at exit 238 following signs.

COLONIAL INN & HISTORIC LODGING
Owner: Colonial Williamsburg Foundation
302 East Francis Street
Williamsburg, VA 23185, USA
Tel: (757) 229-1000, ext 8440, Fax: (757) 565-8444
Toll Free: (800) 447-8679
Double: $150–$700*
63 rooms in the inn, 77 rooms in 28 guesthouses
*Breakfast not included
Open: all year, Credit cards: all major
www.karenbrown.com/vacolonial.html

If not for the charming sign hung under a street lantern, it would be easy to pass right by the intimate Fife & Drum Inn whose single paned glass doorway is its only street front presence. Once past the door a wood stairway handsomely painted and stenciled beckons one up to the second floor landing where one is introduced to the whimsical staging of this lovely inn. Along the wide hallway that transitions from brick to painted plank floors, guestroom doors mimic residential entrances and cleverly effect the illusion of walking down one of Williamsburg's charming alleyways. Just around the corner to the right, the hallway opens on a large room set with wooden tables and chairs that serves as the only public room for guests. Mornings a limited breakfast buffet is set out here from 8 to 9am and at other times one will find beverages and cookies. Guestrooms are decorated with pine reproduction furniture set on stenciled plank floors. Bathrooms are tiled and vary based on the space afforded to accommodate their utilities. Furnished with a chest of drawers, bed and single chair, the rooms are not meant for lingering and with a location right in the heart of old Williamsburg, linger you will not as shops, restaurants, the historic village and the college of William and Mary are all steps away. *Directions:* Take Route 64 east from Richmond, leaving at exit 238 follow signs to Colonial Williamsburg.

THE FIFE & DRUM INN   New
Innkeepers: Sharon & Billy Scruggs
441 Prince George Street
Williamsburg, VA 23185, USA
Tel: (757) 345-1776
Toll Free: (888) 838-1783
9 Rooms, Double: $155–$175
1 cottage
Open: all year, Credit cards: all major
www.karenbrown.com/vafifeanddrum.html

The bed and breakfast experience is handcrafted with style at this charming four-bedroom inn only a short distance from the heart of Colonial Williamsburg. Chair rails, lovely molding, and Williamsburg-blue walls provide an especially warm and inviting ambiance and antiques are used in the furnishings. Fireplaces abound—you'll find one in your bedroom as well as in the inn's public areas. The dining room, known as the keeping room in Colonial days, features Colonial Williamsburg inlaid brick, while the Tavern Room boasts a pool table built in England for the inn. The Williamsburg Suite has a sitting room with fireplace and an attached sun porch, which looks out over a wooded landscape and gardens. In the bedroom there is a queen canopy bed curtained with red Jacobean linen and the bathroom offers all the amenities a traveler would want. The Nicholson Suite offers a sitting room with a fireplace and a deck looking out over a treetop gazebo. The queen bed in this room is canopied and trimmed in red Williamsburg check. A wonderful full breakfast is prepared and served by the innkeepers, who are the most dedicated of hosts. Guests here will experience a delightfully warm and gracious visit to Colonial Williamsburg. *Directions:* Take I-64 east to the Lightfoot Exit 234. Follow 199 east 8 miles to the sixth intersection (second light), which is Jamestown Rd. Turn left onto Jamestown Rd (Rte 5) for 9/10 mile.

LEGACY OF WILLIAMSBURG
Innkeepers: Joan & Art Ricker
930 Jamestown Road
Williamsburg, VA 23185, USA
Tel: (757) 220-0524, Fax: (757) 220-2211
Toll Free: (800) 962-4722
4 Rooms, Double: $135–$185
Open: all year, Credit cards: MC, VS
www.karenbrown.com/valegacy.html

There's a special quality about Williamsburg's bed and breakfasts because the zoning codes do not permit more than four guestrooms, which means that the innkeepers can lavish personal attention on their guests. Such is the case at the Liberty Rose. Sandi greeted me at the door and showed me round the inn with great enthusiasm. The living room and dining room are comfortably furnished in an English Victorian style with lots of places to sit and relax after a day's touring of the historic village. There is a lovely patio at the rear of the home where in good weather it would be a delight to breakfast or relax with a glass of iced tea. Suite Williamsburg is the grandest of the four bedrooms, with a carved ball-and-claw queen four-poster bed, its tester hung with silk and jacquard fabrics, a working fireplace, a sitting area, TV/VCR, and a fancy bathroom with a claw-foot tub and a large black-marble shower. Magnolias Peach also has a queen canopy bed, this time with a fishnet covering so typical of the Victorian style, walls covered with flowered wallpaper, and an adjoining tiny but cozy sitting room. A full breakfast is served either in the dining room at tables for two or in the garden. This inn is a Victorian romance—with all the modern amenities. *Directions:* Take Route 64 to exit 238 to Colonial Williamsburg, following signs to William and Mary College. At the corner of the college and Merchant Square, turn right on Jamestown Road to the inn.

LIBERTY ROSE B&B
Innkeepers: Brad & Sandi Hirz
1025 Jamestown Road
Williamsburg, VA 23185, USA
Tel: (757) 253-1260, Fax: none
Toll Free: (800) 545-1825
4 Rooms, Double: $195–$275
Open: all year, Credit cards: all major
www.karenbrown.com/valibertyrose.html

The Inn at Narrow Passage sits just south of the town of Woodstock and is easily reached using a combination of I-81 and Route 11, formerly known as the Great Wagon Road. Travelers along this route have been coming to the inn since the 1740s and enjoying the large common room with its massive limestone fireplace, pine floors, and comfortable wing chairs. Breakfast is served in the adjoining paneled dining room. The inn's 12 bedrooms, decorated in a simple Colonial style, have well-equipped, functional bathrooms, queen canopied beds, and comfortable chairs for reading. Some of the rooms are located in the original building, some in newer wings where they open onto porches shared by all. Views from the inn are of the Shenandoah River just below and the Massanutten Mountains to the east. There's much to do in this area: fishing, horseshoes, and bird watching right on site, horseback riding, hiking, and canoeing nearby. Burgeoning Shenandoah Valley wineries beckon you to taste their products and antique shops abound all along Route 11. Those interested in the Civil War will enjoy knowing Stonewall Jackson made his headquarters here in 1862 and will want to explore the many historic sites and battlefields nearby. *Directions:* From Washington, D.C. take I-66 west to I-81 south to exit 283 (Woodstock) then travel Route 11 south for 2 miles. The inn is on the corner at the junction of Route 11 and Route 672 (Chapman Landing Road).

INN AT NARROW PASSAGE
Innkeepers: Ellen & Ed Markel
Route 11 South
P.O. Box 608
Woodstock, VA 22664, USA
Tel: (540) 459-8000, Toll Free: (800) 459-8002
12 Rooms, Double: $115–$165
Open: all year, Credit cards: MC, VS
www.karenbrown.com/vanarrowpassage.html

Index

Joshua Wilton House Inn, Harrisonburg, 248

S

KAREN BROWN wrote her first travel guide in 1977. Her personalized travel series has grown to 17 titles, which Karen and her small staff work diligently to keep updated. Karen, her husband, Rick, and their children, Alexandra and Richard, live in Moss Beach, a small town on the coast south of San Francisco. They settled here in 1991 when they opened Seal Cove Inn. Karen is frequently traveling but when she is home, in her role as innkeeper, enjoys welcoming Karen Brown readers.

JACK BULLARD researches for Karen Brown's guides to New England and the Mid-Atlantic. Jack grew up in New England and after completing his graduate education there spent fifteen years in international consulting in marketing and finance, and then ten years as executive director of two Boston law firms. He managed another law firm before owning The Inn at Occidental in the Sonoma wine country north of San Francisco for ten years. He now lives in Newport, Rhode Island and remains close to the world of hospitality—consulting, designing and decorating.

JANN POLLARD, The artist of the cover painting has studied art since childhood, and is well known for her outstanding impressionistic-style watercolors. Jann's original paintings are represented through The Gallery in Burlingame, CA and New Masters Gallery in Carmel, CA. *www.jannpollard.com.* Fine art giclée prints of her paintings are available at *www.karenbrown.com.*

VANESSA KALE produced all of the property sketches and itinerary illustrations in this guide. A native of Bellingham, Washington, Vanessa spent her high school year in Sonoma California. After graduating in Art from U.C. Davis, Vanessa moved to southern California where she lives with her husband, Simon. She works as a project manager for an architectural rendering company, and also as a freelance artist. *www.vanessakale.com.*

Watch for a New Thriller Series
Featuring "Karen Brown"
As Travel Writer & Undercover Sleuth

Author M. Diane Vogt, the creator of the critically acclaimed and popular Judge Wilhelmina Carson legal suspense novels, is writing a new series featuring the exploits of "Karen Brown".

Combine the heroic salvage consultant Travis McGee – from John D. MacDonald's hugely successful Ft. Lauderdale mystery/thriller series with *Under the Tuscan Sun's* Frances Mayes, and that's Karen Brown, clandestine recovery specialist and world renowned travel writer.

Based on actual places and destinations as featured in Karen Brown's guides, join Karen in her travels as by day she inspects charming hotels, and by night she dabbles in intrigue and defeats the world of killers, scoundrels, and scam artists.

The series has been launched with the publication of James Patterson's best selling book, *Thriller*. The short story, "Surviving Toronto" introduces sleuth, Karen Brown.

Quality

Awards coming soon......

Reader feedback will be used to evaluate and award exceptional quality and service for Karen Brown Recommended Properties.

On our website Karen Brown Travelers will have the ability to vote for a property in a number of categories, including but not limited to; best breakfast, location/setting, welcome, comfort/ambiance, value, and romance.

Service

Ambiance

Karen Brown Presents Her Own Special Hideaways

Karen Brown's Seal Cove Inn

Spectacularly set amongst wildflowers and bordered by cypress trees, Seal Cove Inn (Karen's second home) looks out to the distant ocean. Each room has a fireplace, cozy sitting area, and a view of the sea. Located on the coast, 35 minutes south of San Francisco.

Seal Cove Inn, Moss Beach, California
toll free telephone: (800) 995-9987
www.sealcoveinn.com

Karen Brown's Dolphin Cove Inn

Hugging a steep hillside overlooking the sparkling deep-blue bay of Manzanillo, Dolphin Cove Inn offers guests outstanding value. Each room has either a terrace or a balcony, and a breathtaking view of the sea. Located on the Pacific Coast of Mexico.

Dolphin Cove Inn, Manzanillo, Mexico
toll free telephone: (866) 360-9062
www.dolphincoveinn.com